Compensatory Education
for Children
Ages Two to Eight

COMPENSATORY EDUCATION FOR CHILDREN AGES TWO TO EIGHT:

Recent Studies

of

Educational Intervention

PROCEEDINGS OF THE SECOND ANNUAL

HYMAN BLUMBERG SYMPOSIUM ON RESEARCH

IN EARLY CHILDHOOD EDUCATION

Edited by Julian C. Stanley

THE JOHNS HOPKINS UNIVERSITY PRESS

BALTIMORE AND LONDON

Proceedings of the First Annual Hyman Blumberg Symposium on Research in Early Childhood Education were published by The Johns Hopkins University Press in 1972 in both paperbound and clothbound editions as *Preschool Programs for the Disadvantaged: Five Experimental Approaches to Early Childhood Education.*

The Johns Hopkins University Press, Baltimore, Maryland 21218
The Johns Hopkins University Press Ltd., London

Library of Congress Catalog Card Number 72-12355
ISBN 0-8018-1457-X (clothbound edition)
ISBN 0-8018-1461-8 (paperbound edition)

Library of Congress Cataloging in Publication data will be found on the last printed page of this book.

CONTENTS

PREFACE

This volume resulted from the second annual Hyman Blumberg Symposium on Research in Early Childhood Education, ably chaired by Lowman G. Daniels, which was held at The Johns Hopkins University in 1972. On April 1, six leading researchers in the development and evaluation of approaches to educating disadvantaged children presented papers, revised versions of which appear herein. These had been discussed for three hours the previous day by the following 18 persons: Mary Ainsworth, Scarvia Anderson, Edward Ansello, Samuel Ball, Joan Bissell, Mary Blehar, Lowman Daniels, Leo Geoffrion, John Guthrie, Merle Karnes, Michael Lerner, Gail Marchase, Samuel Messick, Susan Rose, Virginia Shipman, Irving Sigel, Julian Stanley, and Roger Webb. Also, Robert Grinder made excellent critical comments concerning the original manuscript.

The annual Blumberg Symposium is financed by the income from a $110,000 endowment created at The Johns Hopkins University in 1969 by the Amalgamated Clothing Workers of America under the leadership of Mr. Jacob Potofsky, General President, and Mr. Sam Nocella, International Vice President. The ACWA pioneered in the development of day care centers for the children of working mothers. The late Hyman Blumberg, whom the symposia honor, was Executive Vice President of the Amalgamated Clothing Workers of America. Of course, the ACWA bears no responsibility for the contents of the symposia.

The Johns Hopkins University and I are indebted to the authors whose papers appear in this volume for the care with which they wrote and revised their reports of important studies in compensatory education of disadvantaged children. Mary Ellen Oliveri prepared the index of names and corrected the page proof. I was especially glad to have had at hand the talents of Nancy Middleton Gallienne of The Johns Hopkins University Press. Joan Finucci made the symposium itself run smoothly. Virginia Grim and Lois Sandhofer provided excellent secretarial assistance.

The first chapter is my brief introduction to the papers, with some critical comments about them. It also includes a few of my "personal opinions" concerning restructuring the public schools so that compensatory education would be less needed than now.

This volume seems a worthy sequel to its predecessor, *Preschool Programs for the Disadvantaged: Five Experimental Approaches to Early Childhood Education*, which was published by The Johns Hopkins University Press in 1972.

JULIAN C. STANLEY
Department of Psychology
The Johns Hopkins University

Compensatory Education for Children for Children Ages Two to Eight

JULIAN C. STANLEY
The Johns Hopkins University
Baltimore, Maryland 21218

I. INTRODUCTION AND CRITIQUE

In this volume the five basic papers and the discussion of them and related points by Anderson continue several of the themes reported from the first symposium (Stanley 1972). These articles are sequels, especially to the chapters by Bereiter, Weikart, and McAfee. As the title of this book indicates, the studies involve children from age two through school grade three, i.e., from Sigel's very young to the oldest of the Follow Through and Karnes's end-of-third-grade children. (Actually, most researchers who start with preschool children also follow their progress into kindergarten and the primary grades.)

All five of the studies are experiments or quasi-experiments, though in some of them controls are tighter than in others. In the work reported by both Bissell and Shipman, assignment to various "treatment" and "control" groups was not manipulated experimentally. Ball and Bogatz, Karnes, and Sigel did set up comparison groups. In all the studies the authors analyzed their data ingeniously. It will become abundantly evident to readers of this volume and its predecessor that adequate experimentation in preschool contexts demands a high order of care and intellect. The various sources of invalidity that Campbell and Stanley (1966) and Bracht and Glass (1968) discuss constantly threaten researchers in the real world of compensatory education; Bissell makes this clear in her provocative warnings about pitfalls encountered when trying to interpret data gathered rather adventitiously in the field.

Through these papers runs the thread of preschool intervention with the hope of improving the educability of children who otherwise might not learn the basic skills, particularly reading and arithmetic, in school. The emphasis is on starting early, at age four or less, and continuing the facilitation as long as feasible. The same question that concerned Bereiter, Weikart, and McAfee in the preceding volume preoccupies Ball and Bogatz, Sigel, Bissell, Karnes, and Shipman: How much educational good will our interventions do in the long run? Attaining precociously skills that would not normally develop until later is a promising beginning, but hovering in the wings is the specter of the fraternal twins, Jimmy and Johnny, one of whom was taught (see McGraw

1

1935) to roller-skate earlier than the other, but both of whom were equally skilled at a later time. Jimmy simply "caught up" with Johnny spontaneously. Thus, Johnny had spent some of his time and energy being made precocious when he might instead have been doing something else that presumably would have been more fun or more permanently effective. Of course, probably there are optimal ages for learning certain skills, but quite likely not "the earlier the better" for most academic skills.[1]

[In a private communication to me, dated 15 August 1972, Ball and Bogatz demurred rather eloquently to the criticism of their study implied in the above paragraph. They wrote:

> It is, of course, proper to assume that we were interested in the question of "How much educational good will our intervention do in the long run?" But our work was not aimed primarily at this, and our rationale is that such interventions as *Sesame Street* are useful if they have good short-run effects. We argue that education, like morphine, is not likely to have a long-term "high" (effect) through a one-shot deal, whether it is mainlined or sent out on VHF. If compensatory education is to have a permanent effect, it must be a constant input (just as living with well-educated parents provides a constant input). In our view, it is unfair to expect 130 hours spread over six months to revolutionize a child's entire life. It might provide some effects which other overlapping inputs could build upon. At the moment, such overlapping inputs are not available for lower-class children. Perhaps a reasonable analogy is to refer to adopted children brought up by advantaged parents vs. adopted children brought up in disadvantaging circumstances. They differ intellectually. Would anyone expect the lower-class adoptees to be like the middle-class adoptees if they spent just a few months of their first 15 years in a middle-class home?

But if 130 hours of rather expensive compensatory effort do not interact later with regular schooling to improve learning appreciably—not "to revolutionize a child's entire life," of course!—how can they be justified? As entertainment superior to the usual TV fare?]

The papers and Anderson's discussion are stimulating and therefore raise a number of other issues that will not be discussed here. Instead, I shall make brief introductory and critical comments about each of the papers in turn, to help get the reader oriented. The critical remarks are not meant to detract from the excellence of the papers, which the reader will readily recognize when he reads them. I then conclude with a "Personal Opinions" section that represents an expansion and extension of one of Anderson's main points. Neither she nor any of the other authors, however, share any responsibility for my suggestions.

---

[1]But also see McGraw (1939). Johnny remained superior "in the degree of bodily coordination" at least until age 22 (personal communication from Dr. McGraw, 4 January 1973). It does not seem possible with these two nonidentical twins to decide how influential the early training of Johnny was.

BALL AND BOGATZ

Ball and Bogatz offer evidence that viewing televised *Sesame Street* helps both the disadvantaged and the advantaged to master basic skills, such as counting to ten or twenty, classifying, and sorting. They ingeniously tease causal inferences from studies in which full experimental control was not possible. For instance, the most disadvantaged children viewed the programs least, but those 164 disadvantaged four-year-olds who viewed them more than five times a week slightly exceeded the advantaged four-year-olds who viewed two to three times a week. This is a modest reversal of the pretest results.

It is possible, of course, that presumably disadvantaged youngsters who view *Sesame Street* often have homes in which more attention is paid to the basic skills than do presumably middle class children who view it less. Clearly, as Figure 2 in their paper shows, those supposedly disadvantaged children who later view the programs most often score essentially the same *initially* as do the middle class ones who will view them "rarely or never." In other words, there are degrees of disadvantage within both the middle class and the so-called disadvantaged groups. How these nonrandomly assigned variations in viewing time within and between groups becloud the interpretation of Ball and Bogatz's results cannot be ascertained from their expository paper in this volume. Interested readers may consult their much longer, more technical reports.

[In a private communication to me dated 15 August 1972, Ball and Bogatz wrote: "You are correct in your comparison, but we think that a more important comparison is the fact that these same disadvantaged children considerably exceeded the middle-class children who viewed *less* than 2–3 times a week. After all, perhaps viewing 2–3 times a week is the most efficient rate and the return drops off subsequently."]

Ball and Bogatz suggest that because children of middle class parents seem to learn well from *Sesame Street*, even though attending nursery school, "perhaps ... their educational input is by no means optimal. ... [W]e may well decide that many children need compensatory education, including a large proportion we fail to recognize when we conventionally think of the term 'compensatory.' " Before accepting that tentative conclusion, however, one must examine carefully the rationale for developing precociously in young *middle class* children skills that most of them will acquire anyway as they go through kindergarten and the primary grades of regular school. Many nursery school educators believe that spending much of a child's early years systematically teaching him things that he or she would probably learn later in home, school, or community may deprive the child of time for other experiences, especially those more directly promoting social and emotional development.

On the other hand, many children are disadvantaged educationally in that without special help they will not acquire such skills. They are the ones for whom compensatory education is essential. This is not to say, of course, that middle class youngsters who enjoy *Sesame Street* should not watch it—especially in preference to commercial television programs—for its various entertainment and skill values. Whether much direct attention should be paid to that group in developing programs, however, is perhaps debatable.

SIGEL, SECRIST, AND FORMAN

Sigel and his associates intervene educationally in systematic ways with two-year-old first-born children from impoverished black families in the inner city of Buffalo, New York. They then study cognitive and affective outcomes. In this volume they report first-year results for nine boys and ten girls, compared with several small control groups. Generally, they are optimistic about the benefits that disadvantaged children this young can gain from a cognitively structured program emphasizing the "development of representational competence, i.e., the ability to deal with representational material." They attempt to do this by "exposing children to distancing behaviors [that] should enhance the development of representational skills" via "an environment in which significant adults are warm, accepting, and sensitive to the child's status." Their approach calls for much one-to-one instructional work in tutorial sessions.

Because of the small number of subjects that can be handled in the desired way and the vast amount of test and other information gathered concerning each of the very young children, it is difficult for Sigel, Secrist, and Forman to make confident statements about outcomes of their study thus far. Many of the same types of reservations that Bissell spells out well in her paper must apply to their report. Especially, recruiting for the program and the comparison group did not produce demonstrably comparable sets of boys vs. girls or experimental vs. control subjects. As in Bissell's study, and most other compensatory education investigations, less attention can be justifiably paid to the tests of statistical significance than to the cogency of the models elucidated and the heuristic value of the hypotheses proposed for more direct, rigorous testing in a later experiment. Sigel and his associates' paper is rich in such models and hypotheses, although perhaps it does not draw enough on the work of other persons researching compensatory education for the preschool disadvantaged. As further background for this paper, see Lewis (in press).

BISSELL

Bissell's discussion of the various Head Start and Follow Through models provides conceptual background for understanding the other papers in this volume and its predecessor. She warns about the limitations of the typical evaluations of such programs and the consequent status of results as tentative hypotheses rather than firm conclusions. Nearly all persons who study compensatory education would benefit from reading her explicit, well-stated caveats. Policy issues loom large in this area. Bissell does, however, ingeniously find and explain certain probable trends in a large body of data that are promising leads to improved programs for the disadvantaged.

KARNES

In her paper, Merle Karnes discusses research by Samuel Kirk, herself, and others at the Institute for Research on Exceptional Children at the University of Illinois. Kirk has been a leading researcher in mental retardation for many years, and Karnes has worked in that area and the more recently devised area of "educational disadvantagement" for a quarter of a century. Indeed, Karnes has more experience in special education than perhaps any other major researcher on the disadvantaged in the country. She brings to her extensive research a wealth of practical background in public school programs.

The central part of her paper is an experiment comparing five methods of compensatory education with children from prekindergarten through the third grade. She concludes that a high degree of structure and emphasis on cognitive skills are most facilitative of gain in Stanford-Binet IQ and other intellectual achievements. "Attention to individual differences, precise planning, inservice education, parental involvement, and on-going evaluation appear to be important components of any preschool program, especially for the disadvantaged and handicapped."

Karnes concludes her important report and survey with fifteen "implications of findings on comparative studies" that are basically optimistic. Most readers will like that happy note, because the need for ways to make disadvantaged youngsters more educable is acute. We must be concerned, however, with the (to me) rather disquieting results depicted in her Figures 4 and 5. It proved readily possible, as in Wiekart's (1972) and other studies, to produce large gains in Stanford-Binet IQ in the prekindergarten year, but by the end of the third grade these had diminished for each of three methods studied that far to an average of some six or seven points. Even that jump, from 94–96 to 100–103, might be considered worth the effort and expense if it were not probable that it represents chiefly practice effects and gains in rapport brought about by interacting with adults in situations analogous to individual testing. This is not to say that any child was coached on Stanford-Binet materials, but instead that one-to-one relationships with adults in preschool programs seem almost certain to make young children function more willingly and effectively when with an individual mental tester than they do initially when tested "cold."

There is always the possibility, too, of statistical regression toward the mean of the group due to errors of measurement, if subjects were apt to be selected because they scored low on intellectual measures related positively to

S-B IQ. Presumably, the initial Stanford-Binet scores themselves were not used for excluding some high-scoring youngsters. Karnes reports that "... children were administered the Stanford-Binet Individual Intelligence Test, Form L-M [i.e., the 1960 version, for which no comparable form exists], and stratified into three groups on the basis of these IQ results (100+, 90–99, 70–89)." But those tested were "75 children who met age (CA 4-0), income, family history, and no previous preschool experience criteria." The last three of these criteria are usually IQ-related, but because races were balanced, 67 percent black and 33 percent white, in each class, it is not clear to what extent higher-IQ youngsters were eliminated. (Karnes reports no other data by race.)

Even if rapport, practice effects, and perhaps statistical regression can account for most or all of the six to seven point retained gain in IQ, the intensive programs might nevertheless have improved school achievement. Karnes's Figure 5 depicts mean reading grade placement scores from three administrations of the California Achievement Test, the last at the end of the third grade. Karnes compares the achievement of the three of her five groups for which such data were available with the following two standards: (1) "grade expectancy based on month of testing and initial mean of IQ of K_1 [one of the three groups]" and "grade expectancy based on month of testing and Test 6 [i.e., last mean IQ of K_1]." By the first of these standards K_1 is four-tenths of a grade equivalent above expectation, and the other two groups are less than two-tenths above. By the second standard K_1 is up to par (GE 3.80), but the other two groups are more than two-tenths of a GE below expectancy. It appears that K_1 is appreciably more successful than the other two groups. (One notes in Figure 4 that the mean IQ of the K_1 children was initially and finally the highest of the three groups by about three points.) Though one might not have strong faith in the GE standards used, they represent the only seemingly pertinent norms available.

One can of course argue, as Karnes and other do, that early intervention probably prevents a cumulative deficit—that even keeping the children achieving up to initial IQ is a victory for such programs. That hopeful stance needs substantiation. See, for example, Coleman et al. (1966), Bereiter (1972), Weikart (1972), and Gray and Klaus (1970) for evidence pro and con.

Karnes's paper contains much material other than these group comparisons. Her observations are based on a vast amount of maturely analyzed experience. They merit close study.

SHIPMAN

Shipman provides an extensive introduction to the Head Start Longitudinal Study being conducted by the Educational Testing Service. She gives background data on the 1875, 3½- to 4½-year-old children, 63 percent of whom are black and 53 percent male. They are at four sites: Lee County, Alabama; Portland, Oregon; St. Louis, Missouri; and Trenton, New Jersey. She also describes the measuring instruments used initially and factor analyses of the scores. Her discussion of problems in conducting such a study under field conditions will be helpful to many researchers.

Also, Shipman has developed a substantial theoretical framework to guide the choice of instruments and procedures. Some readers may consider that it gives too much weight to environmental aspects and too little to abilities influenced by genetics and early development. She does rationalize her emphasis however: "Previous research (e.g., Hess et al. 1968) suggests that it is the process variables which have the greater impact on a child's life; and they certainly have greater theoretical utility than demographic indices for explaining how the environment mediates experience in critical ways. A corollary assumption is that the mother is particularly influential in transmitting to the young child behaviors and adaptations shaped by the environment."

No mention of IQ itself appears in her chapter, and indeed, for reasons outlined elsewhere (her ETS 1968), no measure yielding an IQ score is included in the study. She does, however, allude to basic ability in her discussion of the factor analysis results: "The less clearly defined general ability dimension which was found for the younger, less 'academically' prepared, economically poorer children in the sample may reflect both greater susceptibility to situational determinants and less generalizable information-processing skills. . . . These data . . . suggest that the least able children don't yet have 'g' well enough developed so they can integrate their behavior." But after this brief moment at the periphery of the "nature" area, Shipman reaffirms her "nurture" stance, as the reader may verify on page 188.

She is not the only researcher in this book, or its predecessor, who strongly favors environmental interpretations of mental-test data. Anyone perusing the Index of Names in the two volumes would not suspect that for many years a battle has been raging about hereditability of intellectual ability. Interestingly, Shipman uses the "g" (general intelligence) terminology of one of the early hereditarians, Charles Spearman, without accepting most of its denotations.

Nevertheless, Shipman has produced a report likely to be highly influential on practice and theory. It constitutes an excellent base for the later findings of this important continuing study.

PERSONAL OPINIONS

We do know from the careful research of Carl Bereiter (1972), Gray and Klaus (1970), Merle Karnes (this volume), Oralie McAfee (1972), David Weikart (1972), and others that great expenditures of time and effort have not yet succeeded in permanently elevating IQ's of disadvantaged children much.[2] Large gains the first year are common, but tend not to persist through the primary grades. As noted earlier in my discussion of Karnes's paper, even the modest net gains from age four or so to age nine may be due largely to enhanced rapport, practice effects, and statistical regression. Also, as Bayley (1955) and others have pointed out, IQ's secured for children in the age range from two to four years are developmental quotients only moderately related to later mental ability.

Of course, more effective methods to maintain the gains *may* be developed, but one has to face the possibility that many low-IQ "disadvantaged" children of whatever race will not benefit *enough* from early direct efforts to improve their weakest cognitive abilities. These may be premature. Instead, it may be more effective to capitalize on their intellectual and affective strengths and wait for further development of other underlying abilities.

In my opinion, the educational systems of this country need to be reorganized from the beginning through high school graduation by abolishing school grades (nursery school, kindergarten, first grade, . . . , twelfth grade) and establishing *longitudinal* teaching teams spanning all the various areas from birth—or even earlier!—onward: e.g., language arts, mathematics, science, social studies, the fine arts, physical education, and career education. Then, for example, those children who are not ready for formal reading instruction in the present first grade could be given appropriate experiences until they are ready to begin learning to read, which might not be until age eight or later. From that age onward they could be taught more slowly than the average child until, by the end of what is now high school, they are able to read fairly well. Gone would be "remedial reading" for the considerable number of children who did not profit from the usual reading instruction in grades one to three. (Anderson, on page 205, also calls for fundamental reorganization of schools.)

Perhaps these suggestions will be viewed as heresy by most persons who do research in compensatory education, because nearly all of them are committed to ability-improving approaches, i.e., intervening intensively early rather than fundamentally restructuring the school system itself so that progressing slowly, but in accordance with one's cognitive developmental rates, will not be stigmatizing. It seems to me quite doubtful that most children whose cognitive abilities at age four or five are truly low will learn to read with average or better comprehension by the end of the third grade under any regime now known. This is not to say that far better methods may not be discovered, but to me it seems likely that they will be chemical or nutritional rather than instructional and psychological. Even though heredity may put certain strong restraints on cognitive development, we can probably ex-

[2]Work with even younger children by Rick Heber in Milwaukee has received much favorable publicity, but the outcomes are as yet tentative and controversial. See Page (1972).

pect some major breakthroughs; just what they will be is not yet clear. Intensive work with parents *may* prove to be one of these.

Meanwhile, it would seem highly desirable to restructure the schools to suit the students at all cognitive levels. The present age-grade organization is woefully outmoded. Along with the nongraded longitudinal teaching team structure would come, for the least able students, strong emphasis on "academic *over*achievement." Not only must such students be given careful, detailed attention by teaching teams but also they must be encouraged to make special efforts to learn well. By developing in such children interest, motivation, diligence, conscientiousness, and willingness to work hard and long, the teams can give them a much-needed advantage over somewhat abler youngsters. This obvious way to help academically handicapped children does not seem to have received much attention. Great efforts have been made to improve the academic performance of the so-called "underachiever," usually without much success. It remains to be seen how effectively low-ability children can be made into overachievers.

Another part of their education would be preparation to become parents who foster educational development in their own children. Recently reported good results (e.g., Karnes in this volume) with older children tutoring younger ones suggest that over a considerable period of time educationally disadvantaged boys and girls should be shown how to help young children, in school and at home; while so doing they would be helped systematically to become excellent facilitators of their own children's educational achievement subsequently. As they themselves become well motivated, hard working, and effective in school they should be learning in detail how to pass these academic virtues along to their offspring. (I make no apology to those educational critics who consider such behavior in school deadly sin rather than virtue. My concern here is with slow-learning children in a radically restructured school setting, and for most of them diligence is essential if they are to learn enough to succeed in later life.)

By the above proposal I do not mean to imply that compensatory education studies conducted by well-trained persons should be abandoned. I am, however, pessimistic about their long-term ameliorative possibilities in the present school context. It would seem wise to conduct pilot studies designed to fit the schools far better to children, including the academically disadvantaged.[3] Surely, one learns from reading this volume and its predecessor that

---

[3]Actually, the radical school reorganization proposed earlier in this paper would probably benefit intellectually gifted children as much as it would help academically disadvantaged ones, because the former are usually grossly retarded in their educational advancement within present age-in-grade lockstep schools. Many of the ablest children already know the work of a grade before they enter it, or at least can learn it almost instantaneously. Boredom, frustration, and undesirable intellectual habits often result (see Keating and Stanley 1972; and Stanley, Keating, and Fox [in press]).

there are severe limits to the effectiveness of current preschool intervention efforts. Also, its cost is probably far higher per child than more effective teaching in the greatly restructured school system should be.

REFERENCES

Bayley, N. 1955. On the growth of intelligence. *American Psychologist* 10: 805-18.

Bereiter, C. 1972. An academic preschool for disadvantaged children: Conclusions from evaluation studies. Ch. I (pp. 1-21), in J. C. Stanley (ed.), *Preschool programs for the disadvantaged*. Baltimore: The Johns Hopkins University Press.

Bracht, G. H., and Glass, G. V. 1968. The external validity of experiments. *American Educational Research Journal* 5: 437-74.

Campbell, D. T., and Stanley, J. C. 1966. *Experimental and quasi-experimental designs for research*. Chicago: Rand McNally.

Coleman, J. S., Campbell, E. Q., Hobson, C. J., McPartland, J., Mood, A. M., Weinfeld, F. D., and York, R. L. 1966. *Equality of educational opportunity*. Washington D.C.: U.S. Government Printing Office, OE-38001.

Gray, S. W., and Klaus, R. A. 1970. The early training project: A seventh year report. *Child Development* 41: 909-24.

Hess, R. D., Shipman, F. C., Brophy, J. E., and Bear, R. M. 1968. *The cognitive environment of urban preschool children*. Chicago: University of Chicago.

Keating, D. P., and Stanley, J. C. 1972. Extreme measures for the exceptionally gifted in mathematics and science. *Educational Researcher* 1 (9): 3-7.

Lewis, M. In press. Infant intelligence tests: Their use and misuse. *Human Development*.

McAfee, O. 1972. An integrated approach to early childhood education. Ch. III (pp. 67-91), in J. C. Stanley (ed.), *Preschool programs for the disadvantaged*. Baltimore: The Johns Hopkins University Press.

McGraw, M. B. 1935. *Growth: A study of Johnny and Jimmy*. New York: Appleton-Century.

McGraw, M. B. 1939. Later development of children specially trained during infancy: Jimmy and Johnny at school age. *Child Development* 10(1): 1-19.

Page, E. P. 1972. Miracle in Milwaukee: Raising the IQ. *Phi Delta Kappan* 1(10): 8-10, 15-16.

Stanley, J. C. (ed.). 1972. *Preschool programs for the disadvantaged*. Baltimore: The Johns Hopkins University Press.

Stanley, J. C., Keating, D. P., and Fox, L. H. In press. *Mathematical talent: Discovery, description, and development*. Baltimore: The Johns Hopkins University Press.

Weikart, D. P. 1972. Relationship of curriculum, teaching, and learning in preschool education. Ch. II (pp. 22-66), in J. C. Stanley (ed.), *Preschool programs for the disadvantaged*. Baltimore: The Johns Hopkins University Press.

SAMUEL BALL and GERRY ANN BOGATZ

Educational Testing Service

Princeton, New Jersey 08540

II. RESEARCH ON *SESAME STREET:* SOME IMPLICATIONS FOR COMPENSATORY EDUCATION

It was probably a weak moment when the first-named author unilaterally sent off the title of this paper some months before the paper itself had to be written. At least there was a prolonged pause when we both later set about writing and the second author asked: "And what did you mean by compensatory education?" Well, we did reach consensus, at least as the term relates to preschoolers, but it took awhile.

The first reaction to the question was: "What a silly question. Compensatory means making amends or making up for a loss, so compensatory education is the education you give disadvantaged children. More or less, that is."

Then came the reaction to the reaction. "What about *Sesame Street*? It was telecast throughout the country—not specifically to the disadvantaged. And what if both middle class and lower class children learn a great deal from the program? Does this mean that the program is not compensatory? Does it mean that it is compensatory only if we can somehow persuade middle class children *not* to watch it? Or, does this mean that the middle class too had lacked something that they could be compensated for?" The first-named author did not respond this time. Sometimes it is wiser to cut your losses.

Names and titles are important, as any member of a peer group will tell you. But you do not have to be introduced in order to start a conversation. So without indicating yet what we decided we meant by the term compensatory education, let us present our paper—and then think again about the meaning of the word "compensatory." First, the background to the paper, and this is provided by a brief description of our work over the past few years.

We began our work as independent evaluators of *Sesame Street* in the summer of 1968. At that time the goals for the first year of *Sesame Street* were established. The meetings brought together television writers and producers, authors of children's books, librarians, Madison Avenue executives, educational researchers, child psychologists and psychiatrists, movie moguls, and even teachers of preschool children. These meetings themselves provided compensatory education with the educators learning about the world of research and of television, the academic researchers learning about the world of television and about how young children behave, and the television specialists learning about the wonderful worlds of education and research.

Some goals were selected following those meetings; they were couched in behavioral terms and grouped in four sections:

1. Symbolic Representation (letters, numbers, geometric forms).
2. Cognitive Processes (perceptual discrimination, relational concepts, classification, sorting).
3. The Natural and Physical Environment (animals, machines).
4. The Social Environment (social skills such as cooperation and sharing, community members).

Some of these goals were established as those to be emphasized and were given greater time on the show. They were mainly in the cognitive area of symbolic representation and cognitive processes, and almost all of them were assessed in the first-year evaluation.

Two major principles guided us in the evaluation. First, we felt it important to look for unintended as well as intended outcomes. That is, the goals of the show were important, and we certainly hoped to assess the effects of viewing the show in relation to those goals. But that was not enough. The medical model of evaluation tells us that concentrating on achieving intended outcomes and ignoring side-effects can lead to some horribly wrong overall evaluations—for example, in the original testing of thalidomide (Scriven 1967). So in addition to looking for intended changes in children such as the learning of the alphabet, we also looked for changes in the children's TV viewing habits and in the parents' attitudes toward school.

A second major principle we considered was that interactions might tell us more in an evaluation than main effects. That is, in a worthwhile evaluation we must discover not only if the educational intervention, in general, works (an important question, of course) but also for which children it works best, for which children it does not seem to work, and the conditions under which it operates most efficiently. Too often evaluations have concluded that a new program is of little consequence, when in fact it is a boon to some children and a ruin to others, but when averaged over all children, its effectiveness seems little different from that of the old program.

The application of these two principles in the summative research for Sesame Street caused us to assess at pretest and posttest times not only progress toward some thirty-six primary goals of the show but also transfer effects, home background variables, parental attitudes, and socioeconomic factors. We decided to sample children from middle class suburbia, lower class northern and western urban ghettos, and lower class sections of a southern town; rural children; Spanish-speaking children; children at home and children in Head Start and nursery schools; boys and girls; black children and white children; and three-, four-, and five-year-old children. You will, of course, notice that these categories are not necessarily mutually exclusive.

Initially we tested over 1,300 children in five sites across the country. Then we observed many of them viewing the show, made a content analysis of the show itself, administered a questionnaire to teachers whose classes viewed the show, and assessed the amount of viewing for all the subjects in the study, using four different assessment techniques. When evaluating a program in which side-effects and interactions are considered important, the study has to be wide-ranging, the sampling extensive, and the statistics multivariate (Freeman 1963).

Nonetheless, despite the decision to spread our attention to different groups of preschool children, we also noted that *Sesame Street was primarily intended for disadvantaged children, at home, without benefit of Head Start or similar formal educational experience.* Therefore, our major concentration in the sampling was on this particular subpopulation.

Our experimental design in the evaluation of the first year of *Sesame Street* was much better in prospect than in retrospect. We randomly assigned children to either an encouraged-to-view group or a not-encouraged-to-view group in each of the five field sites. Unfortunately, we had expected, on good evidence, that few children would view unless specifically encouraged to do so. In fact, however, most children viewed the show at least some of the time, irrespective of our assignment to experimental or control conditions. Thus, we were forced to analyze our data in a number of different ways from those originally planned. We think that the analyses we carried out provided convincing evidence to allow us to draw a number of specific and more general conclusions indicating the merit of the show for all groups of children studied. Our report on the first year is available (Ball & Bogatz 1970) and an extensive review of the report is being published under a grant from the Russell Sage Foundation (Cook 1972).

We also carried out a major evaluation of the second year of *Sesame Street*, including a follow-up study of those subjects who were disadvantaged and at home (not in school) during the first year of the show (Bogatz & Ball 1971).

The second year of *Sesame Street* saw an expansion of the show's goals to achieve somewhat wider curriculum coverage and to include more difficult topics in goal areas already established in the first year. For example, classification on the basis of a single criterion was a goal in both years, but in the second year double classification was also included. Similarly, counting from one to ten was extended to from one to twenty, and simple addition and subtraction became goals for the first time in the second year. The replication element in the second year study took us to two new sites where we sampled only at-home disadvantaged children who had not viewed the show in its first year. We were interested in seeing if effects noted in the first year were also seen in the second year, and whether the new and extended goals were achieved. In one site, the only means of obtaining access to the show was through cable, and we assigned cable to only half our subjects. The other site had an ultra high frequency (UHF) television channel that attracted few viewers from ghetto areas unless a special effort was made to encourage viewing a specific show. The result was that in the second-year study the encouraged-to-view (experimental) subjects did view, and a major proportion of the not-encouraged-to-view (control) subjects did not view. Our subsequent analyses of the second-year data were easier to interpret than those of the first-year data. They supported the general finding that the show benefited the viewer over a range of goals; we also found, however, that the new, extended goals were not well learned in comparison to the more basic goals carried over from the first year.

Another aspect of the second-year study was the follow-up of at-home disadvantaged children from the first year. About half of them went on to school in the second year, while the others did not. We tested both these groups of children in October 1970 and May 1971, coinciding with the beginning and ending of the second year of the *Sesame Street* series. We also obtained from the teachers of those who went on to school a ranking of our subjects in relation to the other children in the class on seven criteria. We found that a second year of viewing had positive effects over just one year of viewing, but mainly in the areas of the new, extended goals. Thus, the producers of the show have the dilemma of deciding whether to concentrate on simple and basic goals to the benefit of the younger children viewing for the first time or to put effort into extended goals, thereby benefiting somewhat older children viewing for a second year.

So far we have not been particularly specific about our measures, our field operations, or our results and conclusions. The purpose has been mainly to sketch a general outline upon which to base our implications for compensatory education. As we present the implications, the sketched outline of the evaluation will doubtless be given greater detail, and if the reader becomes really interested there is always recourse to the two reports (Ball & Bogatz 1970; Bogatz & Ball 1971).

We again have to confront the problem of what compensatory education is. One way of looking at it, and the one that we suspect most of us fuzzily use, is to regard compensatory education as education specifically provided for disadvantaged children. Examples would be the Head Start program or Title I programs of the Elementary and Secondary School Education Act. Then, we might legitimately ask: What does our *Sesame Street* research tell us that has implications for such education? Given this approach, there are some major implications.

MEASURES

Perhaps because we were conducting an evaluation pointed toward assessing a number of specific goals, we were interested in using measures that would provide a clear picture of status with respect to a specific goal. At least among the arsenal of tests available for use with young children, we found the situation appalling. Take, for example, items such as: "Put the green marbles in the square box." If the child gets it wrong, is it because he does not know the meaning of "green," "marbles," "square," or "box"? Or, what if the child is given a stimulus triangle and asked if she can find another one just like it embedded in a larger drawing? The child is asked to trace around it. If she cannot perform the task correctly, does this mean that she did not find it, that she has poor motor coordination, or that she does not want to play games with the tester? In one well-known standardized test for five-year-olds, we found that the percentage passing national norms for a particular counting item were lower than we had obtained at pretest with four-year-old disadvantaged children. Then we looked at the administration manual, where we found the instruction for the children was: "We are now going to play a number game. Look at the pictures of the fish bowls at the top of the page. Let's pretend that there are five tables in your class and each table has a fish bowl on it. See the large letters above the fish bowls. These letters are A, B, C, D, and E. Listen carefully. In which bowl do you see just three fish?" What happens to a child who does not understand words like "pretend" and who has never seen a fish bowl?

The point that we are trying to make is this. If we are to develop and improve compensatory education we must have measures that will allow us to learn with reasonable clarity what we are accomplishing. Frankly, our experience as we developed the test battery for *Sesame Street*, and again as we developed our tests for *The Electric Company* (The Electric Battery), was that many tests of young children currently in use are defective: they are unnecessarily difficult to administer; often they lack face, content, and construct validity; and, peculiarly, they seem to assume that if they are individually administered tests they had better involve the tester in making loose subjective and clinical judgments about the child's performance. It does not surprise us, therefore, that our understanding of compensatory education remains at a low level. Science can hardly be expected to flourish without adequate measuring instruments.

RACE

At a time when genetics, race, and education were becoming mixed into a rather emotional stew, we had the interesting experience of meeting poverty groups in order to obtain their cooperation in our evaluation of *Sesame Street*. More than once we were pointedly asked by black community leaders whether we were simply again trying to prove that their children were dumb; and more than once we argued that it was *Sesame Street* we were trying to evaluate and not their children. The fact is that we did collect a lot of data on disadvantaged children, both black and white. It was our intention not to make black versus white comparisons and indeed we kept our resolution during the preparation of our first report. We analyzed the data from our disadvantaged sample in terms of amount of viewing and eschewed the additional, possibly independent, factor of race. Our major reasons were that we had already indicated to those community groups who had cooperated with us that this was the kind of analysis that would take place, and that we were not certain at all that the black disadvantaged in our study were comparable to the white disadvantaged. Thus, we sought to avoid the problem of unfair and invidious comparisons.

After the publication of our first-year study we did look at our data to see if disadvantaged black viewers gained more compared to disadvantaged black nonviewers, and if disadvantaged white viewers gained more compared to disadvantaged white nonviewers. As we surveyed these groupings of the data we were struck by the similarity of the scores of the disadvantaged black children and the disadvantaged white children within each site at pretest, and we were also struck by the similarity of gains made in relation to their degree of viewing. Subsequent multivariate analyses of variance confirmed our impression that among the disadvantaged in our study there were no significant effects due to race.

A curious exception deserves some reflection. Most of our tests were specially developed to assess status and growth on the goals being sought on the show. Here the pretest and gain scores of black and white children were quite similar. However, in the first-year evaluation we also used, at pretest only, a standardized test, the Peabody Picture Vocabulary Test (PPVT), in order better to describe our subjects and as a covariate in covariance analyses of gains. To our surprise, there were systematic differences between black and white disadvantaged children on this test to the degree of about half a standard deviation. In IQ terms there was about a ten-point difference favoring the whites. Note that, of the pictures in the test, only two are of blacks (a spear carrier and a porter). Look too at the specific vocabulary called for. Of course, it could be that our black sample study had a poorer vocabulary than our white sample, but it could also be a function of the test used; this seems a perfectly reasonable assumption, since scores on the other tests did not differ in this way.

In general then, black and white disadvantaged preschool children from within the same testing sites seemed to be quite comparable at pretest and gained similarly, given similar amounts of viewing over the six months of the show. The exception was their present status on the PPVT, and we consider this to be probably a function of the test rather than an indication of lower vocabulary levels by the black children. Thus, apparently serious proposals to use different forms of education for disadvantaged black children than for disadvantaged white children have no substantiation from our *Sesame Street* data. Rather, race was shown to be an unimportant factor in determining the degree to which a child could learn from the show.*

NONTRADITIONAL EDUCATION

The traditional form of education used with preschool children has been to provide small group settings with one or two adults to usually no more than fifteen or so children. Play and fun have often been advocated as an important if not essential element in the process; we can look back to the writings and work of Pestalozzi, Froebel, and perhaps even Plato to show that these ideas are not exactly new. Similarly, experts in early education have usually stressed the need for a close relationship between adult and child for optimal learning to occur.

Sesame Street had objectives that were much more limited than a good nursery school or Head Start program. Nonetheless, the objectives and some of the gains were by no means trivial. We remember the air of somber, sober, and scientific pessimism that pervaded its advisory boards before the show began telecasting for the first time. How could an hour a day on television have much effect? If a teacher in a school all day with her class accounts for so little of the variance of scores among classes (Wolf 1965), how would an object with a mean diagonal measurement of twenty-one inches do better and without personal contact? We were also told that preschoolers have very short attention spans and that disadvantaged preschoolers have even shorter ones.

The facts are that the show was seen to have a marked effect, not only in areas of rote learning of basic skills, such as counting, and in simple contiguity association learning, such as learning the names of letters and numbers, but also in higher areas of cognitive activity, such as sorting and classifying pictorial representations and, as far as we could tell, in attitudinal areas such as attitude toward the race of others. Furthermore, these effects were obtained with boys as well as with girls, yet many studies suggest that boys are the ones who present the majority of the learning problems.

Thus, the implication seems clear that we should put greater effort into nontraditional means of educating young disadvantaged children, not to supplant but to supplement older ways. It also seems clear that the cherished ideas of some educators about what is essential in early education in order for children to learn might not stand close scrutiny. For example, while close emotional ties might be important for learning in the emotional and interpersonal areas, they might not be so important for learning in the cognitive areas.

*Some readers will want to compare these findings with those of Bereiter, Weikart, and McAfee in Stanley (1972). [Ed.]

DELIVERY PROBLEMS

There is a couplet in a song with the words, "Ain't We Got Fun?" which has the interesting social comment that the rich get rich and the poor get children. An analogous problem is that educationally rich middle class parents tend to make use of the educational opportunities that are available for their children, whereas the educationally impoverished lower class tends not to do so. Thus, when *Sesame Street* appeared on the television screen and the educational scene, it quickly acquired a large audience. It was disproportionately larger, though, for the middle class than for the lower class. Furthermore, within the disadvantaged group, it was the most disadvantaged who viewed least. Educators with a sense of social justice similarly note that the ghetto children they would most like to reach are the ones hardest to reach.

In our evaluation of the second year of *Sesame Street*, we assigned children to encouraged-to-view and not-encouraged-to-view conditions. We assessed the amount of viewing for all children, because it was impossible to ensure that all encouraged children would view all the shows, just as it was impossible to ensure that all not-encouraged children would view none of the shows. In fact, the distribution of subjects looked like this:

	Non-viewers	Moderate viewers	Frequent viewers	Total
Encouraged	9	43	78	130
Not-encouraged	99	46	8	153

We were interested in extracting the encouragement effect from the viewing effect, since both effects were somewhat confounded, and since both effects seemed to be positive. We carried out a univariate analysis of covariance on the grand total gain score and obtained the following results: The regression of viewing on total gain was similar for the encouraged and not-encouraged groups. That is, amount of viewing affected both groups similarly.

This regression was significantly different from zero, indicating that amount of viewing was positively associated with gains. There was a definite encouragement effect, irrespective of the amount of viewing.

From other analyses we could conclude that the disadvantaged gained as much as the more advantaged, if they viewed as much. However, the tendency was for them not to view as much. The important question was: What would happen if disadvantaged children were to view the show as much as the advantaged, because of some conscious effort to get them to do so? The answer seems to be that such encouraged viewers will do at least as well as children who view entirely of their own volition. Furthermore, the act of encouragement itself may have beneficial effects. For example, the child's mother is more likely to view with the child and then talk about the show with the child if encouragement to view occurs.

The implication we draw from this is, we hope, now clear. While it is true that the more disadvantaged tend to avail themselves less of educational opportunities, it also seems to be true that a conscious program of encouragement is worthwhile. We should spend money on providing compensatory educational programs; we should also spend money on delivery systems to ensure that those who need these programs receive them.

IQ

We have already discussed the peculiar results obtained with the PPVT in our first-year evaluation (i.e., black disadvantaged children performed less well than white disadvantaged children on this test). In other respects, however, the test proved useful in that it enabled us to describe our sampled children and compare them to those in other studies, and it enabled us to examine, if imprecisely, the moderating effects of vocabulary size on learning.

Soon after the close of the first-year series, a number of unsolicited letters arrived at our office from school teachers and school psychologists in which the thought was expressed that the new groups of children reaching their schools were "brighter" than in the past and that almost invariably the mothers were mentioning *Sesame Street* as the causal agent.

We also realize that the PPVT, despite the fact that it provides IQ conversions, is basically an oral receptive vocabulary test. However, vocabulary is traditionally seen as one slice (though a thin one) of the pie we call intelligence. Therefore, with, I hope, uncharacteristic foolishness we gave the PPVT as a posttest as well as a pretest in the second-year evaluation, both to the follow-up subjects and the new replication subjects. In almost all of our analyses of the second-year data a clear trend emerged. Viewing of *Sesame Street* affected scores on the PPVT, and, therefore, if one had the faith to make the conversion, affected IQ scores. Since teachers commonly misinterpret IQ scores, then children with higher IQ scores on their permanent records might conceivably be treated differently from children with lower scores.

This finding, that *Sesame Street* affects IQ scores as determined by one particular test, is not so different from other studies (though the medium of television has never before been accused of raising the intelligence of the viewer). Compensatory programs can have positive general cognitive effects, just as failure to provide educational programs can have negative ones.

AGE

The final implication we wish to draw, using this model of compensatory education as it applies to preschoolers, deals with age. In our *Sesame Street*

Figure 1.
Pretest and Posttest Scores of 3-, 4-,
and 5-Year-Old Disadvantaged Children

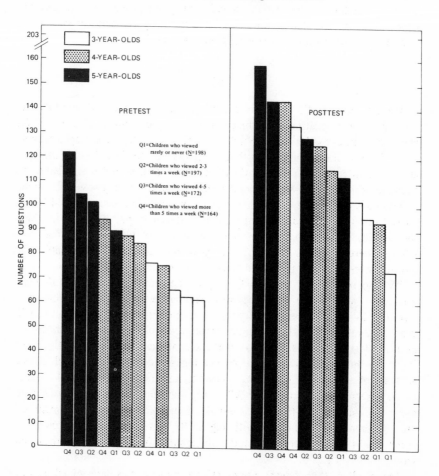

evaluations we studied three-, four-, and five-year-old disadvantaged children. We subdivided each age group by amount of viewing. The results from the *Sesame Street* test battery at pretest and again at posttest are presented graphically in Figure 1. Before *Sesame Street* went on the air, older children almost invariably performed higher on the test than younger children. After *Sesame Street*, however, three-year-olds who watched most (Q4) scored higher at posttest than three of the four-year-old groups and two of the five-year-old groups, although these three-year-olds had pretest scores lower than all five-year-olds and all but one of the four-year-old groups. In other words, the placement of the children along the scale measuring the goals of *Sesame*

Street was very dependent on age at pretest, while at posttest it was much more related to amount of viewing.

If the viewing of *Sesame Street* were not effective and the gains noted in the first-year study among the four viewing groups were primarily a matter of differential growth rates noted at pretest, then the juxtapositions of age groupings at posttest would be difficult indeed to explain.

The implication here is that disadvantaged three-year-olds were quite capable of learning much of the material and many of the skills taught on the first year of *Sesame Street*. Perhaps in compensatory education we aim too low at too high an age level. More positively, perhaps we should think of beginning with younger than four-year-old children, and perhaps we should raise our expectations of what these very young children can learn.

* * * *

An effort has been made in the preceding pages to draw implications for compensatory education, where compensatory education has been defined in terms of disadvantaged children. We did include in our first-year evaluation a group of advantaged middle class children from suburban Philadelphia. We had purposefully chosen a site where we were not studying disadvantaged children, because we were not initially interested in comparing these two groups. Rather, we were making internal comparisons (viewing versus non-viewing) within each group.

However, we were rather surprised by our results. Figure 2 presents pretest and posttest scores of advantaged and disadvantaged children. The frequent-viewing, disadvantaged children not only outgained but surpassed the infrequent-viewing, middle class children. This was the point that interested us, and it was also the point that drew criticism upon us. In one sense the gap between middle and lower class children was being diminished from pretest to posttest; but it should also be noted that the middle class children tend to gravitate to the frequent-viewing groups, whereas disadvantaged children tend toward the less-frequent-viewing groups. Some kind of weighting, therefore might lead us to a different conclusion. We reject, however, the analysis of our data (Sprigle 1971, repeated by Ingersoll 1971), in which nonviewers were included in the comparison in order to show middle class children widening their distance from lower class children. Predictably, lower class nonviewers are going to learn less than middle class nonviewers. Would we argue that Head Start is ineffective because lower class children who do *not* attend are increasingly disadvantaged in comparison with middle class children?

The major point here, however, is not the one we have been presenting. What is worth noting is that the effects of the show can be clearly discerned on middle class, advantaged children too. Note that this group included chil-

Figure 2.
Pretest and Posttest Scores of Disadvantaged
and Advantaged 4-Year-Old Children

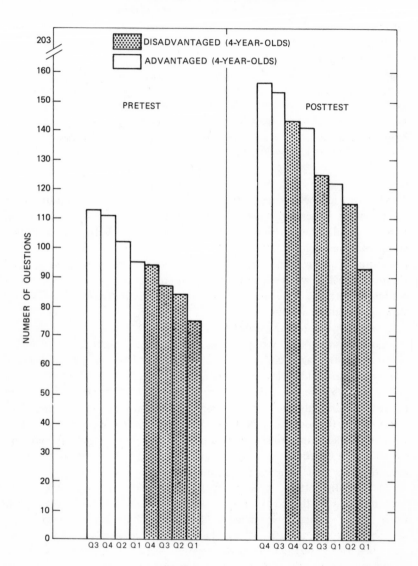

dren attending nursery school. This suggests to us that while for good,
socially responsible reasons we spend much of our time concerning ourselves
at the preschool level with disadvantaged children, we might legitimately be

concerning ourselves with middle class children too. Perhaps even with these children their educational input is by no means optimal.*

If compensatory education is related to what are Webster's Dictionary second and fourth definitions ("to make proper payment to" or "to offset an error, defect, or undesired effect"), then we may well decide that many children need compensatory education, including a large proportion we fail to recognize when we conventionally think of the term "compensatory."

We began by asking: What is compensatory education? We begged the question first by briefly describing the evaluations of *Sesame Street* that we have carried out; then we took one possible definition of compensatory education as extra education for disadvantaged children and drew six implications, assuming the validity of the definition; finally, we took an alternative definition, which suggests that almost all children need compensatory education in some areas, and pointed out the implication for preschool education if this were true. Actually, however, like most semantic arguments, it does not matter which definition we take. Preschool education needs better programs, a greater variety of programs (including nontraditional ones), better delivery systems so that the vast majority of children receive their benefit as opposed to the current minority who do, and better methods of assessing the value of the programs. That may seem to be a rather somber note on which to end this first paper in the series being presented here; but it also carries the message that improvements in all these areas can be effected, for our *Sesame Street* evaluations tell us so. We know, too, that the subsequent papers in this volume will provide heartening examples of progress in early childhood compensatory education—and this means a potential benefit in the education of all young children.

REFERENCES

Ball, S., and Bogatz, G. A. 1970. *The first year of Sesame Street: An evaluation*. Princeton, N.J.: Educational Testing Service.

Bogatz, G. A., and Ball, S. 1971. *The second year of Sesame Street: A continuing evaluation*. Princeton, N.J.: Educational Testing Service.

Cook, T. 1972. Untitled manuscript. A report to be presented on the Educational Testing Service evaluations of *Sesame Street*. New York: Russell Sage Foundation.

*One must consider, however, that most advantaged children will probably in time master the basic skills without special help, whereas a considerable number of the disadvantaged might not. Whether or not precocity resulting from *Sesame Street* permanently benefits middle class children seems to be, as yet, an open question. [Ed.]

Freeman, H. E. 1963. Strategy of social policy research. In H. E. Freeman (ed.), *Social welfare forum*. New York: Columbia University Press.

Ingersoll, G. November 1971. *Sesame Street* can't handle all the traffic. *Phi Delta Kappan* 53(3): 185-87.

Scriven, M. 1967. The methodology of evaluation. In R. E. Stake (ed.), *Perspectives of curriculum evaluation. AERA Monograph Series on Curriculum Evaluation*, No. 1, pp. 39-83.

Sprigle, H. A. March 1971. Can poverty children live on *Sesame Street? Young Children* 26(4): 202-17.

Stanley, J. C. (ed.). 1972. *Preschool programs for the disadvantaged*. Baltimore: The Johns Hopkins University Press.

Wolf, R. M. 1965. The measurement of environments. In *Proceedings of the 1964 Invitational Conference on Testing Problems*. Princeton, N.J.: Educational Testing Service, pp. 93-106. Reprinted in W. H. MacGinitie and S. Ball (eds.), *Readings in psychological foundations of education*. New York: McGraw-Hill, 1968, pp. 186-97.

IRVING E. SIGEL, ADA SECRIST, and GEORGE FORMAN
State University of New York at Buffalo
Buffalo, New York 14214

III. PSYCHO-EDUCATIONAL INTERVENTION BEGINNING AT AGE TWO: REFLECTIONS AND OUTCOMES[1]

Since the advent of Head Start the renewed activity of programming for preschool children and the evaluation of the effects of such programming have reopened Pandora's fabled box. We have learned that the issues in programming and in evaluation are complex, taxing our theoretical and methodological ingenuity and forcing us to reexamine our research and teaching strategies. The state of affairs at this juncture is not only the product of ignorance or naiveté on the part of the investigators, but is equally a result of failures in finding expected outcomes. Beller (in press) has pointed out that this is a good time for reassessment. Reexamination should allow us to profit from past mistakes and, more importantly, may yield clues concerning underlying mechanisms that could explain the variety of results and give shape and continuity to past and future work.

We present this paper with those hopes in mind. Our purpose is to present one model of preschool programming, the Early Childhood Education Project (ECEP), with a brief evaluation of the first year's work. Perhaps more important than our results at this point is a description of the problems we encountered and the successful and unsuccessful solutions we found to them.

The Early Childhood Education Project is an experiment in educational intervention begun with two-year-old, first-born children from impoverished black families in the inner city of Buffalo. This simple statement immediately raises some basic questions. What is intervention? Why intervene? Why work with two-year-old black children?

The frequently used concept of *intervention* rivals *compensatory education* in ambiguity and emotionality. It is difficult to find a broader concept. After all, intervention is what *all* education is about. When illiterate, egocen-

[1]The research reported herein is supported by the Office of Economic Oportunity, Grant #CG8547. Dr. Sigel is the Project Director, Dr. Secrist is the Research Coordinator, and Dr. Forman is the Curriculum Coordinator.

tric, middle class five-year-olds become literate and able to communicate and take the perspective of others, one can argue for the efficacy of the school's intervention. Intervention if so broadly conceptualized leads to heated arguments concerning its true meaning, e.g., good vs. poor school systems. Nevertheless, the right of the school system to exist and to intervene is taken for granted.

Intervention must be defined more carefully, especially for research purposes. For us intervention is considered as a conscious and purposeful set of actions intended to change or influence the anticipated course of development. The ECEP program operationalized a "conscious and purposeful set of actions," by specifically stating the intended change in the course of development. To deliberately set out to change someone immediately engages several crucial moral and value questions. Who has the right to change anyone? What or who gives him that right?

It seems to us that intervention programs operate with some of the assumptions of the medical model. Someone who is sick generally elects to go to a physician, because the disease is not expected to subside without his intervention or treatment. Elimination of the disease is considered desirable and essential for healthy future development. While there may be several factors contributing to the disease, e.g., a specific infection, particular work and housing conditions, or the quality of a personal relationship within the family, the physician will generally concentrate on the factor he feels will do most to eradicate the illness. Usually his judgment is not questioned, or if it is another physician is sought. His right to treat the patient is certainly not at issue.

Educational intervention programs directed at altering the expected course of development are also treatment programs, prescribed for particular classes of people. In recent years, the target populations are minority groups at the poverty level. Using the past as a guide, individuals from these minority groups contributed heavily to the drop-out, unemployed, and welfare rolls. The prescription for alleviation of such dysfunctional social behavior is assumed to be education, but a particular kind of education at a particular time in the child's life. Preschool education is the treatment of choice, with only vague notions as to what kind of program will solve the problem. Other treatment programs are possible, e.g., change the economic system, emphasize change in living practices, or attack the insidious racism that infects our social fabric. These treatments, while no doubt relevant, do not engender the same support as preschool education. Thus, our society has made its choice manifest by assigning relatively large sums to the creation of preschool "treatment" (intervention) centers.

So far the medical and the educational intervention models seem to share many common features. There are, however, some important differences between the two. Whereas the patient has some choice in selecting his physician, that type of choice is less prevalent in intervention programs. Where the physician tends to treat particular illness, the intervention programs have a broader target—the quality of health, education, and family relationships. More important than the target is the objective of the action: in medicine the object is to enable the patient to regain his previous state of health, whereas intervention programs deny the validity of the previous status of individuals similar to the children in question. In effect, the child in an intervention program should emerge different from his parents or previous generations of individuals in his social milieu. Thus, we come head-on to a variety of issues. For what kind of a society are we preparing the children? To what extent are we contributing to cultural alienation? To what extent are linguistic and cognitive skills emphasized at the expense, perhaps, of other areas of life?

Finally, where the physician in his treatment program has some research base for his recommendations, the preschool educator has fragmented bits and pieces on which to make programmatic decisions. Thus, our preschool programs, given objectives and curricula, are operative from a hypothesis testing perspective, with no guarantee of effectiveness in the short run or the long term.

The ethic guiding us, then, has to be similar to that employed in any treatment problem. Parents or guardians have to be aware that they are participants in an educational experiment with no guarantee that all objectives of the program will be fulfilled either in the present or in the future. Parental mandate is a *sine qua non* for working with the children.

What we presented to the parents was a set of intervention objectives that are, in our estimation, consonant with theirs—namely, "making it" in the mainstream of American culture, while at the same time maintaining their black identity. Two major objectives encompass our program, namely, the development of competence in conceptual and symbolic behavior and the development of a sense of personal competence and confidence in oneself. These two objectives are intimately intertwined.

Our program, then, cultivated an environment that maximized opportunities for enhancing intellectual and social competence. Operationally, this meant establishing an appropriate emotional climate which fostered both social and cognitive development.

The effectiveness of a program must be demonstrated by objective measurements relevant to program objectives. Rather than emphasize IQ as a critical criterion, we established an array of procedures (1) to provide information about the children's progress, and (2) to broaden our base of understanding of young children.

As a result of our conviction that the parents or guardians should provide a mandate for the program, discussions were held with the parents prior to enrollment of the children. Some parents rejected our rationale on various grounds. A few felt that the children were too young for such a group program; others believed that the mixing of children's backgrounds was inimical to the development of their own children.

Our position can be summarized as follows: The course of development for poverty children untouched by remedial programs is predicted to become socially pathological and dysfunctional. The remedial program we suggest emphasizes the acquisition of basic cognitive and social competencies whose interaction within the individual might be expected to extend the options a child has in his adaptation to environmental demands.

It should be made clear, however, that the entire burden of modification of subsequent development should not be placed on preschool education. This is but one link in the educational chain. Other efforts, for example, the Follow Through program, are critical extensions (Bissell 1971 and this volume).

CONCEPTUAL FRAMEWORK

In a series of studies beginning in 1965, we discovered that a large proportion of black children from impoverished backgrounds were less competent than their more privileged counterparts when dealing with representational material (Sigel et al. 1966; Sigel & McBane 1967; Sigel & Olmsted 1970; Sigel 1972). These studies revealed that children from impoverished backgrounds had greater difficulty in classification tasks when the task items were colored or black-and-white photographs in contrast to three-dimensional objects. Such discrepancies were found in spite of the fact that the children could label and recognize the pictorial stimuli. The issue becomes, then, not one of recognition, but of *knowledge* that an object can be represented in several modes and still be a member of the same conceptual class. It is easy to confuse recognitory behavior as equivalent to "knowing" or comprehension of equivalence. Not only did these children have difficulty in responding equivalently to pictorial stimuli and their three-dimensional counterparts, they also had difficulty with other tasks involving representational skills, e.g., Motor Encoding from the Illinois Test of Psycholinguistics and Dramatic Play (Sigel & Perry 1968).

A review of the literature does not reveal many data specific to this issue, but some can be reinterpreted to provide further evidence concerning the problem. For example, Kamii and Radin (1969) examined the types of Stanford-Binet items which children in the Perry Preschool Project found difficult and found them to be conceptual items, as compared to the more rote perceptually concrete types. It may be that the reason IQ scores, so often used as an evaluation measure for intervention programs, show a later decline is because the test items involve more conceptual-verbal items than rote-concrete ones. These data suggest then that the generic problem is development of representational competence, i.e., the ability to deal with representational material. This is a capacity basic to any symbolic activity and considered by Piaget (1962) to be intimately related to thought.

Examination of life experiences of children from impoverished and deprived environments suggests that these life experiences reduce the opportunity for representational competence to flourish. For example, Hunt writes that "children of poverty lack opportunities to develop cognitive skills" (Hunt 1969, p. 204). In referring to parent-children interactions he says: "What these parents talk about is also lacking in such conceptual constructions as prepositional relationships, casual explanations, and concepts of space, time, and justice. . . . The parents of the slums not only talk less with their children than do parents of the middle class, but they seldom undertake to discuss with their children matters which prompt them to discern various kinds of relationships among things and people or to use language to describe these relationships" (Hunt 1969, pp. 205–6). It is reasonable to assume that these kinds of experiences may be critical antecedents for the development of representational competence.

If the capacity to represent the environment or to symbolize is a generic human ability and if competence can be affected by certain kinds of life experiences, then a careful examination of experiences that facilitate or preclude representational competence seems in order.

We hypothesize that the most relevant experiences are those that would involve orientation to the environment by anticipation or objectification of temporal, spatial, and causal relationships. It seems to us that certain classes of socializing experiences function to "demand" employment of representational activity. It may well be that the necessary and/or sufficient conditions that set the processes of representation in motion are those that serve to create psychological, spatial, or temporal distance between person and object. These behaviors (social and/or nonsocial), referred to as *distancing behaviors*, are the class of events that create psychological distance between ostensive reality and its reconstruction (Sigel 1972). Thus, the basic hypothesis emerged, namely, exposing children to distancing behaviors should enhance the development of representational skills.

Distancing behaviors, however, will be effective stimulants only if the recipient is motivated to engage and to interact with the significant person or event. Exposure without the prerequisite willingness to participate precludes any effect. To create such a climate necessitates an environment in which significant adults are warm, accepting, and sensitive to the child's status. Adults should be able to listen, appreciate the child's perspective, and be "tuned" into his comprehension level. Thus, the adult must be able to assess the child's developmental level and respond appropriately.

WHEN INTERVENTION SHOULD OCCUR

Representational thought begins to emerge somewhere between eighteen and twenty-four months of age or the period between the sixth stage of the sensorimotor period and the beginnings of preoperational thought (Piaget 1955; Inhelder & Piaget 1964). It is characterized as the mental activity of evoking objects and events which are outside the immediate field of perception. Thus, representational activity extends the perceptual field of the child from the observable present to the past and the future. It involves anticipatory behavior as well as hindsight. The products of representation are symbols and signs which are differentiated from their concrete palpable referents. Somewhere within the eighteen- and twenty-four-month period children become capable of re-enacting past events, such as re-enacting home experiences, e.g., preparing meals in the nursery's housekeeping corner or putting a doll to sleep.

Space does not permit a detailed description of this developmental period; the reader is referred to Overton (1972, pp. 97–100), Ginsburg and Opper (1969), Piaget (1955, 1962), and Inhelder and Piaget (1964). Suffice it to say that this period is of particular significance, since it defines the origins of what becomes adult thought.

Development is a cumulative process. What happens at one stage or period influences the direction that development takes at subsequent stages. It is subsequent to this period that differences in cognitive development seem to occur (Golden & Birns 1968). It seems reasonable to assume that providing additional experiences which help foster and encourage representational thought should contribute to the development of the semiotic function. We made the additional assumptions that an appropriate environment is a necessary condition for fostering representational thought and that the appropriate environmental experiences can be hypothesized as distancing behaviors. The intervention program becomes, in effect, the opportunity to extend the frequency and quality of behaviors deemed relevant to activating and maintaining representational thinking.

These were the reasons that age two was selected as the target period.

MODE OF INTERVENTION

There are many options for intervention, but the choices are basically between individual and group settings. We opted for the latter, in spite of the dearth of information about group educational programs for two-year-old children.

The appropriateness of a group setting was based on a number of premises both theoretical and practical. First, we believe cognitive growth is enhanced by a broad experiential base, with experiences in various contexts and with various materials. A nursery school setting seems appropriate. Furthermore, a nursery school can provide a more intensive and cumulative contact with the social and nonsocial environment than the home. Finally, it provides the opportunity for setting up a sequential set of experiences that can be used to reinforce acquired gains.

TEACHER TRAINING AND CURRICULUM PLANNING

Our next task was to devise a program to meet our objectives. This involved the simultaneous tasks of training teachers and creating the curriculum. None of the teachers had direct experience in working with two-year-olds in a nursery school that had explicit curriculum objectives. It was necessary to orient the teachers to the theoretical system; this required spelling out the concept of representational thinking and defining strategies which would exemplify "distancing." Such an orientation was important in order to provide coherence to the program, to enable the teachers to participate actively in curriculum development, and thereby to employ appropriate teaching strategies.

In-service training is a continual process built directly into the program. Regular staff meetings are held weekly, as well as daily brief reviews of the morning sessions. It is at these meetings that curriculum units are planned and explicated, management problems discussed, and theoretical points argued.

Fostering both group and individual participation became a major challenge because of the array of individual differences. Some children were very articulate and had relatively long attention spans, whereas others demonstrated a fairly low level of socialization. Management procedures, therefore, had to be coordinated to cognitive objectives. The control techniques that were given special emphasis came from research conducted several years ago at the Merrill-Palmer Institute (Hoffman 1960; Sigel 1960). This work basically systematized the influence techniques used by parents to modify the ongoing behavior of their children. The value for our program was the consonance of these techniques with the concept of imposing distance on the child.

THE CURRICULUM

The curriculum contains two coordinated but separate programs. The first is the daily classroom program and the second consists of tutorial sessions.

Classroom Program: Social and Emotional Objectives. The basic objective is to raise the level of socialized behavior. This is done primarily by preventing aggression to others and encouraging sharing and cooperation. Individual and group interactions are used to make the child aware of others and aware of his environment. This implies that the child is simultaneously being encouraged to anticipate future events, to develop higher levels of frustration tolerance, and to verbalize his feelings rather than to demonstrate them by hitting, biting, or pinching. Anticipation and verbalization are essential to imagery and symbolic behavior, so this social objective clearly serves the cause of improving representational competence.

Classroom Program: Cognitive Objectives. All our objectives concern the acquisition of specific relationships and concepts that we believe to be central to representational competence. Furthermore, all objectives demand a particular kind of teacher-child interaction. The teacher must be sensitive to the cognitive possibilities of any situation and must implement the concept of "distance" when directing the child in his activities.

1. *The child must consider things that are not present.* The teacher must challenge the child to think of the non-present. This may take the form of a question, such as asking the child what would happen if an oversized block were placed on an already unsteady tower, or asking the child to imitate the action of a sight seen the day before. The teacher may make requests which force the child to think in past and future terms. For example, she may ask the child to find a spoon to use in the pudding she is going to mix.

The content varies widely, as does the child's mode of response. As often as possible, the teachers attempt to encourage verbal expression rather than simple motor or gestural expression.

2. *The child must search for alternative actions when unable to solve a problem successfully.* Varying the response to a difficult problem situation maximizes the probability of success.

3. *The child must recognize that one object has several different properties.* This objective is intimately related to the second objective. Learning to explore the multiple attributes of a given object is a precursor to problem solving and possibly to classificatory skills. The timing of the teacher intervention is critical and must enable the child to persist and shift to alternatives.

4. *The child must be made aware of temporal and physical relationships whenever possible.* Smaller–bigger, higher–lower, full–empty, dark–light, for example, are simple relationships which categorize objects of all kinds. These relationships can also be part of simple cause and effect conditions. For example, if you flick a switch, a light goes out and it becomes dark. If you pour material into a container, it is no longer empty but full. Categorizations and cause-effect conditions seem to us to be essential components of representational competence.

Incorporating training of this kind into our program was most effectively done by planning mini-lessons suitable for the activity areas of the classroom, such as the kitchen area, sand and water play, transportation and blocks, painting, and manipulative toy area. The following miniature lesson is an example.

The lessons suggested for water play vary according to what is placed in the water bin. Cups and funnels of graduated sizes make more-than less-than comparisons easy to elicit. For example, if a full large cup of water is poured into a small cup, the small cup will overflow but the reverse action leaves the large cup unfilled. Teachers will demonstrate how the sound of a stream of water changes with a change in the height of the fall, or they may help a child discover how a lidded cup can be inverted without loss of water, how an empty cup can float, how a small cup can be inserted into a large cup. Throughout the lesson the teacher emphasizes relationships by pointing, using words for action or states, and requesting observations and verbal responses from the children.

In order to maintain our basic classroom atmosphere of learning by self-discovery and self-initiated action, the teacher plans a list of possible forms of intervention which she enacts only after noting the child's interest. The planned methods give the teacher general objectives and particular suggestions which prevent unnecessary lapses of activity on her part, but she is free to invent when cued by the child's interest.

All major objectives are carried out within the schedule of routine activities, such as free play, juice and rest time, and group activities.

Tutorial Sessions. Each child is seen individually in a one-to-one instructional setting; there the child is exposed to the curriculum units which best represent the distinctive features of the ECEP program. These units once again are designed to provide experiences conducive to the development of representational competence.

Several sets of materials are given to the child in sequence during the course of the year. The teachers' general approach to all materials does not vary greatly. The child is invited, for example, to play with a set of geometric blocks. No particular response is requested. Generally the child will start some type of exploration, e.g., stacking or standing on edge. The teacher watches approvingly and considers her own moves carefully before intervening. When she does so, she tries to elaborate slightly on something the child has already started. For example, the child may roll a large and a small ring, one in each hand. The teacher might show him that the smaller ring fits inside the larger and both can be rolled together. At that point the child may ignore the teacher's elaboration of his response; he may imitate the elaboration once; or he may imitate the elaboration and then generalize it to other materials.

The objective of the teachers in these sessions is to focus on the following: conflict inducement, timely presentation of contrasting material with the intention of stimulating flexibility of thought, orientation to a product, development of reflectivity, sensitivity to the negative instance, analysis and synthesis, and the developing awareness of cause-effect relationships.

ASSESSMENT

An attempt was made to evaluate both cognitive skill and social-emotional development. Cognitive skills were assessed by means of a battery of tests; social and emotional variables were studied by means of narrative observations, rating scales, and observation of test-related behaviors.

Research Design

Cognitive Assessment. ECEP children were compared with non-ECEP children in order to evaluate the effectiveness of the intervention program. A simple pre-post-test design was used. A battery of tests was assembled in order to measure several aspects of cognitive skill. ECEP children were tested twice with essentially the same battery. The first testing (Battery I) was administered upon entry into the program, and the second testing (Battery II) was given at the end of the first academic year. Control subjects were not tested twice, however, because of the high dropout rate in the programs from which the control subjects were chosen. Control subjects were compared to ECEP children on the basis of age at time of testing only.

Subjects. Twenty, two-year-old, first-born black children, ten boys and ten girls, were enrolled in the ECEP program. They were recruited from the inner city of Buffalo, New York, and bussed to the nursery school four mornings a week for two and one-half hours each morning.

Both white and black boys and girls, matched in age to the ECEP children and coming from approximately the same socioeconomic level, were used as control subjects. They were all enrolled in other day care programs and nursery schools in order to make them as comparable as possible to the ECEP group.

Test Battery.[2] **A battery of twenty-five tests was assembled to measure as** many areas of intellectual functioning as was feasible. The areas tested included form perception, classification, language, memory for images, imitation and pantomime, number, and seriation. Most of the tests came from the Bayley and Stanford-Binet scales. Several Piaget classification and sorting tasks were included and a group of tests especially devised by us completed

[2]Descriptions or copies of all tests and instruments used for assessment purposes may be had from Dr. Sigel upon request.

the battery. The complete list and a brief description of each test used will be found in Table 1.

Table 1. Tests Used in Assessment of ECEP and Control Children

LANGUAGE TASKS

1. Bayley V Scale (Naming Parts of a Doll)
2. Bayley Names and Points to Pictures
3. Bayley Z Scale (Understanding Prepositions)
4. Stanford-Binet Picture Vocabulary, Year II
5. Stanford-Binet Understanding Objects by Use (Vocabulary measure)
6. Stanford-Binet Identifying Parts of the Body (Vocabulary measure)

IMITATION AND PANTOMIME TASKS

7. Bayley M Scale (Paper Folding and Copying a Line task)
8. Bayley—Building a Train
9. Pantomime with Four Cue Conditions (Verbal, Pictorial, Object Present, Object to Use)

PERCEPTION AND CLASSIFICATION TASKS

10. Bayley Pegboard
11. Bayley R Scale (Blue Form Board. Circles and squares are alternately inserted into form board.)
12. Stanford-Binet Three Hole Form Board (Circle, square, triangle)
13. Stanford-Binet Three Hole Form Board, Rotated
14. Kagan Embedded Figures (A car, cat and flower are embedded in backgrounds of varying difficulty, 18 trials.)
15. Piaget Large-Small Sorting
16. Piaget Identity Matching (Blocks are matched according to color and size.)
17. Piaget Free Arrangements (Rings, cubes, circles, triangles, squares, rectangles in red, green and yellow. Child arranges them ad lib.)

MEMORY FOR VISUAL AND AUDITORY IMAGES

18. Delayed Response, Simple (A toy kitty is hidden in one of three boxes.)
19. Delayed Response, Invisible Transportation (After kitty has been placed under a box, the position of the box is changed.)
20. Delayed Response, Complex (The box containing the kitty is moved twice before child is asked to find the kitty.)
21. Sigel Memory Matching (The child is shown the picture of an object which he is to remember and pick out from an array of three objects.)
22. Auditory Sequential Memory (ITPA task)
23. Seriation (Five pegs of varying heights, 1 inch gradation are to be placed in ascending order in pegboard.)

NUMBER TASKS

24. Bayley Concept of One, Two
25. Bayley Building a Tower (Cubes are stacked as high as possible.)

Social and Emotional Assessment.[3] This involved the ECEP group only. Rating scales, teacher observations, narrative observations of classroom behavior, and observations of child behaviors occurring concomitantly with test performance were used to obtain information. Frequency data were used and comparisons between boys and girls were made, as well as correlations between observed social and emotional variables and test performance.

Some Preliminary Findings

The results of our first year of data-gathering are not yet completely analyzed. Control subjects are still being examined; therefore, no overall comparisons such as analysis of variance have been done. The comparisons that have been made with control groups are very tentative and done for exploratory assessment only. Much of the fine-grained examination remains to be done.

Cognitive Assessment—Test Results. The ECEP boys and girls were compared on the initial testing (Battery I), on the second testing (Battery II), and on the difference scores between Batteries I and II. Each sex was compared to controls of the same and opposite sex on Batteries I and II. Since the white control group for both sexes was still very small for Battery I, no statistical comparisons for these groups have been made.

Test results are given in Tables 2 through 9. The means for each group and the significance level of the difference between these means are presented for all the tests in Batteries I and II. Significance was tested with the "t" test. Difference score means for the ECEP group are not shown.

1. LANGUAGE TESTS

ECEP boys vs. ECEP girls. There were no significant differences in performance between the ECEP boys and ECEP girls in either Batteries I or II, but differential improvement was seen in the difference scores. Both boys and girls showed significant improvement in the Stanford-Binet Picture Vocabulary. However, in the other tasks the girls showed improvement in the Bayley Names Pictures and the boys improved in the Stanford-Binet Objects by Use. There is a qualitative stimulus difference in these tests; the Bayley test consists of a two-dimensional picture, whereas the Stanford-Binet involves three-dimensional items. The differences between the ECEP boys and girls were not significant overall. The boys showed greater general improvement in the language area.

ECEP vs. Control Ss. ECEP boys were comparable to the black control boys in both batteries but scored lower than the black control girls in Battery I in the Stanford-Binet Picture Vocabulary and the Bayley Z Scale (Under-

---

[3]Descriptions or copies of all tests and instruments used for assessment purposes may be had from Dr. Sigel upon request.

Table 2. Mean Scores of ECEP Males Compared to Mean Scores of ECEP Females in Each Test of Battery I and Battery II

See Table 6 - pg. 41

	Battery I			Battery II		
	Males N=9	Females N=10	p	Males N=9	Females N=10	p
LANGUAGE						
Bayley V Scale	5.00	5.40		5.88	6.30	
Bayley Name Pictures	3.67	3.50		5.44	6.40	
Bayley Z Scale	1.00	1.60		2.11	2.70	
Stanford-Binet Picture Vocabulary	4.44	4.60		10.78	9.20	
Stanford-Binet Objects by Use	1.44	2.40	<.20	3.44	3.40	
Stanford-Binet Identifying Parts of Body	5.11	5.70		6.11	6.70	
IMITATION, PANTOMIME						
Bayley M Scale	2.00	3.20	<.05	2.00	3.50	<.05
Bayley – Building a Train	1.11	1.10		1.56	1.50	
Pantomime with Four Cues:						
Verbal Cue	1.00	0.00		8.00	7.20	<.20
Picture Cue	0.56	0.00		1.11	5.50	
Object Cue	0.00	0.00		0.33	0.90	
Using Object	2.00	2.20		2.11	0.80	<.20
PERCEPTION, CLASSIFICATION						
Bayley Pegboard	3.00	3.00		2.89	3.00	
Bayley R Scale	8.11	7.80		9.00	8.80	
Stanford-Binet Three Hole Form Board	1.67	1.50		1.89	2.00	
Stanford-Binet Three Hole Form Board-Rotated	1.89	1.70		2.89	2.60	
Kagan Embedded Figures	6.89	7.50		9.00	11.20	
Piaget Large-Small Sorting	0.22	0.40		0.11	0.50	
Piaget Identity Matching	1.44	1.60		2.00	0.60	<.05
MEMORY FOR VISUAL AND AUDITORY IMAGES						
Delayed Response (Invisible Transportation)	2.00	1.60		1.77	1.70	
Sigel Memory Matching	2.00	2.50		1.44	2.80	
Delayed Response, Simple	1.78	1.90		2.22	2.00	
Delayed Response, Complex	1.22	1.50		1.44	1.30	
Auditory Sequential Memory	1.33	1.70		2.44	3.40	
Seriation	0.44	1.40	<.05	2.17	1.65	<.20
NUMBER						
Concept of One	0	0.10		0	0	
Concept of Two	0	0		0	0	
Tower-building	4.88	5.80		4.33	5.60	

Note: t test was used to compare groups. p values greater than .20 are not reported.

Table 3. Mean Scores of ECEP Females Are Compared to Mean Scores of Black Female and Black Male Control Subjects in Battery I Tests

See Table 6—pg. 41

	ECEP females N=10	Non-ECEP females (blk.) N=8	p	Non-ECEP males (blk.) N=6	p
LANGUAGE					
Bayley V Scale	5.40	6.25		5.00	
Bayley Name Pictures	3.50	5.75		2.83	
Bayley Z Scale	1.60	2.25		1.17	
Stanford-Binet Picture Vocabulary	4.60	7.50	<.05	3.17	
Stanford-Binet Objects by Use	2.40	2.75		2.50	
Stanford-Binet Identifying Parts of Body	5.70	5.88		3.83	<.20
IMITATION, PANTOMIME					
Bayley M Scale	3.20	2.25	<.05	1.83	<.05
Bayley—Building a Train	1.10	1.00		1.00	
Pantomime with Four Cues:					
Verbal Cue	0.00	3.00	<.20	0.00	
Picture Cue	0.00	2.38	<.20	3.33	
Object Cue	0.00	0.00		0.00	
Using Object	2.20	0.25	<.05	1.33	
PERCEPTION, CLASSIFICATION					
Bayley Pegboard	3.00	3.00		3.00	
Bayley R Scale	7.80	8.38		7.67	
Stanford-Binet Three Hole Form Board	1.50	1.88	<.20	1.83	
Stanford-Binet Three Hole Form Board-Rotated	1.70	1.88		1.33	
Kagan Embedded Figures	7.50	9.25	<.05	6.33	
Piaget Large-Small Sorting	0.40	0.75		0.17	
Piaget Identity Matching	1.60	1.75		1.50	
MEMORY FOR VISUAL AND AUDITORY IMAGES					
Delayed Response (Invisible Transportation)	1.60	1.75		1.17	<.20
Sigel Memory Matching	2.50	3.25		1.33	<.20
Delayed Response, Simple	1.90	1.62		2.50	<.20
Delayed Response, Complex	1.50	1.63		1.17	
Auditory Sequential Memory	1.70	2.25		0.67	<.20
Seriation	1.40	1.63		1.92	
NUMBER					
Concept of One	0.10	0.25		0	
Concept of Two	0	0		0	
Tower-building	5.80	6.37		4.00	<.20

Note: t test was used to compare groups. p values greater than .20 are not reported.

Table 4. Mean Scores of ECEP Males Are Compared to Mean Scores of Black Female and Black Male Control Subjects in Battery I Test

See Table 6 – pg. 41

	ECEP males N=9	Non-ECEP females (blk.) N=8	p	Non-ECEP males (blk.) N=6	p
LANGUAGE					
Bayley V Scale	5.00	6.25	<.20	5.00	
Bayley Name Pictures	3.67	5.75	<.05	2.83	
Bayley Z Scale	1.00	2.25	<.05	1.17	
Stanford-Binet Picture Vocabulary	4.44	7.50	<.20	3.17	
Stanford-Binet Objects by Use	1.44	2.75	<.20	2.50	
Stanford-Binet Identifying Parts of Body	5.11	5.88		3.83	
IMITATION, PANTOMIME					
Bayley M Scale	2.00	2.25		1.83	
Bayley – Building a Train	1.11	1.00		1.00	
Pantomime with Four Cues:					
Verbal Cue	1.00	3.00		0.00	
Picture Cue	0.56	2.38		3.33	
Object Cue	0.00	0.00		0.00	
Using Object	2.00	0.25	<.05	1.33	
PERCEPTION, CLASSIFICATION					
Bayley Pegboard	3.00	3.00		3.00	
Bayley R Scale	8.11	8.38		7.67	
Stanford-Binet Three Hole Form Board	1.67	1.88		1.83	
Stanford-Binet Three Hole Form Board Rotated	1.89	1.88		1.33	
Kagan Embedded Figures	6.89	9.25		6.33	
Piaget Large-Small Sorting	0.22	0.75		0.17	
Piaget Identity Matching	1.44	1.75	<.20	1.50	
MEMORY FOR VISUAL AND AUDITORY IMAGES					
Delayed Response (Invisible Transportation)	2.00	1.75	<.20	1.17	<.001
Sigel Memory Matching	2.00	3.25	<.20	1.33	
Delayed Response, Simple	1.78	1.63		2.50	<.20
Delayed Response, Complex	1.22	1.63	<.20	1.17	
Auditory Sequential Memory	1.33	2.25		0.67	
Seriation	0.44	1.63	<.05	1.91	<.05
NUMBER					
Concept of One	0	0.25		0	
Concept of Two	0	0		0	
Tower-building	4.88	6.38	<.20	4.00	

Note: t test was used to compare groups. p values greater than .20 are not reported.

Table 5. Mean Scores of ECEP Females Are Compared to Mean Scores of Black Female and Black Male Control Subjects in Battery II Tests
See Table 6—pg. 41

	ECEP females N=10	Non-ECEP females (blk.) N=5	p	Non-ECEP males (blk.) N=4	p
LANGUAGE					
Bayley V Scale	6.30	7.00		6.75	
Bayley Name Pictures	6.40	5.00	<.20	6.50	
Bayley Z Scale	2.70	2.00		2.25	
Stanford-Binet Picture Vocabulary	9.20	9.00		10.25	
Stanford-Binet Objects by Use	3.40	3.00		3.00	
Stanford-Binet Identifying Parts of Body	6.70	6.80		6.25	
IMITATION, PANTOMIME					
Bayley M Scale	3.50	3.20		2.00	<.05
Bayley – Building a Train	1.50	1.40		1.00	<.20
Pantomime with Four Cues:					
Verbal Cue	7.20	2.40		0.00	
Picture Cue	5.50	1.40		0.00	<.20
Object Cue	0.90	0.00		0.00	
Using Object	0.80	1.60		0.75	
PERCEPTION, CLASSIFICATION					
Bayley Pegboard	3.00	3.00		3.00	<.20
Bayley R Scale	8.80	8.20		7.50	<.20
Stanford-Binet Three Hole Form Board	2.00	1.60		1.75	<.05
Stanford-Binet Three Hole Form Board-Rotated	2.60	2.60		1.00	<.20
Kagan Embedded Figures	11.20	6.40	<.20	7.75	
Piaget Large-Small Sorting	0.50	0.40		0.00	
Piaget Identity Matching	0.60	2.20	<.05	1.50	
MEMORY FOR VISUAL AND AUDITORY IMAGES					
Delayed Response (Invisible Transportation)	1.70	2.00		1.75	
Sigel Memory Matching	2.80	3.60		2.50	
Delayed Response, Simple	2.00	2.00		2.00	
Delayed Response, Complex	1.30	1.00		1.25	
Auditory Sequential Memory	3.40	3.40		3.75	
Seriation	1.65	3.50	<.001	1.50	
NUMBER					
Concept of One	0.00	0.40	<.05	0	
Concept of Two	0.00	0.20	<.05	0	
Tower-building	5.60	5.60		6.00	

Note: t test was used to compare groups. p values greater than .20 are not reported.

Table 6. Mean Scores of ECEP Females Are Compared to Mean Scores of White Male and White Female Control Subjects in Battery II

	ECEP females N=10	Non-ECEP males (wht.) N=17	p	Non-ECEP females (wht.) N=8	p
LANGUAGE					
Bayley V Scale	6.30	6.35		5.50	
Bayley Name Pictures	6.40	7.30		6.62	
Bayley Z Scale	2.70	3.35		4.25	<.20
Stanford-Binet Picture Vocabulary	9.20	10.12		9.63	
Stanford-Binet Objects by Use	3.40	3.41		3.88	
Stanford-Binet Identifying Parts of Body	6.70	6.41		5.25	
IMITATION, PANTOMIME					
Bayley M Scale	3.50	3.06	<.05	2.63	
Bayley – Building a Train	1.50	1.06		1.25	
Pantomime with Four Cues:					
Verbal Cue	7.20	6.89		10.13	<.20
Picture Cue	5.50	3.18		1.50	<.20
Object Cue	0.90	0.82		0.00	
Using Object	0.80	2.59	<.001	1.13	
PERCEPTION, CLASSIFICATION					
Bayley Pegboard	3.00	3.00		3.00	
Bayley R Scale	8.80	8.82		8.50	
Stanford-Binet Three Hole Form Board	2.00	1.94		2.00	
Stanford-Binet Three Hole Form Board-Rotated	2.60	2.47		2.63	
Kagan Embedded Figures	11.20	11.65		10.63	
Piaget Large-Small Sorting	0.50	0.94		2.00	<.05
Piaget Identity Matching	0.60	2.29	<.001	2.25	<.05
MEMORY FOR VISUAL AND AUDITORY IMAGES					
Delayed Response (Invisible Transportation)	1.70	1.88		1.50	
Sigel Memory Matching	2.80	2.71		3.00	
Delayed Response, Simple	2.00	2.59	<.20	2.38	
Delayed Response, Complex	1.30	1.47		1.25	
Auditory Sequential Memory	3.40	3.71		2.38	
Seriation	1.65	0.92	<.20	2.38	
NUMBER					
Concept of One	0.00	0.36	<.05	0.62	<.05
Concept of Two	0.00	0.12	<.05	0.38	<.05
Tower-building	5.60	5.24		6.88	

Note: t test was used to compare groups. *p* values greater than .20 are not reported.

Table 7. Mean Scores of ECEP Males Compared to Mean Scores of Black Male and Black Female Control Subjects in Battery II

	ECEP males N=9	Non-ECEP males (blk.) N=4	p	Non-ECEP females (blk.) N=5	p
LANGUAGE					
Bayley V Scale	5.88	6.75		7.00	
Bayley Name Pictures	5.44	6.50		5.00	
Bayley Z Scale	2.11	2.25		2.00	
Stanford-Binet Picture Vocabulary	10.78	10.25		9.00	
Stanford-Binet Objects by Use	3.44	3.00		3.00	
Stanford-Binet Identifying Parts of Body	6.11	6.25		6.80	
IMITATION, PANTOMIME					
Bayley M Scale	2.00	2.00		3.20	<.20
Bayley–Building a Train	1.56	1.00		1.40	
Pantomime with Four Cues:					
Verbal Cue	8.00	0.00	<.20	2.40	
Picture Cue	1.11	0.00		1.40	
Object Cue	0.33	0.00		0.00	
Using Object	2.11	0.75	<.20	1.60	
PERCEPTION, CLASSIFICATION					
Bayley Pegboard	2.89	3.00		3.00	
Bayley R Scale	9.00	7.50	<.20	8.20	
Stanford-Binet Three Hole Form Board	1.89	1.75		1.60	
Stanford-Binet Three Hole Form Board-Rotated	2.89	1.00	<.05	2.60	
Kagan Embedded Figures	9.00	7.75		6.40	
Piaget Large-Small Sorting	0.11	0.00		0.40	
Piaget Identity Matching	2.00	1.50		2.20	
MEMORY FOR VISUAL AND AUDITORY IMAGES					
Delayed Response (Invisible Transportation)	1.77	1.75		2.00	
Sigel Memory Matching	1.44	2.50		3.60	
Delayed Response, Simple	2.22	2.20		2.00	
Delayed Response, Complex	1.44	1.25		1.00	
Auditory Sequential Memory	2.44	3.75		3.40	
Seriation	2.17	1.50		3.50	
NUMBER					
Concept of One	0.00	0.00		0.40	
Concept of Two	0.00	0.00		0.20	
Tower-building	4.33	6.00		5.60	

Note: t test was used to compare groups. *p* values greater than .20 are not reported.

Table 8. Mean Scores of ECEP Males Compared to Mean Scores of White Female and White Male Control Subjects in Battery II

	ECEP males N=9	Non-ECEP males (wht.) N=17	p	Non-ECEP females (wht.) N=8	p
LANGUAGE					
Bayley V Scale	5.8	6.35		5.50	
Bayley Name Pictures	5.84	7.30	<.20	6.62	
Bayley Z Scale	2.11	3.35	<.20	4.25	<.05
Stanford-Binet Picture Vocabulary	10.78	10.12		9.63	
Stanford-Binet Objects by Use	3.44	3.41		3.88	
Stanford-Binet Identifying Parts of Body	6.11	6.41		5.25	
IMITATION, PANTOMIME					
Bayley M Scale	2.00	3.06	<.20	2.63	
Bayley—Building a Train	1.56	1.06	<.001	1.25	
Pantomime with Four Cues:					
Verbal Cue	8.00	6.88		10.13	
Picture Cue	1.11	3.17		1.50	
Object Cue	0.33	0.82		0.00	
Using Object	2.11	2.59		1.13	
PERCEPTION, CLASSIFICATION					
Bayley Pegboard	2.89	3.00	<.20	3.00	
Bayley R Scale	9.00	8.82		8.50	
Stanford-Binet Three Hole Form Board	1.89	1.94		2.00	
Stanford-Binet Three Hole Form Board-Rotated	2.89	2.47	<.20	2.63	
Kagan Embedded Figures	9.00	11.65	<.20	10.63	
Piaget Large-Small Sorting	0.11	0.94	<.05	2.00	<.001
Piaget Identity Matching	2.00	2.29		2.25	
MEMORY FOR VISUAL AND AUDITORY IMAGES					
Delayed Response (Invisible Transportation)	1.77	1.88		1.50	
Sigel Memory Matching	1.44	2.71	<.20	3.00	<.20
Delayed Response, Simple	2.22	2.59		2.38	
Delayed Response, Complex	1.44	1.47		1.25	
Auditory Sequential Memory	2.44	3.70		2.36	
Seriation	2.17	0.92	<.001	2.38	
NUMBER					
Concept of One	0.00	0.36	<.05	0.62	<.05
Concept of Two	0.00	0.12	<.05	0.38	<.05
Tower-building	4.33	5.24		6.88	<.05

Note: *t* test was used to compare groups. *p* values greater than .20 are not reported.

Table 9. Means for ECEP Males and Females and *p* Values of the Difference Scores between Batteries I and II

	Males (N=9)			Females (N=10)		
	I	II	p	I	II	p
LANGUAGE						
Bayley V Scale	5.00	5.88	<.10	5.40	6.30	—
Bayley Name Pictures	3.67	5.44	<.10	3.50	6.40	<.01
Bayley Z Scale	1.00	2.11	<.10	1.60	2.70	<.20
Stanford-Binet Picture Vocabulary	4.44	10.78	<.01	4.60	9.20	<.01
Stanford-Binet Objects by Use	1.44	3.44	<.001	2.40	3.40	<.20
Stanford-Binet Identifying Parts of Body	5.11	6.11	<.10	5.70	6.70	<.10
IMITATION, PANTOMIME						
Bayley M Scale	2.00	2.00	—	3.20	3.50	—
Bayley–Building a Train	1.11	1.56	<.05	1.10	1.50	<.05
Pantomime with Four Cues:						
Verbal Cue	1.00	8.00	<.10	0.00	7.20	<.10
Picture Cue	0.56	1.11	—	0.00	5.50	<.05
Object Cue	0.00	0.33	—	0.00	0.90	<.10
Using Object	2.00	2.11	—	2.20	0.80	<.05
PERCEPTION, CLASSIFICATION						
Bayley Pegboard	3.00	2.89	—	3.00	3.00	—
Bayley R Scale	8.11	9.00	<.05	7.80	8.80	<.10
Stanford-Binet Three Hole Form Board	1.67	1.89	—	1.50	2.00	<.05
Stanford-Binet Three Hole Form Board-Rotated	1.89	2.89	<.01	1.70	2.60	<.20
Kagan Embedded Figures	6.89	9.00	<.20	7.50	11.20	<.05
Piaget Large-Small Sorting	0.22	0.11	—	0.40	0.50	—
Piaget Identity Matching	1.44	2.00	<.20	1.60	0.60	<.20
MEMORY FOR VISUAL AND AUDITORY IMAGES						
Delayed Response (Invisible Transportation)	2.00	1.77	—	1.60	1.70	<.20
Sigel Memory Matching	2.00	1.44	<.20	2.50	2.80	—
Delayed Response, Simple	1.78	2.22	—	1.90	2.00	—
Delayed Response, Complex	1.22	1.44	—	1.50	1.30	—
Auditory Sequential Memory	1.33	2.44	—	1.70	3.40	—
Seriation	0.44	2.17	<.20	1.40	1.65	—
NUMBER						
Concept of One	0	0	—	0.10	0	—
Concept of Two	0	0	—	0	0	—
Tower-building	4.88	4.33	—	5.80	5.60	<.01

Note: *t* test for paired comparisons was used to compare groups. *p* values greater than .20 are not reported.

standing Prepositions). This discrepancy was overcome by Battery II. However, they scored lower than both white boys and girls in vocabulary and the Bayley Z Scale on Battery II. ECEP girls initially scored lower than other black girls on vocabulary, but caught up to them by the second testing. However, like the ECEP boys, they scored lower on Understanding Prepositions than both male and female white control groups.

2. IMITATION AND PANTOMIME TESTS

ECEP boys vs. ECEP girls. The girls were significantly superior to the boys in the Bayley M Scale on both batteries.

The pantomime task consisted of asking the child to pantomime a simple action under four sets of instructions, each instruction giving the child a more concrete cue concerning the object to be used in the pantomime. For example, the task "Show me what you do with a pencil" was given as a verbal request, with a life-size picture of a pencil present on the table; the actual object was placed on the table but out of the child's reach, and finally the child was given the actual object to use. Neither sex responded well to the verbal instruction, but the girls showed some tendency to better performance when shown pictures or when looking at the object. The boys, on the other hand, responded more favorably only when given the actual object to use.

The only significant improvement in performance between Battery I and Battery II is shown by the girls in Pantomime with Picture as Cue. Overall, the girls showed slightly greater improvement in this area.

ECEP vs. Control Ss. There were no differences between ECEP and control groups of either sex in the imitation task (Bayley M Scale). ECEP boys performed better than other black females in Pantomime Using Appropriate Object. ECEP females who were lower than other black females in Battery I in that task surpassed them in that task by Battery II. However, white males were better than ECEP females in Pantomime Using Appropriate Object.

Again, boys and girls seem to be responding differentially to a stimulus quality. Girls are able to perform when clued by a two-dimensional picture. Boys show better performance when clued by an actual object.

3. PERCEPTION AND CLASSIFICATION TASKS

ECEP boys vs. ECEP girls. There were no differences in the initial testing, but in the second testing the boys were significantly better at the Piaget Large-Small Sorting Task. Looking at the difference scores between Batteries I and II, one sees that the boys showed significant improvement in the Bayley R Scale on the second testing, whereas the girls improved significantly in the Stanford-Binet Three Hole Form Board. The girls also showed greater improvement in the Kagan Embedded Figures Task than did the boys.

ECEP vs. Control Ss. The only significant difference in Battery I is between ECEP females and black control females. The control Ss scored higher on the Piaget Large-Small Sorting tasks.

In Battery II, ECEP males and females are significantly better than black male control Ss in the Stanford-Binet Rotated Form Board. ECEP males are better than other black males on the Piaget Large-Small Sorting task but they did not perform as well as white males. The white females scored significantly higher than ECEP females on this same task, and both white boys and girls scored significantly higher in Identity Matching than the ECEP group.

Better performance on the Piaget Large-Small Sorting and Identity Matching may be confounded with language skill. A preliminary factor analysis of the test batteries with ECEP children indicates that both of these tests have a sizable language component.

The Piaget Classification Task was given to the ECEP group only. A system of notation has only recently been devised which will allow comparable scoring for the control groups.

The Piaget Classification task consisted of presenting the child with an array of blocks varying in size, shape, and color. The child was asked to group these, and his behavior, following instructions, was videotaped and scored from the tape. Four categories containing twenty-four variables were systematically scored. These categories were: (1) *Non-Grouping Responses*, which included such behaviors as holding, banging, pushing, and random clustering of blocks; (2) *Grouping Responses*, which involved any indication that the child was putting objects together on the basis of similarity or forming a group by stacking (piling one block on another), aligning (lining blocks up horizontally), or taking two blocks and putting them together in consistent fashion; (3) *Decision Responses*, which included exchanging one block for another in order to create a design, scanning and holding blocks to exchange for others, and hesitations; (4) *Completion Responses*, which included any indication that the child was finished with his arrangement. Since this category contained less than five percent of all responses it was not included in the statistical analysis.

Table 10 shows the percentage of each category of response for each sex in both batteries. Clearly, non-grouping responses decrease and grouping responses increase in Battery II for both sexes, but particularly for boys. De-

Table 10. Percentage of Grouping, Non-grouping, and Decisionmaking Responses in Piaget Free Arrangement Task

	Non-Grouping		Grouping		Decisionmaking	
Battery	I	II	I	II	I	II
Males	38	18	33	57	24	20
Females	35	21	43	53	22	21

cisionmaking responses remain fairly constant. Each of the three major responses categories showed some significant changes from Battery I to Battery II for both sexes.

Non-Grouping Responses: Holding, Touching, and Hold-Release decreased significantly for boys. The girls decreased significantly only in Hold-Release.

Grouping Responses: Both girls and boys increase significantly in stacking.

Decisionmaking: While both sexes generally decreased responses in this category, boys decreased significantly in Visual Examination, but girls increased significantly in Adjustments.

The results, while complex, allow us to offer some tentative conclusions. We can infer stages in this classification behavior. Initially, children examine objects and function as if they are learning and becoming acquainted with them as evidenced by the frequency of hesitation responses. At the second testing, six months later, familiarity with similar forms, or perhaps the memory of these forms, enables the children to be less hesitant and more certain in their productions. The most perplexing phenomenon was the prevalence of stacking as the major Grouping Response, as opposed, for example, to aligning or pairing.

4. MEMORY FOR IMAGES

The tasks in this category involve several capacities, for example, language and classification. Image retention seemed, however, to be an underlying similarity that was required for correct performance.

ECEP boys vs. ECEP girls. There were no differences between ECEP boys and girls in the first battery, but in the second testing the boys were significantly better at the Delayed Response Task and the girls at Seriation.

ECEP vs. Controls. ECEP males scored significantly higher in the Delayed Response Task and in Seriation in Battery I than the black male control group, but this difference disappeared in Battery II. The boys scored significantly better than the white males in Seriation and Train Building (Battery II), but both white boys and girls did better than ECEP boys in the Sigel Memory Matching task. Black control girls were significantly higher in Seriation than ECEP boys, as were the ECEP girls.

There were no differences in Battery I between ECEP girls and black control girls, but in Battery II ECEP girls were significantly better in Seriation than this control group and were better in tower-building than white boys.

5. NUMBER CONCEPT

There were no significant within-group differences. White boys and girls scored higher than ECEP children in both the concept of one and two.

OVERVIEW OF TEST RESULTS

Since the control groups are small and material is still being gathered, much of the data are still exploratory and we shall examine the scores for suggestions as to differences. If one compares the total number of tests in which ECEP scored higher than any given control group, relative to the total number of tests in which they scored lower than that given control group, a general picture of improvement becomes clear.

ECEP females did better on a greater proportion of tasks when compared to black control females. In Battery I, ECEP females scored lower than black control females in 21 out of 26 tasks, a difference in proportion significantly better than chance. In Battery II, ECEP girls now scored higher in 14 and lower in 8, a proportion *not* significantly different from chance.

Similarly, ECEP boys improved in Battery II relative to black control females. In Battery I ECEP scored lower than black control females in 20 out of 26 tasks, a difference in proportion significantly different from chance. In Battery II, ECEP males scored higher in 14 out of 29 tasks, a proportion not significantly different from chance.

Comparisons with white control groups were not done for Battery I, but there was no overall difference between ECEP females and white females or males in Battery II. ECEP males, on the other hand, were no different from black male control groups over all of Batteries I and II, but performed significantly lower than white males. In Battery II, ECEP males scored higher in 7 tasks and lower in 22 than the white male control groups, a proportion significantly different than expected by chance.

ECEP children showed significant strides in Battery II, as evidenced by their catching up to or overtaking the black control groups in Language, Pantomime, Seriation, and Train-Building. It should be noted that Pantomime, Seriation, and Imitation are given special emphasis in the classroom curriculum; these are the major areas, other than language, where improvement was noted.

In general, ECEP children did not perform as well as the white control group in Language, Identity Matching, the Sigel Memory Matching task, and Number Concept. An argument might be made that language skill may be the basic differentiator, since a preliminary factor analysis of the test batteries indicates that both the Identity Matching and the Sigel Memory Matching Task are highly correlated with verbal ability.

There may be an interesting sex difference concerning differential response to three- vs. two-dimensional stimuli. Both sexes improved in vocabulary, but girls raised their scores in Naming Pictures (two-dimensional stimuli) and boys improved in Objects by Use (three-dimensional stimuli). Furthermore, ECEP males, who usually scored below black female controls, were superior to the black females in both batteries in Pantomime Using Appropriate Object (three-dimensional stimulus). Again, ECEP females did better than black female controls in Pantomime Using Appropriate Object, a result consistent with the classroom program. In that same task they scored lower, however, than white males. This may be related to a difference in developmental rate. Response to the concrete three-dimensional stimulus may appear before appropriate responses to the more abstract and less immediate two-dimensional stimulus. While the evidence is conjectural at this time, it seems to be a difference worth further investigation.

At this time, the test results support the conclusion that the classroom intervention program was effective. The improvement over the black control groups shown in Battery I argues to that point.

SOCIAL AND EMOTIONAL ASSESSMENT, PRELIMINARY RESULTS

I. TEST-RELATED BEHAVIORS

As the child was being given the tests of Battery I, a variety of attentional, motivational, verbal, and manipulatory behaviors which occurred as a function of specific tester behaviors were recorded. Thirteen tester behaviors involving giving instructions, presenting test materials, and giving the child reinforcement and personal attention were systematically observed. Thirty-six child behaviors, such as looking at the tester or material, handling items, wandering, and staring, were observed in relation to the tester behaviors which were presumed to be probable elicitors. One tester behavior and two child behaviors were recorded every five seconds throughout the test sessions. Two to four observers recorded these behaviors with an overall agreement of 85 percent.

Of these tester-child behaviors, only six tester and twenty child behaviors occurred with enough frequency to warrant statistical treatment. Three types of responses were analyzed: (1) Attentional and Interpersonal Responses, (2) Orientation and Manual Responses to Materials, and (3) Verbal Responses. Comparisons along these dimensions were then made between the children who scored in the first and fourth quarters of the test battery.

A. Attentional and Interpersonal Responses

It was found that high and low scorers seem to differ in their orientation to the material and to the tester. Low scorers stare away while being watched and sit still during instructions and throughout the test sessions. High scorers smile when material is presented and smile at the tester throughout the session more than low scorers do.

Boys appear more distracted than girls, as evidenced by staring away from either the tester or the task, but there are some indications of greater dependence, as seen in boys going to the teacher's lap while girls went close to the tester. Also, boys seem to smile more than girls during instructions. This latter observation is particularly interesting since it is the high scorers rather than the low scorers who smile more during instructions, and it will be recalled that the high scoring group contains more females than males.

B. *Orientation and Manual Responses to Test Materials*

The differences in this category reflect the nature of high- versus low-scoring groups and indicate one possible source of this difference. Obviously correct and incorrect gestural responses, such as pointing to the correct picture or placing a form into the correct slot, differentiate high- from low-scoring groups. In addition, low scorers show greater absence of responding. Low scorers engage in more tactile manipulation of material during instructions and throughout all tester-child combinations. This may indicate some impulsiveness, since instructions were given with the command not to touch the material until told to do so. It may also be an indication of a more primitive mode of response to the material, since tactile manipulation was defined as random touching and fingering rather than any exploratory constructive handling of the materials.

There is some indication that high scorers look at the materials more than low scorers, although boys appear to look more than girls as a group, even though boys require more orientation to the materials. This may be a confounding factor in the looking response. While boys respond to the initial instructions with the correct gesture more often than girls, the girls improved very significantly when their instructions were repeated. Girls were also better at piling blocks and aligning them laterally.

C. *Verbal Responses*

Girls and high scorers clearly verbalize more in general and respond correctly to test questions, whereas boys remain silent rather than make errors.

In summary, then, the high scorers, who are predominantly female, are a more active group, enjoying the task as evidenced by the smiling differences or perhaps reflecting greater interpersonal ease. They sit still more than the low-scoring group only when instructions are repeated, indicating once again perhaps a response to a personal demand from an adult or possibly need for achievement.

The low scorers, who are predominantly male, seem to show less motivated interaction with the materials, stare away, and engage in tactile manipulation of materials as opposed to an exploratory response.

When we look at the boys' versus girls' behaviors, irrespective of their scoring status, we find that the boys are quiet, more unresponsive, less verbal, and less drawn to test materials; they require more orientation. The girls are more restless, more verbal, and better at piling and aligning blocks.

Thus, we find that there is some obvious relationship between performance and attendant behaviors. As one examines these results, one should be cautioned to realize that some of the attendant behaviors and performance are confounded. However, there are indications that the attendant test behaviors seem to be in the service of test performance rather than just as a concomitant of this.

II. RATING SCALES

Teachers were asked to rate the child's behavior in the classroom according to a bipolar scale of social-emotional dimensions, originally devised by Emmerich (1971). The bipolar scales include twenty-one pairs of adjectives such as the following: withdrawn, involved; expressive, restrained; sensitive to others, self-centered; and active, passive. The teacher rated the child on a point scale where a rating of four indicated no difference between the two poles of the dimension.

The teachers were randomly assigned a different group of five children to rate each week during the school year. The ratings done from November 1969 to January 1970 were pooled and called Scale 1. Those from February to May 1970 were pooled and designated as Scale 2. The reason for the division is that we wanted to see if any differences existed between the beginning and the end of the year; this arbitrary division divided the data into two approximately equal groups of scales.

The median rating for boys and girls on Scale 1 vs. Scale 2 was not significant when individual dimensions were examined, but very interesting changes in teacher ratings between Scale 1 and 2 should be noted.

In Scale I, based on the early part of the year, the girls were very decidedly seen as more productive, powerful, and active than boys. Girls outranked boys in nineteen of the twenty-one dimensions, which is a significant difference. Girls were ranked as more involved, vulnerable to frustration, rebellious, expressive, sensitive to others, dominant, active, constructive, purposeful, aggressive, academically motivated, socially secure, energetic, stable, socially assertive, independent, rigid, and happy. Boys outranked girls only very slightly as more relaxed and more masculine. Of the nineteen categories in which girls were seen as possessing more of that particular quality, only four are usually construed as undesirable attributes, i.e., vulnerable to frustration, rebellious, rigid, and aggressive to others. In terms of stereotyped sex-role typing, males are usually seen as more dominant, active, rebellious, vulnerable to frustration, energetic, and assertive. All of these characteristics were given to the girls in Scale 1.

In Scale 2, however, the position of the girls versus the boys changed considerably. Now the girls were seen as ascendant in only eleven categories, a difference which is no longer significant. Eleven of the categories in which girls were ranked higher than boys are the same as Scale 1: dominant, constructive, purposeful, academically motivated, stable, social, assertive, independent, and rigid. Judging by Scale 2, the girls have become more tolerant of frustration and more relaxed than the boys.

At least in the view of teachers, the boys have made considerable strides in adjusting to the school situation. By Scale 2, they outranked the girls in being more involved, rebellious, expressive, sensitive to others, active, aggressive, socially secure, energetic, and happy. Only two of these categories, rebellious and aggressive, are construed as negative qualities; both of them, at least in stereotyped sex-role typing, are attributed to males more often than females.

Some preliminary analyses of the relationship between performance on each of the test batteries and rating on social-emotional dimensions were made. Contingency coefficients were computed to determine the relationship between test performance and teacher-rated social-emotional dimensions. Several significant relationships appeared.

Both males and females who scored above the median on the constructive and socially secure dimensions scored significantly higher on cognitive tasks in the first testing. Furthermore, in the second testing, males who were identified as above the median on social dimensions received higher test scores. At .10 and .20 significance levels, males and females who were seen as happier, more academically motivated, and purposeful in the classroom performed better in the initial testing. The more relaxed and flexible males also obtain higher scores in Test Battery I. The girls who were viewed by the teachers as being energetic, assertive, independent, aggressive, dominant, social, and involved also received higher scores on this initial battery.

III. *TEACHER OBSERVATION SCHEDULES*

The teachers were also required to make certain specific observations of classroom behavior and to record these observations once a week. Most of the behaviors that were observed centered around imitation, performance in puzzles and games, signs of independence or dependence, and social and emotional variables similar to those on the rating scale but asked in terms of specific classroom behaviors. For example, "Did child ask for help to solve problems or to complete a task?" "Did child imitate your gestures in an imitation game?"

Teachers were randomly assigned five different children each week, so that all the children were observed at least once a week by one of the teachers. Observations were scored "frequently" (seen daily or several times a day), "sometimes" (seen two or three times a week), or "rarely" (seen not at all or once a week).

The observations for November through February were averaged to obtain one score for winter. Scores for March to May were averaged to obtain one score for spring.

Results:

Three categories of behaviors were analyzed for male-female differences: (1) Social and Emotional Behaviors, (2) Imitation, and (3) Performance.

1) *Social and Emotional Behaviors.* The pattern of results for boys and girls was similar, although the frequency of the behaviors was higher for girls than for boys in both Winter and Spring Observations.

In the Winter Observation, all categories of response except two occurred with greater frequency for girls. Those two exceptions were *Throwing Objects* and *Watches Others.*

In the Spring Observation, the frequency of behaviors in this category declined, both sexes decreasing significantly in *Watches Others* and *Follows Children*, and boys decreasing significantly in *Throwing Objects* and taking a sizable drop in *Takes Turns* and *Follows Teacher.*

There were only two instances in which boys and girls went in reversed directions in the Spring Observation. Boys increased in the frequency of *Seeks Help*, and girls decreased. Boys increased in the frequency of *Helps Others* and girls decreased. *Attentiveness* and *Aggressiveness* were the most stable behaviors for both sexes, but again girls were considered to be slightly more aggressive and more attentive than boys.

2) *Imitation Behaviors.* The pattern of results repeats that of the Social Emotional Behaviors as far as the Winter Observation is concerned. Girls imitate more often than boys. However, there is an almost complete reversal at the end of the year. In the Spring Observation, boys increase imitative behavior in all categories—*Imitates Teacher, Imitates Language, Imitates Actions.* Girls decreased in all categories, significantly so for *Imitates Actions.* Boys showed the greatest increase in *Imitates Language.*

3) *Performance*. Once more, a consistent pattern emerges. Girls are more interested in puzzles and put them together correctly more frequently than boys. Both sexes increase in interest and accuracy in the Spring Observation, but the girls still have the higher frequency of behaviors in this area.

Summary:

Girls were rated by their teachers as more active in almost all areas of classroom activities in both the Winter and Spring Observations. The major exception was *Throwing Objects*, and this declined for boys in the Spring Observation.

Both sexes seem to gain in independence, as evidenced by reduced following of other children and the teacher, decreased watching of others, and (for girls) a decrease in seeking help.

Boys increase in frequency of imitation of the teacher and other children, while girls decreased their behaviors in the imitative category.

IV. *NARRATIVE DATA*

Narrative observations of the child's classroom behaviors were tape recorded every other month from late October to the end of June. All of the regular school activities, such as free play, juice, rest time, and guided games, were considered to be a set of observations. Each child was observed in each of the school activities for a ten-minute period, and a complete set of observations was made on each child every other month.

A coding system for analyzing these reports was devised. The codes categorized the child's behavior into *Interaction with People* and *Interaction with Objects*. Six major kinds of behavior were coded concerning *Interaction with People*: General Social Interaction (parallel versus solitary play, cooperation, etc.), Defense-Offense Behaviors, Help-Seeking, Help-Giving, Imitation, and Pretend. Four major kinds of behaviors were coded concerning *Interaction with Objects*: Gaining Objects, Handling Objects, Construction, Puzzle Completion and Seriation Tasks, and Location of Objects in Space. Occurrences of anticipation, persistence, and language were looked for in all categories.

Only one analysis has been completed so far. Ninety-one items subsumed under the *Interaction with People* and *Interaction with Objects* categories were compared for male-female differences. Comparisons were made for four time periods: November–December, January–February, March–April, and May–June. An overall comparison across all time periods was also done.

The data consisted of frequency of a particular behavior per minute of observation. The *t* test was used to compare the groups.

Results:

Reciprocal Behaviors. Boys clearly were more cooperative. They began the year significantly more cooperative and remained so.

Defense-Offense Behaviors. Boys defended possessions and directed their aggression to objects and things more than girls. They defended their possessions more than girls in three of the four time periods, going from a passive defense (remonstrance but no physical contact) to active physical defense of possessions in time period four. Averaged over the year, boys were significantly more aggressive. The only item in this category in which girls showed a higher frequency than boys was in *Defends Self*.

Help-Seeking and Help-Giving. In the beginning of the year boys gave help spontaneously and sought help more often than girls for interpersonal problems and in order to complete a task. These behaviors showed no appreciable sex differences after March, although boys maintained a slight superiority in seeking help for interpersonal reasons across the four time periods. There was some indication that girls were more task-oriented than boys earlier in the year.

Teacher-Child Interactions. In interactions that were initiated by the teacher, a difference in complying to teacher demands stands out clearly. Girls complied with demands, instructions, and requests more than boys; boys refused to comply more often. This difference was maintained throughout the year. Although significance levels of the differences ranged only from .20 to .10, girls had the higher mean for compliance and boys had the higher mean for refusals in nine out of nine comparisons.

There was some indication of teacher by child's sex interaction. In March–April, the teacher gave significantly more positive reinforcement to girls, yet refused offers of help from girls more often. This is confounded, however, by the fact that girls offered to help more often.

Child-Teacher Interactions. These interactions were child-initiated; girls initiated all the interactions where any male-female differences occurred. They made more bids for attention, offered more help, and had their demands acceded to more often than boys.

Interaction with Objects. Boys interacted with objects at fairly low levels of sophistication. They collided with objects and engaged in more random tactile manipulation, but in the last observation period boys completed puzzles or seriated without error more often than girls.

Anticipation and Language Behaviors. Any indication that the child planned ahead or was aware of an outcome before it occurred was coded as an instance of anticipation. All differences in this area showed boys to have the higher mean. They had the higher mean in six out of six comparisons, and the anticipation was observed in all modalities: visual, motoric, and verbal.

In the beginning of the year, boys used inarticulate screams, gestures, and cries more often than girls; in the fourth observation period, girls were observed as having more articulate speech than boys and using words and sentences.

Summary

There were clear sex differences in classroom behavior. Boys were more cooperative, defended their possessions, and were more aggressive to people and objects than girls. Boys sought help for interpersonal reasons and to complete a task more than girls, but both sexes showed a decline in help-seeking behaviors. Boys exhibited more negative responses to teacher-instigated interactions of all kinds. Boys appeared to have more immature interaction with objects earlier in the year than the girls, but completed puzzles without error more often than girls at the end of the year. This may reflect interest rather than skill. A difference in language was also noted; the boys were more inarticulate than the girls in the early part of the year, and the girls used more articulate speech by the end of the year.

Girls, on the other hand, were more compliant to demands, requests, or offers of assistance made by the teacher. These responses were consistent throughout the year. Girls also initiated more interactions with teachers and had more of their demands complied with than boys.

SUBJECTIVE IMPRESSIONS

The quantitative results provide only some of the outcomes of our program. Various aspects of the program could not be systematically evaluated because of limitations of time and money as well as unavailability of adequate methodology. Eventually some of these gaps will be filled by case history analysis.

Few, if any, of our children had difficulty separating from their mothers. They entered this new environment joyfully and enthusiastically. Although the mothers were in the classroom the first few days of school, the children gravitated toward the materials in the classroom. The significance of this case of separation is difficult to interpret. It may be due to varied experiences with adult caretakers and to the high valence of the room and the other children. The fact is that with this group the separation was not an overt issue.

Engagement with the materials varied from intense concentration to flighty sporadic involvement. In spite of limited use of expressive language, the children seemed to understand the language of the teachers. Further, the children made their wants known.

The relationship with the teachers tended to be comfortable but not intense. The children seemed relatively self-sufficient and would seek comfort and help when hurt or frustrated. We did not notice strong ties to adults. In fact, toward the middle of the year, we experimented with teacher withdrawal from some of the usual stations and observed the children's unsupervised behavior. We were impressed with the length of time constructive play behavior was sustained under these conditions.

Relations of children to each other also were highly varied, with consistent and stable friendship patterns emerging. There were enough instances of cooperative play to suggest that stereotyping of two-year-olds' social interaction as individualized and noncooperative is an overgeneralization.

Many of the children were highly variable in the degree of which they would respect productions of peers. There were those occasions when a child would destroy the production of another, grab materials, and disregard the "rights" of other children. This type of imperialism subsided, but what is most interesting is the observation that these behaviors were not consistent patterns.

Some children tended to hoard materials, as if the possession of an object functioned as a security blanket. Reluctance to surrender an object, even if not used, was observed. This possessiveness raised problems of management. If the object functions as a "security blanket," how does the teacher handle this without provoking undue anxiety in one child and still facilitate the concept of possession and surrender of what is, in effect, public property?

The relationship of the individual to his possession in a nursery school environment is of particular significance when one of the objectives of a program is to facilitate the understanding of the value of another's product and possession.

Over the year, the children not only increased in fluency and comprehensibility of language expression but also in the complexity of their messages. Our program encouraged language production in the service of reporting events and actions and in requesting materials from children and adults. However, no corrections or explicit imitations of adult language were done. Hence, gains in accuracy, fluency, and complexity seem to have occurred in relation to relevant encouragements and inducements to use language in lieu of grabbing, hitting, or other physical methods. Of course, increase in age also accounts for these changes. The program, however, did contribute when we take note of the fact that opportunity and encouragement for verbal expression were consistently expected in our program.

An interesting sidelight on this issue is reflected in the teachers' reporting that the children talked more on the way home than they did in the classroom. We pondered this and concluded, after more observation, that the reason may well be that in the classroom the children were very task-oriented, involved with actions on the materials, whereas in the bus materials were not available and the children did not have such distractions.

Another area in which considerable variability was observed was in attention span and involvement with materials. The children could and did get involved in activities and persisted for some length of time. These activities included handling small manipulative objects, building with blocks, or even symbolic play, especially in the doll corner.

In effect, the experience with this two-year-old group demonstrated that our knowledge base for working in a psychoeducational context with these children is sparse. Solace or guidance could not be found in the literature. Experimental work within a group psychoeducational context for children of this age is virtually nonexistent. Consequently, we depended heavily on our observations for teaching us what to do.

Were the goals we set for ourselves realistic? At this point and with the data we have, the answer is an unqualified yes. It is feasible to establish group nursery half-day programs for children as young as two. This is in contrast to the traditional concept which raised not only questions about age at entrance but also number of days per week. We have everything to indicate that our children successfully handled a four-day week and have every reason to believe they could assimilate a five-day week as well.

To conclude on a note of smug self-satisfaction would be misleading. There are a number of problem areas that need identification and further study, and so let us turn to these.

PROBLEM AREAS

One of the major problems facing us involves evaluation. Techniques of assessment and assessment tasks do not exist in great abundance. Most of them are embedded in intelligence tests, many are perceptual or motor types and do not allow for explicit testing of behavioral outcomes predicted from our program. This problem faces many of us in research in this area. We were not interested in measures limited to IQ scores. Hence, we had to construct some tests specifically for this project. Admittedly, these measures are new and do not have the necessary validation to argue for their psychometric purity. Rather, they are first efforts. The need for measurement procedures continues to be great.

In this regard, however, our experience has raised considerable doubt as to the validity of traditional psychometric procedures. We have found that at least in the numerical and language areas, performance in the classroom does not relate to performance in the testing situations. Children frequently failed items in the formal situation (e.g., concept of one) which they understood in the classroom context. This suggests an interesting problem concerning the contextual basis of knowledge and the degree to which measurement for very young children should follow the same format as for older children.

When do we know when a child knows? is the basic issue that emerges. If he can respond only in one context and not another, what does this tell us? We are not convinced that this issue is resolved with psychometric reliability, but rather that it indicates the contextual basis of knowledge. In effect, the child is not able to transcend the situational supports that are integral to his knowledge base. From a theoretical and practical perspective, such information is very telling of the child's cognitive status.

Another set of evaluation issues relates to the tasks and the formal test situations. Many of the problems are self-evident (e.g., boredom, fatigue, and strangeness). What of the particular variables themselves? For us, the decision was to test for variables that were directly relevant to the primary mission of the study. There was no time for developing procedures, nor were there measures already specifically developed for our program. Thus, the procedures employed are in fact crude efforts. The only solution was to create *all* new measures prior to the onset of the program. The problems are horrendous, not only in terms of operationalizing our conceptualizations but also in demands of time and money. Thus, there is no question in our mind that our assessments are approximations containing error. To employ only the true and the tried (e.g., Stanford-Binet) shifts the nature of our assessment to global procedures, and this is a choice we did not want to make.

Formal testing, however, also leaves much to be desired. Such procedures do not provide any explanatory bases for obtained change. What is needed is a careful monitoring of transactions that occur from Time 1 to Time 2. To carry out such a process involves a heavy input of observational data-gathering because we are observing a complex, systematic network in which the teacher, the child, other children, and materials interact in varying degrees and on various levels. The complexity of the setting demands a very careful conceptual analysis defining the relevant variables. We are in the process of analyzing data gathered over a one-year period. To date, we can say nothing except that the effort was strenuous and we hope it will prove productive. It is, we believe, a necessary task if we are to provide a rational base for making statements about sources of behavioral change.

Since children are rapidly aging organisms, disentangling developmental effects from program effects becomes a major question. Employment of control groups is one method of dealing with the problem. Control groups in other settings should be monitored with equal degrees of intensity, however. Few programs are able to mount this effort and few have done it with some success. There is much more work to be done, because all programs have method problems for which they cannot be faulted. This seems to be the challenge in this field of research. Our methods are not geared to such multivaried problems.

A particularly confounding element is one that is characteristic of the populations usually involved in such evaluations. Many middle-class situations have some stability of family and living arrangements. In many of the social groups serviced by these programs, however, shifts and changes in family and living patterns are frequent and contribute sources of error beyond the control of research techniques.

That such problems are characteristic of all longitudinal studies is obvious, but when the project under study is involved in defining sources of change, then the research task is even more complicated. It is not always feasible to have random assignments, control over psychological and sociological factors, and cohorts of children and of teachers for tightly controlled replications.

If asked, Is the program a success? we would have to first ask for criteria of success. Judging by the morale of the children, attendance, and involvement in program activities, there seems little doubt that the children enjoyed their time in nursery school. The parents seemed satisfied and are eager for the program to continue until the children enter kindergarten. Parenthetically, in regard to parents we were surprised to learn that some of the mothers went back to work or to school once their children were in the program. Whether this is coincidental or a direct result of our program will have to be examined. If returning to school or work is directly related to the program, a justification for the program is provided in and of itself from the parental perspective.

Turning now to objective criteria, we are still analyzing the data. It seems clear that the children are showing expected gains in the various competencies under consideration. Further work here is planned; in a year we shall be in a better position to make definitive statements.

Our experiences indicate the great need for more methodological ingenuity in order to grasp the significance of the experience for these children.

Another major source of error in research of this type lies in the execution of the program. The research objectives and the derivative program objectives may be explicit and articulated via precise instructional media. The application of these materials, however, is the responsibility of the teacher. Variation in teacher motivation and resourcefulness in executing the program can account for variability in outcome. Of course, teachers are not robots, so in programs calling for individual judgment they are prone to vary.

A related issue is the fact that not every child is equally exposed to every phase of the program. The only way to test the degree to which children are receiving a given amount of stimulation is to intensify procedures and to increase sample size; on the other hand, this requires more teachers and hence contributes to teacher variability as a source of error. The trade-off here can only be surmised at this point. Obvious as these issues are, our job is to try to create procedures for their solution. We hope in the near future to provide more specific suggestions along this line.

A final area of concern involves the interactive play of forces that influence the outcome. Specifically, we are referring here to such considerations as the pattern of relationships among affective and cognitive variables. As we have seen from our own data, attentional variables seem to be related to performance on our assessment procedures. Thus, the level of performance may well be attenuated by concomitant behaviors not wholly examined.

The issues are complex. Although the aim of this paper was to describe in some detail the workings of ECEP, we could not avoid mentioning some methodological concerns that plague us all.

These are but some of the issues we pondered and struggled over with varying degrees of success. The solutions often are partial and ephemeral, especially those related to interpersonal factors. Ongoing monitoring seems to be the most effective solution.

The more precise research issues, then, are still before all of us. We are not pessimistic, but neither are we naive enough to believe that simplistic solutions are possible. Rather, the solution resides in a lot of hard work and thinking, embedded in the firm conviction that we are engaged in a mammoth task that will tax our patience, endurance, and creativity. Since the experimental research model of the laboratory is not appropriate, we must search for a model that is realistic and tuned into the social realities, and this is often far from the ideals of research-design textbooks. For all researchers in this field, the first problem is to work at conceptual model-building. Models that integrate discrepant data and that generate provocative as well as practical hypotheses are essential to progress.

Research in preschool education poses a major challenge to social scientists. It is difficult, taxing, and rewarding. We believe it has a unique set of problems that cry for solution.

REFERENCES

Beller, E. K. In Press, *Research on Teaching Organized Programs in Early Education.* Rand McNally.

Bissell, Joan S. 1971. Implementation of planned variation in Head Start. Washington, D.C.: U.S. Office of Child Development, Department of Health, Education and Welfare, April.

Emmerich, W. 1971. *Disadvantaged children and their first school experiences: Structure and development of personal and social behavior in preschool settings.* Princeton, New Jersey: Educational Testing Service, November.

Ginsburg, H., and Opper, S. 1969. *Piaget's theory of intellectual development: An introduction.* Englewood Cliffs, New Jersey: Prentice-Hall.

Golden, M., and Birns, B. 1968. Social class and cognitive development in infancy. *Merrill Palmer Quarterly* 14: 139–49.

Hoffman, M. L. 1960. Power assertion by the parent and its impact on the child. *Child Development* 31: 129–43.

Hunt, J. McV. 1969. *The challenge of incompetence and poverty.* Urbana, Illinois: University of Illinois Press.

Inhelder, B., and Piaget, J. 1964. *Early growth of logic in the child: Classification and seriation.* New York: Harper and Row.

Kamii, C., and Radin, N. L. 1969. The retardation of disadvantaged Negro preschoolers: Some characteristics found from an item analysis of the Stanford-Binet Test. *Psychology in the Schools* 6: 283–88.

Overton, W. F. 1972. Piaget's theory of intellectual development and progressive education. In J. R. Squire (ed.), *A new look at progressive education.* Association for Supervision and Curriculum Development, Washington, D.C., pp. 88–116.

Piaget, J. 1955. *The child's construction of reality.* London: Routledge and Kegan Paul.

—— 1962. *Play, dreams and imitation in childhood.* Trans. by C. Gattegno and F. M. Hodgson. New York: Norton.

Sigel, I. E. 1960. Influence techniques: A concept used to study parental behavior. *Child Development* 31: 799–806.

—— 1972. Distancing hypothesis: Revisited. An elaboration of a neo-Piagetian view of the development of representational thought. Paper presented at third annual Western Symposium on Learning. Bellingham: Western Washington State College.

Sigel, I. E., Anderson, L. M., and Shapiro, H. 1966. Categorization behavior of lower and middle class Negro preschool children: Differences in dealing with representations of familiar objects. *Journal of Negro Education* 35: 218–29.

Sigel, I. E., and McBane, Bonnie. 1967. Cognitive competence and level of symbolization among five year old children. In J. Hellmuth (ed.), *The disadvantaged child*, vol. 1. Seattle, Washington: Special Child Publications.

Sigel, I. E., and Perry, C. 1968. Psycholinguistic diversity among culturally deprived children. *American Journal of Orthopsychiatry* 38: 122–6.

Sigel, I. E., and Olmsted, P. 1970. Modification of cognitive skills among lower class black children. In J. Hellmuth (ed.), *The disadvantaged child*, vol. 3. New York: Bruner, Mazel.

JOAN S. BISSELL

U.S. Department of Health, Education and Welfare *

Washington, D.C. 20202

IV. PLANNED VARIATION IN HEAD START AND FOLLOW THROUGH[1]

Beginning in the mid-1960s, the federal government undertook a number of systematic experiments to explore the efficacy of various alternative approaches for delivering educational and social services. Two of the largest federal efforts in systematic experimentation were the programs of Planned Variation in Head Start and Follow Through.[2] In this chapter the history of each program, the models of early childhood education included in each, the problems involved in evaluating each program, and the patterns of results found in the first major evaluations are described.

PROJECT HEAD START

A brief history of Project Head Start will serve to place the Planned Variation experiment in perspective. During the early 1960s an increasing number of psychologists and educators began to study the effects of early experiences on human development. Much research suggested that preschool compensatory education might be an important step for disrupting the cycle of poverty experienced by large numbers of Americans. Combined with powerful social and political factors, this notion led to the authorization of Project Head Start in 1965. Among its comprehensive objectives were the following:

---

*Now at Laboratory of Human Development, Graduate School of Education, Harvard University, Cambridge, Massachusetts 02138.

[1] Many individuals in the Office of Child Development, Office of Education, local communities, and the Stanford Research Institute are responsible for the successful operation of the Planned Variation studies. The author, who was involved with these studies as a member of the staff of the Department of Health, Education and Welfare, wishes to acknowledge all those dedicated individuals whose extensive efforts were the basis for this chapter.

[2] Both Head Start and Follow Through are comprehensive programs, including the following components: health, nutrition, education, psychological and social services, and parent involvement. The Planned Variation studies focus most directly on the educational and parental involvement components of the programs.

- improving the child's health and physical abilities;

- fostering the emotional and social development of the child by encouraging self-confidence, spontaneity, curiosity, and self-discipline;

- promoting the child's mental processes and skills, with particular attention to conceptual and verbal skills;

- establishing patterns and expectations of success for the child in order to create a climate of confidence for his future learning efforts;

- increasing the child's capacity to relate positively to family members and others, while at the same time strengthening the family's ability to relate positively to the child;

- developing in the child and his family a responsible attitude toward society and fostering constructive opportunities for society to work together with the poor in solving their problems;

- increasing the sense of dignity and self-worth within the child and his family.

Although these objectives have continued to guide Head Start, the program has evolved considerably since its inception. Most early Head Start centers were varied, hastily assembled adaptations of the adjustment-centered nursery schools long attended by middle-class children. Tested and generally accepted curricula for providing enriched experiences to children of the poor simply were not available in 1965. Since that time, there has been a proliferation of preschool models for disadvantaged children based on different educational theories and methods.

Impact of Head Start

Evaluative studies concerning the effects of Head Start have been conducted since the program's beginning. Similar evaluations have been undertaken by other preschool programs, and the findings from the two groups of studies have been basically alike. Typically, studies have shown increases on general ability and achievement tests immediately after participation in both summer and full-year preschool programs. Participant children generally have performed better than nonparticipants immediately after the program, with the differences small in absolute magnitude but "statistically significant." Although most evaluations have demonstrated immediate increases, the magnitude of gains has been large in only a few cases. The increases have been greatest when programs were of longest duration, when program objectives were well-formulated and focused on the domains evaluated, and when the participating children's initial level of performance was low. In addition to reporting gains on measures of intellectual functioning, some evaluators also have reported immediate positive effects on children's attitudes, motivation, and social behavior as rated by teachers (Grotberg 1969).

Follow-up evaluations, however, have indicated that the immediate advantages to participant children generally diminish by the end of the first or second year in public school. What seems to happen is that the increases in rate of development promoted during the preschool year on measures of ability and achievement are not sustained during the early elementary grades. Rather, the rate of growth during these years is somewhat less for participant than for nonparticipant children. The result is that usually by the end of first grade, although in a few cases not until the second or third grade (Beller 1969; Engelmann 1970; Bereiter 1972; Weikart 1970, 1972), poor children who have had preschool experiences perform approximately on a par with their peers who have not, and both groups perform below national norms.

The usual explanation for the "leveling off" in rate of development by participant children is that public schools are unable to support the increments in children's growth which occur during participation in Head Start and other preschool programs. As Datta (1969, p. 14) explained: "It may be naive to expect a child to continue to progress rapidly in a classroom where the teacher may be responsible for 30 or more children, may be primarily concerned with maintaining order and perhaps convinced that most of her students have little potential."

An equally plausible explanation for the failure of preschool gains to be maintained is, of course, that the skills taught in preschool programs generally relate to functions which are specific to the preschool years and which have very little transfer value to later behaviors.

Basically, the findings after several years of preschool compensatory education are inconclusive. A few Head Start programs and experimental preschools have produced relatively large and lasting improvements in the measured cognitive achievement of low-income children. But the majority of Head Start and other compensatory preschool programs, although producing small immediate gains, have not produced lasting increases in children's intellectual development.

The current situation regarding knowledge of the effects of preschool programs is problematic. On the one hand, little conclusive information exists about the total range of the effects of programs or the processes which underlie these effects. On the other, the federal government's involvement in education and child care programs for preschool children continues, as does the interest of state and local governments, industries, and groups of parents.

HEAD START PLANNED VARIATION

The Head Start Planned Variation Study was undertaken in 1969 to study several well-formulated approaches to preschool education in a variety of settings. In conjunction with Follow Through it explores such issues as:

- the processes involved in implementing various early intervention programs;

- the nature of experiences provided by different early intervention programs;

- the effects of different intervention programs on Head Start children and their families;

- the contributions of intervention programs during the preschool years versus during the primary grades;

- the benefits of continuous, sequenced intervention following the same educational strategy over several years.

The purpose of conducting these studies is *not* to identify one or two "best" approaches to compensatory education. Rather, the goal of the Planned Variation studies is to provide local communities with information about a range of educational alternatives, both in terms of specific program elements which can be combined in an eclectic fashion and in terms of total "program packages."[3]

Head Start Planned Variation Models

In order to be included in the Head Start Planned Variation study, an early education model had to meet the following criteria:

- It must have represented a well-formulated, previously tested strategy for preschool education.

---

[3]It is important to note that both the Office of Child Development and the Office of Education wish to promote good educational practices in general. Neither prescribes that curriculum "models" be adopted by local communities. The Planned Variation studies are intended only to provide information about a variety of educational approaches.

- The sponsor of the model must have been implementing a program for elementary school children based on the model's principles as part of the Follow Through program.[4]

On the basis of these two criteria, eight preschool models were selected to participate in the first year of the Head Start Planned Variation study. During that year, each model was implemented in two communities where the sponsor had already been operating Follow Through classes. It is the results of that first-year study that are summarized in this chapter.[5] Brief descriptions of the eight models included in the first year of Planned Variation in Head Start are as follow:[6,7]

A pragmatic action-oriented model, sponsored by the Education Development Center in Newton, Massachusetts, was inspired by the English Infant Schools. Perhaps the unique feature of this approach is its great emphasis on self-development, for teachers and schools as well as for children. Its objective is to fashion classroom environments responsive to the individual needs and styles of children and teachers. It is an advisory and consultant system which encourages schools and teachers to experiment with diverse avenues for fostering children's self-respect, respect for others, imagination, curiosity, persistence, openness to change, and ability to challenge ideas.

The academically oriented preschool model is sponsored by Wesley Becker and Siegfried Engelmann of the University of Oregon. This model is based on the premise that low-income children are academically behind middle-class children. In order to "catch up," it is assumed that they must learn essential skills at a faster rate than middle-class children "naturally" learn these skills. Consequently, the model promotes academic learning in reading, arithmetic, and language through structured drills and reinforcement techniques. Small

[4]A program sponsor refers to an individual, a group, a university, or a private corporation that directs a specific model.

[5]In the two remaining years of the Head Start Planned Variation study, the eight models were extended into additional communities and four new models were added. Data from the second and third years are not yet available.

[6]The descriptions are taken from Klein and Datta (1970), Maccoby and Zellner (1970), Gordon (in press), and the author's own observations.

[7]Montessori projects were not included, due to problems in accommodating Montessori training requirements to staff training procedures in the Head Start and Follow Through Planned Variation programs. Montessori projects have been included, however, in other federally funded comparative evaluations of preschool models (Di Lorenzo et al. 1969; Karnes et al. 1969; Miller & Dyer 1970).

study groups of five to ten children are organized by teachers according to ability levels in order to facilitate presentation of patterned learning materials and to elicit constant verbal responses from children.

The behavior analysis model was developed and is sponsored by Don Bushell of the University of Kansas. The goal of the program is to teach children both subject matter skills, such as reading and arithmetic, and social skills through systematic reinforcement procedures using a token system and individualized programmed instruction. Bushell does not see the token system as precluding the possibility that learning itself can be rewarding for a child. The tokens are used only to support the child's early learning efforts until he reaches a level of mastery that will allow him to enjoy a new skill for its intrinsic reward.

The Bank Street College model, developed and sponsored by the Bank Street College of Education in New York City, represents a "whole-child" approach in which the ultimate objective is to enable each child to become deeply involved and self-directed in his learning. By functioning as consistent adults that children can trust, by being responsive to individual children's needs, and by sensitizing them to sights, sounds, feelings, and ideas, Bank Street teachers help children build positive images of themselves as learners. These teachers build on classroom events initiated by children as well as planning activities, such as cooking, block-building, and socio-dramatic play— activities characteristic of traditional, middle-class nursery schools.

The Florida parent-educator model, developed and sponsored by Ira Gordon of the University of Florida, insures home instruction as well as classroom instruction by involving parent-educators. A parent-educator is a mother from the local community who works in the classroom as a teacher's aide and with parents in their homes. The curriculum used in the model is cognitively oriented and based generally on the theories of Piaget, although it is flexible and varies according to the needs of particular individuals and classes.

The Tucson early education model, originally designed by Marie Hughes, is sponsored by the University of Arizona. The model was first developed for Mexican-American children and, therefore, concentrates on facilitating the transition from Spanish to English and on the more general development of language competencies. The model attempts to promote intellectual skills, motivation, and social skills through providing children with freedom to choose activities, through fostering cooperation among children, and through systematic positive reinforcement from teachers.

The responsive model, designed and sponsored by Glen Nimnicht of the Far West Laboratory for Educational Research and Development, is focused on helping children develop both a positive self-image and intellectual abilities through use of a responsive environment which consists of self-pacing and self-rewarding materials. These materials emphasize problem-solving skills, sensory discrimination, and language ability; they provide immediate feedback and enjoyment from learning itself. The model is best distinguished by its classroom environment, which is structured so that as a child freely explores he will make discoveries and thereby learn.

The cognitive model, developed and sponsored by David Weikart of the High Scope Educational Research Foundation, is a cognitively oriented preschool program, primarily derived from the theories of Piaget. The model emphasizes the importance of home-training sessions with mothers and of decisionmaking roles for teachers. Teachers plan detailed lessons and activities; they are given continual assistance from classroom supervisors.

The clustering of educational approaches, each of which is distinct in many ways, requires detailed analyses of program content if it is to be meaningful. Although clustering on the basis of systematic classroom observations is likely to be more accurate than clustering simply on the basis of programs' stated orientations and procedures, the latter approach was the only feasible way to categorize first-year Planned Variation models. Thus, clustering on the basis of programs' stated emphases was undertaken (in the absence of an assessment of the validity of the resultant categories), primarily to provide a convenient method for reducing data to manageable proportions. The three categories into which models were grouped by the Stanford Research Institute are the Preacademic, Cognitive Discovery, and Discovery approaches.

The *Preacademic* programs are the Engelmann-Becker academically oriented and the Bushell behavior analysis models. Both foster development of preacademic skills, such as number and letter recognition, reading, writing, and instructional language; their techniques include use of systematic reinforcement.

The *Cognitive Discovery* programs are the Florida parent-educator model, the Tucson early education model, the responsive model, and the Weikart cognitive model. Each promotes the growth of basic cognitive processes, such as categorizing, differentiating, abstracting, and inferring, by providing continuous verbal accompaniment to children's sequenced exploration.

The *Discovery* programs are the EDC pragmatic action-oriented model and the Bank Street College model. Both foster learning as part of the humanistic growth of the "whole child" by encouraging such experiences as free exploration and self-expression. They place heavy emphasis on the child's sense of self-worth, of trust in adults and the world, and respect for others.

Head Start Planned Variation Study

It would require numerous lengthy chapters to describe adequately the methodological shortcomings in the Head Start (and Follow Through) Planned Variation research designs. Nevertheless, the major problems in the studies will be enumerated here in order to provide the reader with a framework for interpreting the evaluation findings.

The basic design of the Planned Variation studies is not a classical "experimental" design, since sites throughout the country were not randomly assigned to preschool models and children were not randomly assigned to model and "control" classes within sites. This problem is what Datta (1971) has called "the soft underbelly of the mega-studies: the inability to over-recruit and assign children to treatments or sites to treatments at random or in keeping with sound design principles" (p. 5). Without random assignment it cannot be assumed that groups in different models are comparable upon entry into the program and, therefore, that apparent model effects are attributable to true effects of the models rather than to characteristics of self-selected participants. Although a variety of statistical procedures can be used to adjust scores of Planned Variation and comparison children to minimize effects of initial group differences, ". . . there is simply no logical or statistical procedure that can be counted on to make proper allowances for uncontrolled preexisting differences between groups" (Lord 1967, p. 305). Given this limitation, the Planned Variation studies should be used primarily to generate hypotheses that can be tested in rigorous small-scale experiments, rather than to establish definitive conclusions.

Another major experimental design problem relates to a recurrent issue in longitudinal studies—sample attrition. Since attrition rates have been particularly high in the Planned Variation studies, the possibility of large biases in resultant samples must be considered. At some Planned Variation sites the missing data level exceeds 50 percent for certain tests. Since many children do not remain in the evaluation sample from the beginning to the end, the generalizability of the evaluation results is suspect. In addition, differential attrition rates among models jeopardize the validity of measured differences between them. Although statistical corrections can again be made, the only conclusions which one can draw with some assurance are those dealing with patterns of growth among the select children who continued to participate in particular models.

Other critical problems in the Planned Variation studies concern the measurement instruments used in the evaluations. When the studies were designed, criterion measures representing common objectives of the various models and having reasonably adequate reliability and validity were selected for inclusion in the evaluations. This led to a heavy weighting of instruments assessing cognitive achievement. For some models, the measurement instruments represented a reasonably fair set of criteria for evaluating their effects, although the full extent and variety of effects may have been underestimated. For other models, while the measures that were used tapped some of their objectives, goals in other domains were not measured, due to the unavailability of reliable, validated tests in these domains. In general, the Planned Variation evaluations focus attention primarily on the limited range of program outcomes related to cognitive achievement.

Even in the measurement of cognitive achievement, the Planned Variation instruments have serious limitations. All measures of cognitive achievement include, to some extent, elements of general ability, general achievement, and specific skills. Although the most adequate criteria for measuring program effects are those concentrating on general achievement and specific skills, most instruments used in the Planned Variation batteries were heavily weighted with measurement of general ability.

A large number of additional methodological problems range from possible floor and ceiling effects on test instruments and questionable test administration and scoring procedures to missing data, nonrepresentativeness of projects, appropriateness of the units of analysis used in the evaluation, etc. Instead of elaborating these problems in detail here, we will move on to a description of the two studies in an attempt to pull out of them the patterns of preliminary results which, regardless of methodological flaws, appear to be important hypotheses for further study.

The objectives of the first-year Head Start Planned Variation study were: (1) documenting implementation of the eight different models; and (2) undertaking preliminary analyses of program effects.[8] The first-year evaluation was carried out by Stanford Research Institute.

Measures of Implementation

The process of model implementation was documented in several ways. Each sought to answer the question: To what extent do the classrooms embody the teaching strategies and concepts advocated by their respective models?

Two methods of describing implementation relied on reports prepared by Office of Child Development consultants and by model sponsors. These reports

---

[8]The primary objective of the first-year evaluation was to document implementation. In future years, the focus will shift to measurement of effects—both immediate and sustained—with assessment of children continuing through the end of the third grade. The reason for this two-stage approach was to enable models to achieve satisfactory implementation before extensive program impact comparisons were made.

concerned the success with which various classrooms were implemented, the level of performance of different teachers, and the efforts of sponsor representatives to train, guide, and support teachers. A third method relied on information collected in teacher questionnaires. A fourth method of documenting implementation was based on analyses of the actual experiences provided for children in the different models. This information was derived through systematic observations using the Stanford Research Institute Classroom Observation instrument. The instrument addresses such questions as: How is time allocated in the classroom? What materials are used? What do the adults do? What do the children do? How are children grouped? What control systems are used? What is the affective environment? (Stanford Research Institute 1971a, p. 114).

Measures of Growth among Children

In the first year of the Head Start Planned Variation study, assessment of growth among children included measures of cognitive functioning, achievement, response styles in coping with tasks, and personal-social development.[9] Initiative and curiosity were not tapped, due to the unavailability of validated, standardized tests in these domains. Thus, due to the state of the art in measuring young children's development, it was not possible in the first year of the Head Start Planned Variation study to measure all the significant concerns of all the programs.[10]

The first instrument measuring growth among children, a test of *academic achievement*, was a combination of six subtests from the New York University (NYU) Early Childhood Inventory. It tested knowledge related to specific areas, including science, mathematics, letters, numerals, and shapes.

The second and third measures, the Preschool Inventory (Caldwell 1967) and the Stanford-Binet Intelligence Scale, were included as two of the best available measures of *general cognitive development*. Both are complex measures, however, and scores on them reflect numerous motivational and cultural experience factors as well as general learning ability (Zigler & Butterfield 1968).

The fourth measure was the Hertzig-Birch scoring of the Stanford-Binet. It is used to analyze the way a child responds to the Binet. A child may pass or fail an item in several ways. He may give a work response, for example, either by doing what is specifically required by the task (a delimited response), or

---

[9] Personal-social development was evaluated through clinical case studies prepared by a team of psychologists at the University of Maryland under the direction of Dr. Laura Dittmann. The results of these studies are described in Dittmann et al. (1970).

[10] An extensive effort has been made to develop a battery assessing numerous domains for the second- and third-year evaluations of Planned Variation in Head Start.

by doing things which extend beyond the limits of the task (an extended response). In either case, his response may be verbal or nonverbal. A child also may give a nonwork response in any of several ways: he might provide an irrelevant verbalization instead of engaging in task-directed activity (substitution) or he might not respond at all (passivity).[11] The Hertzig-Birch scoring provides a description of a child's *style of coping with cognitive demands*.

The fifth instrument, a measure of another component of response style, was the Maccoby *Motor Inhibition Test* (Maccoby et al. 1965). It requires a child to perform several tasks twice, once at his natural speed and once as slowly as he can. The difference between the two scores is considered a measure of his capacity to inhibit movement.[12]

Measures of Changes among Parents

The analysis of changes among parents included an assessment of *mother-child interaction styles*. This domain was included because: (1) previous research showed a strong relationship between the nature of mother-child interactions in a structured situation and children's success in both laboratory problem-solving tasks and in school (Hess et al. 1968; Bee et al. 1969; Hess et al. 1969), and (2) an objective of several Planned Variation models was to involve the parents in the program, particularly the mother, teaching her new techniques for interacting with her child in learning situations.

The Eight-Block Sort Task developed by Hess and Shipman (1965) was administered to study mother-child interaction. The task involves sorting eight blocks into four groups defined by two criteria. The blocks differ according to several attributes—height, mark, color, and shape. Only two of these attributes are relevant to the sorting task: height (tall or short) and mark (X or O painted on the top).

The mother teaches the child to sort the blocks on the basis of height and mark. Next, the child is asked to sort the blocks this way and to explain the basis for the sorting. While the mother and child interact freely in this standardized situation, several questions are explored. Among them are: How does the mother communicate information to her child? How does the mother structure the learning situation? In particular, does she provide her child with task-relevant information? How does she monitor and regulate the child's behavior? How are the child's performance and the mother's behavior related?

---

[11]Hertzig et al. (1968, pp. 13–15).

[12]Maccoby's original measure was adapted for use in the Head Start Planned Variation study.

Another parent measure was a questionnaire developed by Stanford Research Institute. The items contained in the questionnaire tapped several areas, among them:

- the extent of parental involvement in the Head Start program;

- parents' attitudes toward schools and toward other situations influencing their lives;

- the things parents liked best about the Head Start program;

- the differences parents thought Head Start made in their lives.

THE SAMPLE

The sample in the first-year Head Start Planned Variation study included (1) children in the eight Planned Variation models, implemented in several classes in two communities each, and (2) children in "regular" Head Start comparison classes, generally in the same communities as the Planned Variation classes.[13]

The total number of children in the sample was 2,647. Of these, 1,569 were in Planned Variation classes and 1,078 were in "regular" Head Start comparison classes. The children came from northern (5.3 percent), eastern (23.4 percent), southern (42.7 percent), central (21.2 percent), and western (7.4 percent) states. Most (72 percent) were between four and one-half and five and one-half years old at the beginning of the Head Start program in the fall, although they ranged in age from three to six and one-half years. The sample included approximately half girls and half boys.

The ethnic composition of the sample was approximately 55 percent Black, 25 percent White, 7 percent American Indian, 2 percent Puerto Rican, and 1 percent Mexican-American. (No information was available on the remaining 10 percent of the sample.) This represents a composition fairly similar to that of the national Head Start program.[14]

The majority of parents in the sample had attended only grade school (43.1 percent) or had attended high school but had no additional formal

[13]In five cases comparison classes were in other communities, since samples of non-Head Start children were not available in the same communities.

[14]In the 1969 national Head Start program, 51 percent of the children were Black, 23.4 percent White, 2.3 percent American Indian, 6.6 percent Puerto Rican, 8.8 percent Mexican-American, 0.5 percent Eskimo, 0.2 percent Oriental, and 1.0 percent of other ethnic groups, with no information available on 6.2 percent.

schooling (49.5 percent). The most frequently reported employment of the heads of households was as an unskilled laborer (43.8 percent).

With respect to age, sex, ethnicity, and family background, children in the Planned Variation classes and children in the "regular" Head Start classes were essentially alike for the groups as a whole. There were, however, marked variations in these characteristics within given sites.[15]

IMPLEMENTATION FINDINGS

The first-year data on implementation, like the other findings, are subject to critical methodological shortcomings and are highly tentative. No attempt was made to estimate inter-rater reliability in implementation ratings or to calibrate ratings across different observers. Still, some preliminary patterns are noteworthy as hypotheses for further study.

Table 1. Ratings of Teacher Implementation by Sponsors

Period	Teacher ratings	Preacademic models	Cognitive Discovery models	Discovery models[a]
Fall 1969	High	10%	3%	0%
	Medium	42%	21%	21%
	Low	48%	76%	79%
	N	19	28	14[a]
Spring 1970	High	55%	31%	44%
	Medium	45%	38%	13%
	Low	0%	31%	44%
	N	19	33	16[a]

[a]Reflects only the Bank Street model.

One measure of implementation made use of reports prepared by program sponsors and Office of Child Development consultants. Table 1 presents the ratings of teacher implementation given by sponsors in the fall and the spring. These ratings indicated that:

[15]Variations within given sites in these characteristics appear not to have been dealt with adequately by the evaluators in the data analysis.

- Most teachers began the year in October rated low on implementation, although the majority had been given two weeks or more of preservice training.

- By the end of the year, a large number of teachers had achieved ratings of high or medium implementation. Thus, many of them appeared to make substantial progress during the year.

- It appeared that there was a relationship between curricular approach and success of implementation, such that:

  1) In both the fall and spring, the largest proportion of teachers rated high or medium in implementation was in the Preacademic models.

  2) The proportions of teachers rated high for implementation in the Cognitive Discovery and Discovery programs were about equal, but more teachers were rated low in Discovery programs.

At the end of the year, sponsors were asked to predict the performance of teachers during the second year of Planned Variation. Preacademic sponsors predicted that virtually all their first-year teachers would perform as program exemplars by the next year. Cognitive Discovery and Discovery sponsors predicted slower rates of improvement, with little or no change for some teachers.

These data suggest that the changes in teacher behavior required by Cognitive Discovery and Discovery models may take a good deal of time to occur and may not realistically occur in *all* Head Start teachers. Some intrinsic characteristics of these models might explain this phenomenon. Most of them require the internalization of a broad theory of child development. They require a teacher to initiate and respond to a large array of naturally occurring events in insightful, supportive ways which foster children's growth in numerous domains. Implicit in the Discovery models—especially in the EDC pragmatic, action-oriented model—is the notion of few precise specifications for teacher behavior or curriculum content. The EDC (and to a lesser degree the Bank Street) model is an advisory and consultant system which enables schools to move toward goals that are determined to a large degree by the particular community. In contrast, the Preacademic models are closer to "packages" specifying discrete and highly explicit preplanned components in their daily operation.[16] It appears that these kinds of differences influence

---

[16]The distinction between "package program" and "consultant systems" is taken from Gordon (1972).

the relative ease with which Head Start centers can implement a new model in a short time and the respective ratings on implementation among the models.

Another important pattern suggested in the study concerned the relationship between a teacher's background and ratings of her performance. There was essentially no relationship between years of education and success in implementation for Planned Variation teachers. There was, however, a relationship between teacher's background and rating of performance in the "regular" Head Start comparison classes. This finding is especially noteworthy, since the teachers in Planned Variation classes had, on the average, less previous academic training than teachers in the "regular" classes. Planned Variation classes had fewer teachers with bachelor degrees or further training (33 percent) than did "regular" classes (45 percent) and more teachers who had attended only high school or junior college (67 percent in Planned Variation and 54 percent in "regular" classes). The relationships between background and success in implementation suggest that sponsors' technical assistance may have provided the "know-how" that teachers ordinarily gain through academic training and experience.[17]

The sponsors' and consultants' reports pointed to specific issues involved in implementing new early education models. For example, one recurrent issue in the reports was that the models required complex changes in teacher behavior. In the fall, one consultant reported:

"The teacher is telling, rather than helping, the child discover (a difficult task for many teachers, yet a major component of this model). I'm not sure the teachers know what 'exploration and discovery' means. I think they think *they* discover for the child."

Similarly, new teacher-aide relationships had to be worked out: "The relationship between the teacher and assistant teacher is not implemented. The assistant teacher is used more for clean-up chores than as an assistant teacher. According to the model, the assistant teacher is supposed to plan with the teacher and work out different responsibilities in terms of the program."

The reports also suggested external factors related to ease of implementation. Successful operation was more likely to be reported in sites where:

- Head Start facilities and materials were at least adequate. Some sites were subject to disruption due to heating, plumbing, and lighting breakdowns and slow procurement of necessary equipment, while others enjoyed well-arranged, well-lighted, well-maintained, and well-equipped quarters.

[17]It is important to note that the measures of training dealt only with level of training and not with area of specialization.

- The Head Start program itself was stable. Some Planned Variation sites were disrupted by internal dissension, racial tensions, conflicts between the operating agency and other groups, and delays in funding, while other sites had stable, well-organized staffs that worked together as a team and related well to other agencies.

- Teachers felt that the sponsor had something to offer, because the sponsor's field staff functioned as helpful educational consultants (almost independent of model content) or because the model content was something they really could use.

Observations in select classes provided additional, especially interesting information about implementation. These are among the first data describing the actual experiences that children have in educational programs based on a range of different models. They indicate a large amount of diversity in the kinds of preschool experiences which can be provided for children.

In areas of primary importance to models, children's experiences reflected models' stated orientations. In these areas, models generally could be distinguished from one another and from "regular" Head Start classes. In areas of lesser importance to the models, there was considerable overlap in the nature of children's experiences in the various programs.

For example, the observations showed the following about program content:

- Academic activities involving numbers, letters, and language training occurred most frequently in Preacademic models.

- Social Studies activities as well as puzzles and games teaching such things as colors, sizes, and shapes occurred most frequently in Cognitive Discovery models.

- Expressive, role-playing activities such as doll play and fantasy occurred most frequently in Discovery programs and "regular" classes.

- "Regular" Head Start classes included a relatively large component of cognitive training—as much as model programs except in the areas of primary concern to the models.

In addition to demonstrating a considerable correspondence between models' stated orientations and their actual content, the classroom observations added to the evolving picture of natural variations in "regular" Head Start classes. They demonstrated diversity, for example, in the frequency of academic language experiences provided to children (ranging from occurrence in 3 percent to 27 percent of the observation periods in "regular" classes), in puzzle and game experiences (ranging from occurrence in 4 percent to 23 percent of the periods observed), in the frequency of active indoor games (ranging from occurrence in 0 percent to 11 percent of the periods), and in the frequency of individualized instruction (ranging from occurrence in 0.2 percent to 7 percent of the observation periods in "regular" classes).

GROWTH AMONG CHILDREN AND PARENTS

Measures of participants' growth, even more than those on implementation, must be viewed as hypotheses for further study rather than as conclusions. The implementation study demonstrated that successfully establishing models in new sites generally involves an extensive training effort for sponsor field representatives, for teachers, and for communities. This suggests that measures of participants' growth in early stages of implementation may not represent levels or patterns of growth which may appear after two or three years of a model's operation. In addition, the lack of random assignment of sites to models and of children to Planned Variation and comparison classes within sites means that apparent model effects might actually be due to preexisting differences between subjects participating in the various Head Start models.

Cognitive Measures

Keeping in mind the limitations in the data, let us examine the measures of children's performance. The data showed that on the measures of *academic achievement* and *general cognitive* development the mean gains of all the Head Start children—in both model and "regular" classes—were larger than those attributable to usual maturational development in these children.[18] These gains were distributed across all classes, suggesting a measurable effect on participating in a Head Start program on children's cognitive development.

Another preliminary finding was that children in Planned Variation classes made larger gains than children in "regular" Head Start classes on both cogni-

[18]Changes greater than those attributable to usual maturational development in these children were derived by comparing the gains children made during the year with expected gains based on the fall scores of same-ethnicity cohorts who were the same age in the fall as were the Planned Variation children in the spring. It is important to recognize that this technique allowed for possible confounding of *Sesame Street* effects with Head Start effects.

tive measures. The differences were quite small, however, and valid inferences must await replication.[19]

In order to compare growth among children in the different models, classrooms identified as high in implementation were studied. On both the measure of academic achievement and the measure of general cognitive development, trends suggesting largest gains in the Preacademic and Cognitive Discovery models emerged.[20]

Important suggestive patterns also emerged concerning the education and experience of teachers. In "regular" Head Start classes, children's gains on the two cognitive measures were related to teachers' professional background: children whose teachers had the most academic and practical experience made the largest gains. This relationship did not exist for children in model programs. The pattern supports the notion derived from the implementation study that sponsors' technical assistance may provide the "know-how" teachers ordinarily gain through academic training and experience.

Response Style Measures

The response style measures of *motor inhibition* and *styles of coping with cognitive demands* suggested consistent and important effects of Head Start programs in areas previously little studied. Each of the measures suggested changes manifesting increases in "response inhibition" in task situations. The increases were greater than those attributable to maturation alone and showed differences among programs consistent with their orientations.

On the Maccoby *motor inhibition* measure (Maccoby et al. 1965) children gained significantly. They were better able to inhibit motor responses in the spring than in the fall, and the increases could not be attributed to maturational effects alone. The mean increases were approximately equal in model and "regular" Head Start classes.

The Hertzig-Birch measure of *styles of coping with cognitive demands* included two parts. One was an assessment of the nature of a child's nonwork responses to the Stanford-Binet—what he did when he failed to work at the Binet task. This measure itself included two components—substitutions and

[19] A major problem in Stanford Research Institute's data analysis procedure was the use of the individual child as the unit of analysis. Since children were not assigned randomly to classrooms and "treatments" were administered to classrooms of children, the appropriate unit of analysis for testing the significance of treatment effects is the classroom. As with other methodological shortcomings, this will simply be noted here and, despite the flaws in them, the data will be explored to determine what patterns exist.

[20] The sample size in this comparison (children in well-implemented classes of the different models) was small, including only 20 classes—10 Preacademic, 8 Cognitive Discovery, and 2 Discovery.

Table 2. Measures (Mean Score) of Children's Nonwork Responses to the Stanford-Binet

Period	Component	Preacademic models	Cognitive Discovery models	Discovery models	All model classes	All "Regular" classes	Total
Fall 1969	Substitutions Verbal	0.93	1.18	1.03	1.06	1.35	1.20
	Nonverbal	2.27	2.66	1.71	2.24	3.18	2.67
	Passivity	6.56	2.57	2.85	3.70	3.04	3.40
Spring 1969	Substitutions Verbal	0.72	0.26	0.47	0.45	0.40	0.43
	Nonverbal	1.70	0.59	1.12	1.06	1.00	1.03
	Passivity	9.32	2.96	2.75	4.54	3.21	3.93

Table 3. Measures (Mean Score) of Children's Nonwork Responses
to the Stanford-Binet

Period	Component	Preacademic models	Cognitive Discovery models	Discovery models	All model classes	All "Regular" classes	Total
Fall 1969	Delimited Responses Verbal	29.62	27.73	30.21	29.06	28.41	28.76
	Nonverbal	25.17	34.16	39.46	36.22	37.47	36.79
	Extended Responses Verbal	0.58	0.49	0.56	0.54	1.15	0.81
	Nonverbal	2.75	2.56	1.83	2.36	2.96	2.64
Spring 1969	Delimited Responses Verbal	28.35	24.27	27.54	26.44	26.24	26.35
	Nonverbal	38.89	40.02	41.10	40.09	39.46	39.81
	Extended Responses Verbal	0.15	0.10	0.11	0.12	0.16	0.14
	Nonverbal	0.52	1.11	0.89	0.88	1.23	1.04

passive behaviors. Substitutions occur when the child offers an irrelevant verbal or nonverbal response instead of engaging in task-related activity. Passive responses are those in which the child simply does not respond. There were relatively large mean decreases in all programs in substitutions, and mean increases in all except Discovery programs in passive responses (see Table 2).[21] These changes were larger than could be accounted for by maturation alone. Especially large increases in passive responses were found in Preacademic programs.

The second part of the Hertzig-Birch described components of a child's approach when he *worked* at Stanford-Binet tasks. This measure again included several aspects—delimited and extended responses, both verbal and nonverbal. Delimited responses are those which are restricted to the defined requirements of the task. Extended responses are those which go beyond the limits of the task; they are spontaneous, unsolicited elaborations in action or speech. Scores on these measures indicated relatively large mean decreases in all programs in verbal and nonverbal extended responses (the data are presented in Table 3).[22] Again, the changes could not be accounted for by maturation alone.

These findings are extremely important because they suggest both a generalized effect of Head Start and a specificity of effects in an area not examined heretofore. Although there is a wealth of data in these response style measures, at least one consistent pattern of changes not attributable to maturation alone can be found in them. The consistent theme from the several measures is an increased *"response inhibition" in situations much like those children will encounter in elementary schools*. These changes suggest that the children have learned what a question is and what an "appropriate" answer is, and that they have learned to focus their attention on the "essential" components of school-like tasks.

Within the model programs, a striking specificity of effects was manifested. Particularly noteworthy is the fact that the Preacademic programs produced the largest *increases in passivity*—the situation where a child simply provided no response whatsoever to an item. These findings may reflect the

---

[21] We can evaluate the meaning of decreases in substitutions by looking at data on other children's styles of response to Stanford-Binet tasks. Hertzig et al. (1968) found that a lower number of substitutions was made by middle-income than low-income children, suggesting that decreases in the Head Start sample are in the direction characteristic of middle-income children's styles of response.

[22] Hertzig et al. (1968) found that middle-income children were likely to make at least one verbal spontaneous extension during administration of the Stanford-Binet. It is difficult to interpret the decrease in extended responses in the Head Start sample, however, since the measure used in the evaluation was the total number of extended responses given by a child (not whether he made at least one extension—the measure used by Hertzig et al.).

orientation of these programs which emphasizes the child's responding only with *correct* verbal responses in the classroom situation.

Mother-Child Measures

The measures of *mother-child interaction styles* suggested changes generally consistent with the cognitive measures. These changes, like others reported in this chapter, were important because they suggested growth in areas not previously reported for Head Start. Several mother-child interaction dimensions were examined using the Hess and Shipman Eight-Block Sort Task. This task requires: (1) a mother to teach her child a particular method of sorting eight blocks and (2) the child to sort the blocks in this manner and explain the basis for the sorting. The following components of mothers' and children's behavior were studied:

- maternal verbal communication—the total amount of task-related communication from mother to child;

- maternal task description—the specific information about performing the task given by the mother to the child;

- maternal regulation—amount of verbal praise (high score) and blame (low score) provided a child by the mother;

- child verbal responsiveness—the extent to which the child discussed the task with his mother;

- child success—the child's success in sorting the eight blocks correctly and in explaining the sorting.

The mother-child interaction data for all the Head Start children suggested that maternal verbal communication, maternal praise regulation, child verbal responsiveness, and child success all increased from fall to spring. In the spring, mothers talked more to their children and children talked more to their mothers. The largest change from fall to spring, however, was in children's success scores. These scores may reflect both the effects of Head Start on learning skills and the consequence of changes in mother-child interaction patterns. The increases in all the areas were larger than expected from the estimates of typical maturational changes among low-income children made by Stanford Research Institute (1971a).

Mothers of children in model and "regular" Head Start classes changed about equally in their styles of verbal interaction. Children in model programs, however, had slightly greater increases in success on the sort task than children in "regular" classes. This parallels the finding of slightly greater gains for these children on other measures of cognitive functioning.

Within model classes, the largest gains on maternal dimensions were made by parents of children in Cognitive Discovery and Preacademic classes. Gains in maternal use of praise were particularly high in the latter. In addition, children in Preacademic classes made the largest increases on the child success measure. Like the earlier reported findings on cognitive functioning, these trends suggest generally positive changes in areas congruent with models' orientations. Any suggestions of maternal changes are particularly important, of course, because changes in a mother's behavior may be transmitted to other children in the family, promoting their growth as well as the growth of a particular Head Start child.

Parental Questionnaire

Another parent measure, the questionnaire, showed interesting variations among Head Start classes. In response to the question, "What difference has Head Start made in your own life this year?", a large number of parents in "regular" programs answered in terms of babysitting and day-care facilities. In model classes, parents were more likely to emphasize changes in the parent-child relationship and in the child's and the parents' self-development. The answers to this question are given in Table 4. They reflect a correspondence between models' orientations and parents' responses.

Parents were also asked, "What are the things you liked most about Head Start?" Again, a clear match between models' orientations and parents' answers was suggested here. In general, the parents of children in Preacademic programs stressed academic performance and learning improvements. In other models, parents placed relatively more emphasis on the relationships among children and between teachers and children. These findings suggest that the developmental goals held for children and their families by Planned Variation models are shared by parents of participant children. There is, of course, an inextricable confounding of possible model effects and initial attitudes of parents, since children were not randomly assigned to models. Again, given the design limitations in the study, the best we can do is present the results and suggest further research attempting to disentangle this matrix of confounded variables.

An additional set of questions tapped parental contact and involvement with Head Start. Responses suggested more participation on the part of parents in "regular" than in model programs. In view of the significance of this dimension to the Head Start program, the finding suggests the importance of sponsors' seeking ways in which parents can be involved participants within the framework of specific preschool models.

Table 4. Response to Parent Questionnaire Item:
"What difference has Head Start made in your own life this year?"
(%–Percentage of responses; percentages not listed are below 10%.)

Response category	"Regular" classes	Preacademic models	Discovery models	Cognitive Discovery models	Parent-Educator model[a]
16	11.3%	16.9%	15.2%	14.8%	13.9%
91	15.7	14.6	16.8	12.6	
45		12.4	11.2		11.1
21		14.6		12.6	
22			11.2		13.9
14					13.9
93				12.6	
13			10.4		

Legend: 16 Relationship to my own child.
91 Head Start acts as baby-sitting or day-care service.
45 Opportunity for learning.
21 Relationship with teachers, school, or other adults.
22 Parent self-development learning.
14 Relationship between teacher and child.
93 No change.
13 Child's self-development and self-concept.

[a]Data from the Florida parent-educator model were analyzed separately, due to the importance of these variables to the model.

SOME INTERPRETATIONS OF THE FINDINGS

As is clear to the reader, few pieces of data have been presented to illustrate the patterns and results summarized in this discussion (the same is true in the Follow Through discussion). The reader interested in a fuller picture of the first-year Planned Variation data is referred to Stanford Research Institute's evaluation reports. This author found many highly questionable procedures in the data-analysis techniques used in the evaluation, and has attempted to identify patterns of results which are not simply artifacts of the analytic technique. Among the problems in Stanford Research Institute's procedures are the fact that the data-analysis unit was the child and not the class; transformation of scores to obtain measurement scales was done with individual student scores rather than by classroom; adjustment for initial differences among groups of children was wholly inadequate. Given this situation, the author has found it impossible to present most of the numerical data in a way that would not prove misleading to readers. Personal communications with Stanford Research Institute staff identified the patterns of results presented in this chapter as ones which did not appear to be artifacts of the main data-analysis procedures (i.e., patterns which also emerged through supplemental analyses). In general, the author has attempted to summarize potentially important patterns of results, particularly those that have not been identified heretofore in evaluations of early education programs. In view of the questionable data-analysis procedures, these are presented simply as hypotheses which warrant further exploration in rigorous studies.

In concluding this discussion, it is important to review the findings from previous comparative evaluations of preschool intervention programs. When the Head Start Planned Variation study was undertaken in 1969, two patterns of program effects had been documented in research projects involving a limited set of preschool programs attended by children in particular locations. One comparative evaluation (Weikart 1969, 1972) had demonstrated an *equality of effects* of well-implemented programs: three different preschool curricula, all with highly trained teachers and careful program supervision, had resulted in approximately equal gains in children's cognitive performance and academic achievement.

Several other comparative evaluations (Di Lorenzo et al. 1969; Karnes et al. 1969 and this volume; Miller & Dyer 1970) had yielded findings consistent with the notion of a *specificity of effects*. In each of these comparisons, programs with particular emphases and well-formulated objectives in specific areas did indeed result in somewhat larger growth in these areas than did other programs.

The first-year Head Start Planned Variation findings suggest that a global appraisal supports the equality of effects pattern, but more differentiated analyses point to a pattern of specific effects. Equal effects of well-implemented curricula were reflected in the fact that although there were some differences among models, the more striking findings concerned the similar magnitude of changes in all well-implemented classes. At the same time, a specificity of effects was manifested, such that programs with well-formulated objectives in particular areas appeared to yield changes in participants consistent with program orientations. This specificity was suggested particularly on measures of achievement and cognitive functioning and on measures of response style.

The measures of growth among participants in the second and third years of the Head Start Planned Variation study should help to further clarify these patterns. Measures of such additional domains as motivation, persistence, curiosity, and initiative, and more differentiated information in the areas of cognitive and language development will be collected. These measures should contribute to the emerging picture of changes which occur among participants in preschool compensatory education programs and should serve to test the highly tentative results presented in this chapter.

PLANNED VARIATION IN FOLLOW THROUGH

History of Follow Through

Project Head Start, undertaken by the federal government in 1965, focused national attention on the importance of experiences in the early years of life for promoting children's optimal development. The need for a Follow Through program to accompany Head Start and to continue compensatory education into the early elementary grades was recognized as Head Start evaluations reported time and again that children made large gains in achievement during the preschool year, but that increases in their rate of development usually were not sustained when they entered the public school system. The importance of a Follow Through program was also suggested by a few scattered studies which demonstrated that continuation of compensatory education into kindergarten and the early elementary grades did appear to sustain or further increase preschool gains (Beller 1969; Erickson et al. 1969; Karnes et al. 1969, and this volume).

Designed to extend Head Start services from preschool into the primary grades, Follow Through was begun as a pilot venture in the fall of 1967. Its purpose was spelled out clearly in Section 222(a) of the Economic Opportunity Act, P.L. 90–92, which authorized: "A program to be known as 'Follow Through' focussed primarily upon children in kindergarten or elementary school who were previously enrolled in Head Start or similar programs and designed to provide comprehensive services and parent participation activities . . . which the Director finds will aid in the continued development of children to their full potential."

Follow Through was to be a comprehensive program providing for the educational, emotional, physical, medical, dental, and nutritional needs of elementary school children previously enrolled in Head Start. Parents were to participate actively in major decisionmaking and day-to-day operations involved in the development and conduct of the program at the local level. Although authorized under the Economic Opportunity Act, Follow Through was to be administered under a delegation of authority from the Office of Economic Opportunity to the U.S. Office of Education in the Department of Health, Education and Welfare.

Early in Follow Through's history the decision was made that it should be an experimental program designed chiefly to produce information which would be useful if the program was expanded to nationwide service proportions. As a result, Follow Through undertook a strategy of planned variation to assess the effectiveness of a variety of different approaches for working with disadvantaged children and their families in a number of different cultural and environmental settings throughout the country. During the 1970–71 school year, the Stanford Research Institute undertook the first national evaluation of Follow Through. The tentative patterns of results summarized in this chapter are based on that evaluation.

The number of communities involved in Follow Through rose from 39 serving 2,400 poor children during the 1967–68 school year to 174 serving 60,000 poor children during the 1970–71 school year. Of the 60,000 children from low income families enrolled in Follow Through projects during 1970–71, approximately 15,000 were in kindergarten, 22,400 in first grade, 15,300 in second grade, and 7,300 in third grade.

Half of the children in each Follow Through project are expected to be graduates of full-year Head Start or similar preschool programs. The Follow Through project in a particular community typically begins with the earliest grade in a school (kindergarten or first grade) and progressively adds a higher grade each year as the original Head Start children advance up to the third grade.

At the local level, Follow Through, like Head Start, has been shaped by the program's focus on improving the child's "life chances," not simply his chances to succeed in school. In order to fulfill this broad mandate, projects have emphasized a variety of aspects of the child's development, including his academic achievement, confidence, initiative, autonomy, task persistence, and health. Project personnel have worked with a range of institutions which influence the child's continued growth, including families, schools, community health services, welfare departments, and other social service agencies.

Follow Through Approaches

In the school year 1969–70, during which the Stanford Research Institute first-year evaluation was undertaken, Follow Through included fourteen different approaches which qualified for inclusion in the evaluation. These approaches, as well as the remaining approaches which will be included in subsequent evaluations, were considered to be promising methods for working with disadvantaged children and families and were unique in some significant ways.[23] Nevertheless, as with the Head Start Planned Variation models, the sponsors share common orientations. All of them seek to develop children's learning abilities. All are convinced of the importance of individual and small-group instruction and frequent interchange between children and concerned adults. All attempt to make learning interesting and relevant to the child's cultural background. All believe that the child's success in learning is inseparable from his self-esteem, motivation, autonomy, and environmental support, and all attempt to promote successful development in these domains, while fostering academic goals. The sponsors differ among themselves chiefly in the priorities which they assign to these objectives and in the sequences and methods through which they pursue them.

Several of the sponsor approaches are complementary and have been operated in combination by various Follow Through communities. Some approaches, for example, are primarily concerned with parental involvement and community control, while others place primary emphasis on the curriculum, the teacher, and the classroom (Stanford Research Institute 1971b, p. 3).

The fourteen different approaches in the first-year Follow Through evaluation were categorized by Stanford Research Institute into five groups on the basis of their primary emphasis in working with disadvantaged children and their families. These five categories are the Structured Academic approaches, the Discovery approaches, the Cognitive Discovery approaches, the Self-Sponsored approaches, and the Parent-Implemented approaches. As in the case of the Head Start Planned Variation study, this clustering of approaches on the basis of stated commonality of emphasis was not validated through empirical program descriptions. Despite the shortcomings in this approach to clustering programs, Stanford Research Institute's categories will be used in this summary, since no alternative clustering procedures have yet been developed, and since the first-year data were analyzed by the Stanford Research Institute on the basis of these categories.

[23] Subsequent evaluations will include the six additional Follow Through approaches, bringing the total number of approaches to twenty.

The Structured Academic approaches (the first sponsor group) place heavy emphasis on teaching academic skills and concepts within the classroom through programmed instructional techniques. As in the Head Start Preacademic models, each of these approaches uses an analysis of the components which makes up desired behavioral objectives to guide a careful sequencing of learning experiences and a consistent use of external reinforcement. Highly structured educational environments are used by all these sponsors to "engineer" accelerated rates of learning, although they vary among themselves in the specific curriculum content, in the degree of individualized learning, in the respective roles played by teachers, parents, and materials, and in the emphasis placed on the child's initiative and autonomy. The five approaches in this group are:[24]

The behavior analysis model, sponsored by Don Bushell, Jr., Support and Development Center for Follow Through, University of Kansas. In this approach, teachers use a token system of positive reinforcement and individualized programmed materials to teach social skills (such as taking the role of the student) and academic skills in the areas of language, reading, writing, and mathematics; parents are hired to work in the classroom alongside teachers as behavior modifiers and tutors.

Individually prescribed instruction and the primary education project, sponsored by Lauren Resnick and Warren Shepler, Learning Research and Development Center, University of Pittsburgh. These approaches provide an individualized, sequenced program of instruction for each child which teaches him academic skills and concepts in the areas of language, perceptual motor mastery, classification, and reasoning. Diagnostic tests determine each child's strengths and weaknesses and are used by the teacher to prescribe instructional materials; positive reinforcement is given continually for success in learning.

The language development-bilingual education approach, sponsored by Juan Lujan, Southwest Educational Development Laboratory. This approach was originally designed to meet the educational needs of poor Spanish-speaking children (it is currently being adapted for use with French and other non-English-speaking children as well) and teaches mathematics, science, and social studies in the children's native language, while simultaneously teaching English as a second language; its methods include extensive use of structured drill techniques, reliance on materials relevant to the children's native background and experiences, and development of oral language prior to written language.

[24]More detailed descriptions of the models in each sponsor group can be found in Maccoby and Zellner (1970).

The mathemagenic activities program, sponsored by Charles Smock, School of Education, University of Georgia. Of central importance to this approach is the emphasis on children's learning-by-doing in a sequentially structured environment designed to teach skills and concepts in mathematics, language, science, social studies, art, music, and physical education; children learn through self-initiated, inductive solving of problems which are finely sequenced to assure both advances in understanding and a high level of positive reinforcement.

The systematic use of behavioral principles program, sponsored by Siegfried Engelmann and Wesley Becker, Department of Special Education, University of Oregon. The primary focus of this program is on promoting skills and concepts essential to reading, arithmetic, and language achievement through structured rapid-fire drills and reinforcement techniques using rewards and praise to encourage desired patterns of behavior; small study groups of five to ten children are organized by teachers according to ability levels in order to facilitate presentation of patterned learning materials and to elicit constant verbal responses from children.

The basic goal of the second group of sponsors, the Discovery approaches, is to promote the development of autonomous, self-confident learning processes in children, rather than simply transmitting specific knowledge and skills. Although, like the Structured Academic approaches, they focus on children's classroom experiences, their emphasis is not on teaching a programmed sequence of materials, but rather on promoting exploration and discovery in an environment which is responsive to the children's own initiative. Heavy emphasis is placed on intrinsic motivation and the gratification children derive from mastery itself. Cognitive growth is seen as only one component of the child's total ego development, inseparable from a positive self-concept, curiosity, independence, and the ability to cooperate with others. The three Discovery approaches are:

The Banks Street College model, sponsored by Elizabeth Gilkeson, Bank Street College of Education. By functioning as consistent adults that children can trust, by being responsive to individual children's needs, and by sensitizing them to sights, sounds, feelings, and ideas, Bank Street teachers help children build positive images of themselves as learners; they introduce themes of study and play relevant to classroom life, encourage children to explore various media, support children's making of choices and carrying out plans, and help them use language to formulate ideas and feelings in order to promote self-confidence, environmental mastery, and language expressiveness.

The Education Develpoment Center model, sponsored by George Hein, Education Development Center. This approach fashions classroom environments responsive to the individual needs and styles of children and teachers in accordance with the "open classroom" concept which has revolutionized British primary schools over the last several years; it is an advisory and consultant system which encourages schools and teachers to experiment with diverse avenues for fostering children's self-respect, respect for others, imagination, curiosity, persistence, openness to change, and ability to challenge ideas.

The responsive environment model, sponsored by Glen Nimnicht, Far West Laboratory for Educational Research and Development. In this approach, children are free to set their own learning paces and to explore the classroom environment, which is arranged to facilitate interconnected discoveries about the physical environment and the social world. The two primary objectives, helping children develop a positive self-image and promoting their intellectual ability, are achieved through use of self-correcting games and equipment which emphasize problem-solving skills, sensory discrimination, and language ability, and which provide immediate feedback and enjoyment from learning itself.

The third group of sponsors, the Cognitive Discovery approaches, are less systematically similar to one another than those in either the Structured Academic or Discovery groups. In general, they promote the growth of basic cognitive processes, such as reasoning, classifying, and counting, through highly directed teaching of specific academic skills, through children's autonomous discovery, and through constant engagement of children in verbal activities. Proponents of these approaches share a willingness to be eclectic and to include diverse program elements in their curricula. The four approaches in this group are:

The cognitively oriented curriculum model, sponsored by David Weikart, High Scope Educational Research Foundation. Derived from the theories of Piaget, this model fosters children's understanding of five intellectual domains (classification, numbers, causality, time, and space) through experimentation, exploration, and constant verbalization on the part of the children, through planning of detailed lessons on the part of the teachers, and through extensive observation and assistance on the part of supervisors. A home-teaching program provides an opportunity for parents to become directly involved in the education of their children.

The Florida parent-educator model, sponsored by Ira Gordon, University of Florida. In addition to providing ways to improve classroom organization and teaching patterns, this model trains parents to supervise learning tasks in the home in order to increase their children's intellectual, personal, and social competence. A key element in the program is hiring mothers of Follow

Through children as parent-educators who function as teacher's aides in the classroom and who work with other mothers in their homes. The curriculum is flexible and varies according to the needs of particular individuals and classes, but there is an orientation toward the theories of Piaget.

The interdependent learner model, sponsored by Don Wolfe, New York University. In this model, learning occurs principally in structured small-group instructional "games" where children of different ability levels teach one another and become relatively independent of the teacher. The verbal transactions between children, which are implicit in the process, are a direct stimulus to language development, experiences in phonic blending and decoding skills stimulate reading ability, and language-math-logic games such as Cuisenaire rods and matrix boards promote mathematical understanding.

The Tucson early education model, sponsored by Joseph Fillerup, University of Arizona. Major objectives of this model are to promote language competence, intellectual skills necessary for learning (e.g., the ability to attend, recall, and organize), positive attitudes toward school and learning, and skills in particular subject areas, such as reading and mathematics, and in social interaction. Methods emphasize individualized experiences and interests as well as the frequent use of positive reinforcement by teachers.

The fourth group of sponsors, the Self-Sponsored approaches, are similar to one another in unique characteristics of sponsorship rather than in the educational processes they employ. All the projects in this group are Self-Sponsored, meaning that the local school district staff has played the role of architect and implementer of the Follow Through project.[25]

The fifth group of sponsors are also similar in characteristics of sponsorship, in this case each of them being Parent-Implemented and not having a secondary affiliation with a particular instructional model. These projects may differ considerably from one another in the approach and style of their educational tactics, but all share a commitment to high levels of parent participation in policy-making, program planning, and classroom operation.

FOLLOW THROUGH EVALUATION

The purpose of the Planned Variation strategy in Follow Through, like the Head Start Planned Variation strategy, is to develop information about the design and implementation of educational programs intended to overcome the educationally harmful effects of poverty on young children. In order to

[25] All self-sponsored projects are from the initial group of districts that joined the Follow Through experiment in 1967–68, before the Planned Variation strategy was undertaken.

begin providing this information, the Stanford Research Institute evaluators of Follow Through examined the impact of different approaches on the children enrolled, their parents, and their teachers. The evaluation also described classroom processes in various different approaches, a procedure intended to shed light on the relationships between educational environments and their patterns of effects.

The design of the Follow Through study, like the Head Start Planned Variation study, is not that of a controlled experiment, since neither communities, schools, classrooms, nor children are randomly assigned to either "treatment" or "control" groups, or to a specific approach within Follow Through. The effects of the program on participants are measured through comparisons with nonparticipants whose family and community characteristics approximate those of Follow Through children. In most cases, these comparison classrooms have been located in the same school district as the associated Follow Through project, although in some cases comparison groups have had to come from neighboring communities. Two critical problems which have confronted the Follow Through evaluation are: (1) the difficulties in locating comparison groups which match the Follow Through groups in characteristics related to educational success and (2) the lack of assurance that selected comparison classrooms represent "conventional" educational environments. The fact that participation as a comparison class may itself lead to changes in a school, the possibility that comparison groups participate in other special impact programs designed to help disadvantaged children, the possible diffusion of effects from Follow Through to comparison classes, and the general difficulty of finding appropriate comparison groups in the absence of random assignment to treatments are major problems in this study, as in the Head Start Planned Variation study. Again the author has concluded that in view of the inadequate statistical adjustments on the part of the evaluators and the other methodological problems with the study the patterns of results from the first-year Follow Through evaluation are best seen as hypotheses for further research rather than as definitive conclusions.

The evaluation considers the first year of any sponsor's participation in the program and the first year in a new school district as implementation years. The patterns of findings in this chapter concern the efficacy of "mature" Follow Through projects during the 1969–70 school year, defined as those in their second or third year of operation during that school year. Of the twenty Follow Through approaches, fourteen were in at least their second year of operation during 1969–70 and, therefore, were included in the evaluation. Only sponsor *groups* were contrasted with one another in this evaluation (as in the Head Start Planned Variation evaluation), since the differences among approaches in the sequences through which they pursue various objectives suggested to the evaluators that children should participate in them for the full duration of Follow Through (i.e., through the third grade) before comparisons among individual approaches are made.

Measures of Children, Parents, and Teachers

The instruments in the 1969-70 evaluation were primarily concerned with assessment of:

- children's academic achievement in reading, language skills, arithmetic ability, and related areas;

- children's attitudes toward school and learning;

- children's interpersonal feelings toward teachers and classmates;

- parents' participation in Follow Through and other educational programs, their feelings of efficacy in relation to their own lives, the school, and the community, and their support for their children's educational progress;

- teachers' classroom practices and their educational goals and expectations for Follow Through children;

- the nature of Follow Through projects as described in sponsors' ratings and systematic classroom observations.

Children's academic achievement was measured through a battery consisting of items drawn from the following instruments:

Lee-Clark Reading Readiness Test
Metropolitan Readiness Test
Early Childhood Inventories, New York University
Preschool Inventory
Stanford Achievement Test
Metropolitan Achievement Test
Comprehensive Test of Basic Skills
Wide Range Achievement Test
Individual items contributed by sponsors

Children's attitudes toward school and learning were assessed through questions focusing on:

- how children felt about learning from books;

- what they thought about coming to school in the morning;

- how they felt about learning new things.

Children expressed their feelings by marking one of three faces in a test booklet—a smiling face (feeling good), a neutral face (feeling neither particularly good nor bad), or a frowning face (feeling bad).

Children's interpersonal feelings were studied through questions about their feelings toward their teacher and their classmates. Again, children responded by marking a smiling face, a neutral face, or a frowning face, and these responses were considered indices of good, indifferent, or bad feelings.

In each of these domains, growth in children was measured through comparisons of changes in Follow Through participants and nonparticipants. In addition, different Follow Through approaches and different subgroups of children were examined through analysis of changes in terms of sponsor groupings of programs, extent of Follow Through services received, prior enrollment in Head Start, and income level of family.

Attitudes of Follow Through and non-Follow Through parents were also examined in the evaluation. Although different Follow Through approaches vary in the nature of their emphasis, all of them consider parental participation of definite importance. Attitudes of parents were measured through interviews which focused on several dimensions, including the amount of support given in the home to the child's academic activities, the parents' feelings of self-esteem and effectiveness in dealing with schools, and the parents' awareness of, participation in, and satisfaction with Follow Through.

The relationships between participation in Follow Through and classroom practices and educational goals of teachers were also studied in the evaluation. These relationships were examined in a questionnaire encompassing the following areas:

1. Demographic information and background.
2. Classroom practices.
3. Availability and use of equipment and materials.
4. Educational goals for children.
5. Information and attitudes about home visits and parent participation in the classroom.
6. Knowledge about Follow Through, manner of involvement with the program, and opinions about its effectiveness.
7. General assessment of children's progress.

A final area of primary concern—describing the nature of different Follow Through projects—was carried out through sponsors' ratings of sites and through systematic classroom observations. Sponsors' ratings included an overall assessment of each project and an assessment of individual teacher's performance along dimensions important to the model. Structured classroom observations provided additional descriptions of various Follow Through approaches. The classroom observation instrument, also used in the Head Start Planned Variation study, was used to record such things as classroom activities, classroom atmosphere, and the interactions among children and teachers. These observations were collected only in the eight Follow Through approaches that were also included in the Head Start Planned Variation experiment.

The Sample

The 1969–70 sample included school districts in which the Follow Through program had been fully operating for at least one previous school year. Children in these districts participating in Follow Through classes either began their public school experience in Follow Through classes or began public school in "conventional classes" and then entered Follow Through classes. Since Follow Through is designed to assess the impact of continuous, systematically coherent educational programs, children whose entire schooling was in Follow Through classes are of primary concern here; information in this chapter deals primarily with them, their families, and their teachers.

The evaluation sample contained 2,623 children who participated in mature Follow Through classes in kindergarten and a comparison group of 1,303 non-Follow Through kindergarten children. It also contained 1,119 children from mature Follow Through first-grade classes (in school districts having no kindergarten) and a comparison group of 753 first graders from non-Follow Through classes.

Of the Follow Through children in the sample, most on whom information was available had received a full array of services prescribed by the Follow Through guidelines. Almost one-third (30 percent) were from families that definitely fell below the Office of Economic Opportunity (OEO) poverty line, approximately one-quarter (27 percent) from families that did not meet the OEO poverty definition, and the remainder (approximately 43 percent) from families for whom fine-grained family background data were not available. The majority (60 percent) of the Follow Through children had participated in Head Start or equivalent preschool programs. Although the poverty distributions for the Follow Through and non-Follow Through samples were similar, a considerably smaller proportion of the non-Follow Through children (approximately 30 percent) had attended Head Start or equivalent compensatory preschools. Follow Through and comparison samples differed slightly in average age of children, education of parents, and ethnicity. Generally, Follow Through children were somewhat younger and were from families of slightly higher educational attainment than non-Follow Through children, with the median level of education completed by Follow Through parents in the high-school range, but the median educational attainment of comparison parents close to eighth grade. The proportion of White children was lower in the Follow Through sample, of Black children was approximately equal in the two, and of non-Black minority children was higher in the Follow Through than the comparison sample. On other demographic variables, including family size and the occupation and income of the head of the household, the Follow Through and non-Follow Through samples were essentially similar.

As must be obvious to the reader, the large amount of missing data on the demographic variables and the differences between the Follow Through and non-Follow Through samples on these variables are extremely problematic. For large numbers of Follow Through and non-Follow Through children, fine-grained family background data were not available. This means that the data that are available should be considered as providing potentially biased descriptions of sample characteristics and not representative descriptions of the entire sample. The fact that Follow Through families appear to have been somewhat better educated than non-Follow Through families is, nevertheless, especially noteworthy. This difference makes many of the results in the evaluation suspect, since apparent patterns of growth may well be due to intital differences between Follow Through and non-Follow Through samples and not to program effects. The Stanford Research Institute evaluators did not adjust for initial differences in their statistical analyses. Thus, once again the methodological shortcomings in the evaluation make it useful primarily for generating hypotheses rather than for drawing conclusions.

Growth among Children

Findings concerning the growth of Follow Through children, as in the case of Head Start, must be considered *highly tentative* hypotheses pending further, more rigorous research. Nevertheless, despite all the caveats expressed throughout this chapter, the evidence collected during 1969–70 on a sample of 5,800 children—in kindergarten in some school districts and first grade in others—does suggest that Follow Through is accomplishing some of its intended objectives. Although the children in the evaluation are scheduled to participate in Follow Through projects for two to three more years (through completion of third grade), the evaluation suggested several important patterns after children had participated for one to two years in the program.

In both the kindergarten and first-grade samples, the evaluators found that Follow Through children made somewhat larger fall-to-spring gains in achievement test performance than did non-Follow Through children.[26]

[26]The evaluators again used the child rather than the classroom as the unit of analysis, although the classroom is the appropriate unit. This error is likely to have produced inflated estimates of statistical significance. Therefore, measures of statistical significance are not reported.

When the sample was broken down into subgroups, it was found that the largest achievement gains among Follow Through participants (relative to nonparticipants) in both kindergarten and first grade were made by children whose families were definitely below the OEO poverty line, children who had participated in Head Start, and children receiving the full range of program services.

In general, the findings on the achivement battery suggest that the Follow Through objective of promoting school achievement was realized during the 1969–70 school year. Follow Through children slightly surpassed non-Follow Through children in their rate of growth on school achievement measures at both kindergarten and first grade, with the largest differences between Follow Through and comparison children found for the especially important subgroup of children from families definitely below the OEO poverty line.[27]

The achievement gains of children were also examined separately for the five sponsor groupings. In both the kindergarten and first-grade samples, Follow Through children in the Structured Academic approaches made particularly large gains. Two limitations must be kept in mind when interpreting sponsor group comparisons, however. They are: (1) the fall scores of children participating in the various approaches differed considerably, so that "error effects" might have affected gain scores in some approaches more than in others, and (2) the various programs had been operating in school districts for different periods of time in the fall of 1969, a factor which should be reduced in importance in future years. Despite these limitations, the pattern of relatively large achievement gains made by children in the Structured Academic approaches in both kindergarten and first grade is noteworthy, since it suggests a match between the orientations of programs and the growth of children in them.

Like the achievement battery, measures of children's attitudes toward school and learning showed slight changes favoring Follow Through children in both kindergarten and first-grade samples. The largest shifts in attitudes toward school and learning were made by Follow Through children whose families were definitely below the OEO poverty line. Children in this category showed increments slightly greater than those of comparison children at both grade levels. Examination of changes by sponsor groupings showed that differences favoring Follow Through children at *both* kindergarten and first grade occurred only in Discovery and Cognitive Discovery classes. These findings provide another suggestion of a match between program orientation and children's growth. In this case, approaches in which children's affective and

---

[27]Again, it is important to point out that the evaluators did not utilize statistical controls to adjust for initial differences between parents in levels of educational attainment. This means that the superior growth rates among Follow Through children may have been related not to program effects but to their having better-educated parents than non-Follow Through children.

motivational growth are considered to be of critical importance appear to be those in which growth in these areas occurs consistently.

Table 5. Interrelationships between Gains on Achievement Tests and on Attitudinal Measures for Follow Through Children by Sponsor Category (Kindergarten and First-Grade Samples)

Sponsor Category	N	r
Structured Academic	14	0.08
Discovery	15	0.64
Cognitive Discovery	16	0.72
Self-Sponsored	15	0.39
Parent-Implemented	3	0.86[a]

[a]The correlation for Parent-Implemented projects is unreliable due to the small sample on which it is based.

A striking pattern of interrelationships emerged in the data concerning growth in achievement and in attitudes toward school and learning. In the Discovery and Cognitive Discovery approaches, there was a strong association between gains in achievement and positive shifts in attitudes toward school. In contrast, achievement gains and attitudinal changes appeared to be independent of one another in the Structured Academic approaches. These different relationships, presented in Table 5, are especially noteworthy in the context of the educational philosophies which underlie the different approaches. The Discovery and Cognitive Discovery approaches typically view the child's ego development as a complex of inseparable components—problem-solving skills, a positive self-image, positive attitudes toward learning, expectation of success, independence, initiative, critical thinking, and the ability to get along with others—in which cognitive development and academic achievement are inextricably tied to other processes. In contrast, the Structured Academic approaches typically define behavioral objectives which address specific skills and are to be achieved through sequenced and highly focused steps that intentionally separate processes into discrete components. On the basis of these differences, one would predict that relatively strong interrelationships would emerge between changes in achievement and attitudes in the Discovery and Cognitive Discovery approaches and relatively weak interrelationships would emerge in the Structured Academic approaches. Precisely these differential relationships did appear in the data—another suggestion of a possible match between program orientation and children's growth.

Measures of children's interpersonal feelings toward teachers and other children, unlike the achievement and attitude measures, did not show consistent patterns of growth favoring Follow Through children and did not appear to differentiate among the various Follow Through approaches.

In summary, children in Follow Through showed slightly greater gains in school achievement during the 1969–70 school year than did their non-Follow Through counterparts. This was true for the entire sample, with the largest differences among Follow Through children whose families were below the OEO poverty line, children who also participated in Head Start, and children who received the full range of Follow Through services. Follow Through participants showed positive changes during the school year in their attitudes toward learning and school, and their growth in this area was slightly larger than that of comparison children at both grade levels. In each of these areas, however, it is important to consider the possibility that apparent effects are actually due to self-selection of atypical families into the Follow-Through program or to selective "experimental mortality." The evaluators did not explore whether the Follow Through children who persist in the program are atypical of low-income children, despite the fact that attrition rates in the program are generally high. Neither did the evaluators examine differential biases among Follow Through models related to children's home backgrounds or to variations in attrition rates. Needless to say, these limitations are critical.

Parental Attributes

Differences between parents of Follow Through and non-Follow Through children were examined through interviews tapping numerous dimensions of family life and parental awareness of and participation in school activities. In terms of family life—parent-child mutual help, home reinforcement of school-child relationships, and parents' confidence in their control over the majority of external events in their lives—few significant differences emerged between the two groups of parents. With respect to parental awareness of, participation in, and feelings of control over school activities, however, consistent differences favoring parents of Follow Through children were found. Differences showed that Follow Through parents were more aware of their children's school programs, more likely to visit school and work in classrooms (for pay or as volunteers), more likely to talk to teachers and other school staff, and more convinced of their ability to influence school programs than parents of non-Follow Through children. Since adjustments were not made to control for preexisting differences between Follow Through and non-Follow Through parents, this finding is, of course, extremely difficult to interpret.

Teacher Attributes

Another area examined in the evaluation was the relationship between participation in Follow Through and teachers' practices and attitudes. In general, teachers, paraprofessional aides, and other school staff who were involved in Follow Through viewed the program as very helpful to children, as something they would like to continue participating in, and as a positive influence on both their instructional practices and their feelings about what is possible in working with disadvantaged children. Follow Through teachers differed from non-Follow Through teachers in many ways. They were, for example, more likely to consider such activities as home visits by the teachers and other school personnel as highly important activities for the school to perform. While only half of the non-Follow Through teachers reported home visits at all and the median number of visits among them was less than 1.0, 77 percent of the Follow Through teachers reported home visists and their median number of visits was 9.0.[28] Similarly, Follow Through teachers were more likely to place a high value on direct parent participation as classroom volunteers and aides than were non-Follow Through teachers. When asked whether they thought parental involvement in classroom activities should increase, remain the same, or decrease, Follow Through teachers were more supportive of increased parental participation than were non-Follow Through teachers. In addition, Follow Through teachers showed markedly greater satisfaction with the progress of their students than did non-Follow Through teachers at the same grade levels. Again, the lack of adjustments by the evaluators in the data analysis to control for initial differences between Follow Through and non-Follow Through teachers and parents make the findings difficult to interpret.

Descriptions of Follow Through Projects

As part of the description of the processes involved in implementing different Follow Through approaches, sponsors were asked to rate a number of their classes and teachers according to the congruence between classroom activities and the specifications of the approach. Sponsors who made such ratings judged the majority of their projects included in the evaluation to be high in implementation status. This was a valuable piece of information because it suggests that it is possible to achieve successful implementation within the relatively short period of two or three years.

Additional evidence on implementation came from systematic classroom observations in a subset of projects representing Structured Academic, Discovery, and Cognitive Discovery approaches that were also in the Head Start Planned Variation experiment. These observations showed that most adult-child communication in Follow Through classes focused on the *individual* child or a *small* group of children, a finding which suggests success among Follow Through projects in achieving one of their important objectives. Consistently more adult communication was addressed to *large* groups of children

---

[28]The evaluators did not indicate the respective teacher:child ratios, including paraprofessional personnel, in Follow Through and non-Follow Through classes.

in non-Follow Through than in Follow Through classes.[29] The classroom observations also demonstrated that differences in the orientations of sponsors elaborated in their own descriptions are reflected in objective measures of actual classroom activities. The finding is important because, like similar findings from the Head Start Planned Variation study, these are among the first data suggesting that early childhood education programs differ not only in the rhetoric of program publications but also in the day-to-day experiences they provide for children. The potential importance of this finding is further enhanced by an additional pattern of results: the kinds of activities found most frequently in classrooms were consistent with the student changes identified.

It was found, for example, that approaches which emphasized academic skills, highly structured learning, and frequent reinforcement in their program descriptions—Structured Academic approaches—actually provided numerous daily experiences congruent with these emphases, including:

- frequent directed learning activities in such areas as reading, mathematics, and language development;

- large amounts of positive praise and corrective feedback;

- frequent direct requests from teachers to children aimed at eliciting particular responses.

In accordance with their objectives and curriculum content, these programs appeared to be associated with the greatest gains of any approaches in academic achievement among both kindergarten and first-grade children.

In contrast, approaches based on educational philosophies that emphasize the interrelationships between children's exploration, independence, affective development, and cognitive growth—the Discovery and Cognitive Discovery approaches—were characterized in classroom observations by relatively frequent

- use of table games through which children learned by discovery;

- "active learning" experiences in arts and crafts and science;

- requests from teachers to children which were designed to encourage a wide range of possible responses.

---

[29] Again, the evaluators did not give information on the respective teacher-child ratios in Follow Through and non-Follow Through classes.

Apparently in congruence with the activities they provided, the Discovery and Cognitive Discovery approaches appeared to be associated with the largest consistent increments in Follow Through children's attitudes toward learning of any programs. In addition, associations were found between children's growth in achievement and in attitudes toward school and learning in these approaches.

The variations in classroom experiences provided by the different approaches and the apparent associations between children's experiences and their measured growth are noteworthy for several reasons. First, they begin to provide objective information for decisionmakers, school administrators, teachers, and parents about the variety of educational experiences available to young children. This information is a first step in the development of a "menu of alternatives" from which communities and parents can choose what best fits the needs of their children. Second, the data suggest that variations in children's experiences in a natural setting are associated with variations in patterns of development. In Follow Through approaches where children's experiences consisted of large amounts of academic learning activities, growth appeared to occur consistently in the area of academic achievement. In programs which provided experiences that simultaneously promoted the development of children's intellectual skills, attitudes, and self-concept, growth appeared to occur in attitudes toward learning as well as in achievement, and growth in these two areas appeared to be interrelated. Due to the experimental design shortcomings in the Follow Through evaluation, it is, of course, impossible to determine the extent to which these associations reflect "effects" of Follow Through programs, "self-selection" by families into Follow Through programs having orientations consistent with their own values, or a combination of these factors.

CONCLUSIONS

The results from the Head Start and Follow Through Planned Variation studies, although highly tentative and subject to the numerous caveats described in this chapter, appear to provide important future directions for research on the relationships between school experiences and children's growth. Among the major patterns emerging from the two studies are the following:

1. Participants in Head Start and Follow Through make slightly greater gains in achievement and cognitive development during the school year than do nonparticipant children.

2. Examining the general magnitude of gains in academic achievement and cognitive and attitudinal growth among Head Start and Follow

Through children suggests an *equality of effects* of well-implemented educational programs.

3. Differences *among* Planned Variation approaches in both Head Start and Follow Through suggest a *specificity* of effects, such that in programs with specific objectives and well-formulated strategies to achieve these objectives somewhat more growth is found in areas related to these objectives than is found in these areas in other programs.

4. Systematic observations in Planned Variation classrooms suggest that approaches differ in actual practice in accordance with their published descriptions. In areas of primary importance to different approaches, children's experiences generally reflect models' stated orientations. Measured student changes appear to be consistent with the differences among models identified in these observations.

In summary, the first major evaluations of the Head Start and Follow Through Planned Variation programs provide preliminary information about the variety of educational experiences available to young children. Future evaluations of the two programs will describe patterns of growth in different educational approaches after children have participated in them continuously for several years. If evaluators are able to overcome and adjust for the numerous methodological shortcomings which plague the studies, both will have the potential of providing significant milestones in our understanding of the relationships between school experiences and children's growth.

REFERENCES

Bee, H. L., Van Egeren, L., Pytowicz, A., Nymar, B., and Leckie, M. 1969. Social class differences in maternal teaching strategies and speech patterns. *Developmental Psychology* 1: 726–34.

Beller, E. K. 1969. The evaluation of effects of early educational intervention on intellectual and social development of lower-class, disadvantaged children. Pp. 1–39, in E. Grotberg (ed.), *Critical issues in research related to disadvantaged children*. Princeton, New Jersey: Educational Testing Service.

Bereiter, C. E. 1972. An academic preschool for disadvantaged children: Conclusions from evaluation studies. Ch. I (pp. 1–21), in J. C. Stanley (ed.), *Preschool programs for the disadvantaged*. Baltimore: The Johns Hopkins University Press.

Caldwell, B. M. 1967. *The preschool inventory*. Princeton, New Jersey: Educational Testing Service.

Datta, L. 1969. A report on evaluation studies of Project Head Start. Paper presented at annual meeting of American Psychological Association, Washington, D.C.

—— · 1971. Three going on four: A progress report on the Head Start Planned Variation study as an approach to research in early childhood education. Paper presented at the annual meeting of the National Association for the Education of Young Children.

Di Lorenzo, L. T., Salter, R. T., and Brady, J. J. 1969. *Prekindergarten programs for educationally disadvantaged children.* Washington, D.C.: U.S. Office of Education, Department of Health, Education and Welfare.

Dittmann, L. *et al.* 1970. *A study of selected children in Head Start,* College Park, Maryland: Institute for Child Study, College of Education, University of Maryland.

Engelmann, S. 1970. The effectiveness of direct instruction in IQ performance and achievement in reading and arithmetic. Pp. 339–61, in J. Hellmuth (ed.), *Disadvantaged child,* vol. 3. New York: Brunner/Mazel.

Erickson, E. L., McMillan, J., Bonnell, J., Hoffman, L., and Callahan, O. 1969. *Experiments in Head Start and early education: Curriculum structures and teacher attitudes.* Washington, D.C.: U.S. Office of Economic Opportunity.

Gordon, I. J. 1972. An instructional theory approach to the analysis of selected early childhood programs. *Yearbook of the National Society for the Study of Education.*

Grotberg, E. H. 1969. *Review of research 1965–1969 on Project Head Start:* Washington, D.C.: Office of Child Development, U.S. Department of Health, Education and Welfare.

Hertzig, M. E., Birch, H. G., Thomas, A., and Mendez, O. A. 1968. Class and ethnic differences in the responsiveness of preschool children to cognitive demands. *Monographs of the Society for Research in Child Development* 33(1), whole.

Hess, R. D., and Shipman, V. C. 1965. Early experience and the socialization of cognitive modes in children. *Child Development* 36: 869–86.

Hess, R. D., Shipman, V. C., Brophy, J., and Bear, R. 1968. *The cognitive environment of urban preschool children.* Chicago: Graduate School of Education, University of Chicago.

—— · 1969. *The cognitive environment of urban preschool children: Followup phase.* Chicago: Graduate School of Education, University of Chicago.

Karnes, M. B., Hodgkins, A. S., Teska, J. A., and Kirk, S. A. 1969. *Research and development program on preschool disadvantaged children: Investigations of classroom and at-home interventions.* Washington, D.C.: Office of Education, U.S. Department of Health, Education and Welfare.

Klein, J. W., and Datta, L. 1970. *Head Start planned variation study.* Washington, D.C.: Office of Child Development, U.S. Department of Health, Education and Welfare.

Lord, F. 1967. A paradox in the interpretation of group comparisons. *Psychological Bulletin* 68: 304–5.

Maccoby, E. E., Dowley, E., and Hagen, J. 1965. Activity level and intellectual functioning in normal preschool children. *Child Development* 36: 761-70.

Maccoby, E. E., and Zellner, M. 1970. *Experiments in primary education: Aspects of Project Follow-Through*. New York: Harcourt Brace.

Miller, L. B., and Dyer, J. L. 1970. *Experimental variation of Head Start curricula: A comparison of current approaches*. Washington, D.C.: U.S. Office of Economic Opportunity.

Stanford Research Institute. 1971*a*. *Implementation of Planned Variation in Head Start: Preliminary evaluation of Planned Variation in Head Start according to Follow-Through approaches (1969-1970)*. Washington, D.C.: Office of Child Development, U.S. Department of Health, Education and Welfare.

———. 1971*b*. *Longitudinal evaluation of selected features of the national Follow Through program*. Washington, D.C.: Office of Education, U.S. Department of Health, Education and Welfare.

Weikart, D. P. 1969. A comparative study of three preschool curricula. Paper presented at annual meeting of the Society for Research in Child Development, Santa Monica, California.

———. 1970. Longitudinal results of the Ypsilanti Perry Preschool Project. Ypsilanti, Michigan: High/Scope Educational Research Foundation.

———. 1972. Relationship of curriculum, teaching, and learning in preschool education. Ch. II (pp. 22-66), in J. C. Stanley (ed.), *Preschool programs for the disadvantaged*. Baltimore: The Johns Hopkins University Press.

Zigler, E., and Butterfield, E. C. 1968. Motivational aspects of changes in IQ test performance of culturally deprived nursery school children. *Child Development* 39: 1-14.

MERLE B. KARNES
University of Illinois
Urbana–Champaign 61820

V. EVALUATION AND IMPLICATIONS OF RESEARCH WITH YOUNG HANDICAPPED AND LOW-INCOME CHILDREN

The interest of the Institute for Research on Exceptional Children (IREC) at the University of Illinois in young handicapped and disadvantaged children dates back to the late forties. At the start of this period, Samuel A. Kirk, then director of IREC, with supporting funds from the National Institute of Mental Health, U.S. Public Health Service, and the Illinois State Department of Public Instruction in cooperation with the Champaign public schools and Lincoln State School and Colony, launched a five-year pioneer research project with young mentally retarded children, the majority of whom were from low-income families. The author considers herself to be most fortunate to have been enlisted to direct the educational program.

The purpose of this early, foresighted study (Kirk 1958) was to determine the effects of preschool training on the development of mentally retarded children. Uniquely, one experimental group was located in a community setting and the other experimental group in an institution for the mentally defective. Contrast groups were identified for both of the above groups. According to Kirk (1958, p. 9), the three major questions the research purported to answer were:

1. Does preschool training of mentally retarded children displace the rate of development of such children as compared to children who do not obtain the benefits of early training?

2. Does the rate of growth at the preschool age continue at an accelerated rate, or does it return to the original rate of development during the primary school years?

3. Are the results similar for children living in different environments, such as their own homes, foster homes, or institutions for the mentally deficient?

As an aside, this project was the first in the College of Education at the University of Illinois to obtain outside funding. In this day and age when

109

federal funding is more or less taken for granted, it is interesting to recall what a stir this project made locally, because up to that time outside funding was virtually nonexistent.

The treatment efforts were focused on enhancing the social and mental development of young educable mentally handicapped children ages three through six with Binet IQs ranging from 45 to 80. The children (N=81) were examined prior to the experiment, at regular intervals during the preschool period, at the termination of the preschool project, and at the regular intervals following the preschool period. Follow-up for some children continued as long as five years after they left the preschool.

Briefly, the overall results of the experimental project indicated positive changes. Seventy percent of the children demonstrated accelerated rates of development and retained these gains, according to follow-up data. Children who remained at home without benefit of preschool experience either maintained their previous rate of development or decreased their rate of development. Generally, the greater the change in the environment of the child, the greater the change in rate of development. As is true of most preschool projects to date, "summative evaluation" (Scriven 1967) characterized the research design.

One finding that is of particular interest to those who are concerned about the irreversibility of the effects of prolonged deprivation associated with being a member of a low-income family is that Kirk's community contrast children demonstrated an accelerated rate of growth after they entered first grade at age six. Kirk concluded that age six might not be too late to initiate an educational program for children similar to those included in this project. This finding is of particular interest since these children either maintained their rate of development or showed a decrease during the preschool years.

While none of the subjects of this study has graduated from a university with a graduate degree at the master's level, as did one of Skodak's and Skeels' (1945) subjects, there have been dramatic cases in Kirk's study. Notably, one institutionalized child who was placed in an adoptive home and moved to the community experimental class has graduated from a university with an above-average record and is currently a public school teacher at the secondary level.

When one reads Kirk's report (1958) of this early study, which was initiated a quarter of a century ago, one cannot but be discouraged that progress to date has been so slow. For example, Kirk made a plea for what has come to be known as "formative evaluation" (Scriven 1967) to help guide the discovery of better ways of meeting the individual needs of children and to determine why some children make progress and some do not. Kirk (1958, p. 205) pointed out in his final report, "These results, though affirmative, do not tell the whole story. They do not tell us what kinds of children, and under what circumstances these children, made the most progress. They do not tell us why some children did not make progress." In spite of his plea, we are just now getting around to developing formative evaluations of our programs.

Kirk also pointed out the need for environmental changes outside the boundaries of the classroom, especially for those children who are psychosocially deprived. He felt that a total impact was a necessity to bring about changes in the environment conducive to helping the handicapped child develop his potential. Even prior to Hunt's (1961) monumental contribution in the form of a book dealing with intelligence and experience, Kirk (1958, p. 212) pointed out that the findings of his study in regard to the concept of fixed intelligence suggested that although the contention was true within limits, an enriched environment during the preschool years can accelerate the rate of intellectual growth.

The Kirk approach to preschool educational programming modified traditional models. In his preschool, a great deal of attention was given to the specific needs of the individual child. There was a real attempt to gear instruction to the cognitive development of the child. The teacher-pupil ratio was 1 to 4, and in some instances tutoring was provided for individual children. Although language development was deemed to be of great importance in the cognitive development of the children, there was no instrument available to determine the child's strengths and weaknesses in psycholinguistic areas. Thus, there was no assistance to the teacher pointing the way to developing an individualized instructional program which would help the child ameliorate his weaknesses. It was at this time that the need for the Illinois Test of Psycholinguistics was conceived and its development initiated.

Despite the fact that an entire book detailing this program has been made available, there is little evidence that service programs utilized the findings of this study. Over the years, many researchers have plowed the same field and have come up with relatively the same findings. Certainly, efforts to determine whether preschool programs for young handicapped and/or disadvantaged children are beneficial or not have been made repeatedly. Further efforts to answer that yes-or-no question would seem to be a sheer waste of time and financial resources.

The most important criticism that can be leveled at Kirk is that he failed to deliver his message to the field. It is obvious that a written report is not sufficient to narrow the gap between research and practice. One need that comes through loud and clear is that researchers in the field must develop viable ways of disseminating their research findings and evaluating the delivery systems, so that we can be assured that the people who need new knowledge the most will have ready access to it.

The institutional preschool program initiated by Kirk in 1948 has continued to operate over the years. The community preschool program, as is typical of so many research projects, died its natural death as soon as the funds expired. Despite the fact that the community preschool was a part of the Champaign public schools and that the present author became director of special education in the Champaign schools and remained in that position for twelve years, she was never able to sell the idea of the community's supporting a preschool such as Kirk's, even though the results of providing preschool for young mentally retarded children were well documented and were known to the constituents.

Although Illinois continues to be one of the leaders in special education, it was not until July 1971 that legislation was enacted to make mandatory by July 1972 special education for handicapped children at the preschool years down to age three. Presently, the University of Illinois has the only training program in preschool education of the handicapped in the state. In addition, there is an on-going demonstration project for the multihandicapped supported by the Bureau of Education for the Handicapped. Both are under my direction. Also connected with the demonstration project is a well-developed delivery system which will be described later in this chapter.

To better understand the development of these programs, it may be helpful to trace their history. In the fall of 1965 I joined the staff of the Department of Special Education and the Institute for Research on Exceptional Children at the University of Illinois to become the overall director of a research program on preschool disadvantaged children, supported for a period of three years by the Cooperative Research Branch of the U.S. Office of Education. Other researchers in this center over the first three years were Samuel Kirk, Carl Bereiter, Siegfried Engelmann, Ernest Washington, Bernard Farber, Michael Lewis, and David Harvey. At the end of the three-year grant period, I continued my work under grants from the Office of Economic Opportunity, the Office of Child Development, the Bureau of Education for the Handicapped, and the office of the Illinois Superintendent of Public Instruction.

The research during the first three years fell into two broad categories: (1) sociological research focused on those social variables in lower-class families which were expected to affect intellectual and educational development (Farber et al. 1969), and (2) educational research focused on developing and testing various curricular interventions for the disadvantaged child (Kirk 1969; Karnes 1969; Bereiter and Washington 1969). This paper concerns itself primarily with the programmatic research on curricular interventions. Essentially, the research was directed toward answering these four major questions:

1. What kind of intervention is most effective?
2. How long must intervention be continued to stabilize effective functioning?
3. What is the most strategic age for intervention?

4. Can an effective educational intervention be implemented by mothers in the home and by paraprofessionals functioning as teachers in the classroom?

WHAT KIND OF INTERVENTION IS MOST EFFECTIVE?

In 1965 I undertook a study to determine the differential effects of five preschool interventions. Assessment of differences was evaluated through batteries of standardized tests administered prior to the intervention, following the preschool year, and at the end of the kindergarten year. In addition, the effects of three of these programs were evaluated over a five-year period.

The classroom programs in the five model preschool intervention studies were chosen on theoretical as well as practical bases. One major consideration was degree of structure along a continuum from the traditional nursery to the highly structured preschool. The nature of teacher-child interaction was considered to be the critical dimension of structure: as the specificity and intensity of this interaction increased, so did the degree of structure. Two programs (Traditional $[K_2]$ and Community-Integrated) represented the less structured end of the continuum; a third (Montessori) embodied an established theory which included much that can be identified with a child-centered or traditional approach and a methodology which incorporated considerable structure; the fourth (Karnes $[K_1]$) and the fifth (Bereiter-Engelmann $[B-E]$) programs fell at the highly structured end of the continuum.

Comparability was initially sought by identifying 75 children who met age (CA 4-0), income, family history, and no previous preschool experience criteria. In addition, children were administered the Stanford-Binet Individual Intelligence Test, Form L-M, and stratified into three groups on the basis of these IQ results (100+, 90-99, 70-89). Children were then assigned to classes such that there was comparability of IQ, sex (50 percent-50 percent), and race (67 percent Black and 33 percent White). Finally, each class unit was randomly assigned to a particular intervention group—B-E (1 class), K_1 (2 classes), K_2 (2 classes).

During the second year of the project the above procedures were followed, resulting in comparable groups assigned as follows: B-E (1 class), Montessori (1 class), and Community-Integrated (a total of sixteen children assigned to middle-class community preschools). A multivariate analysis of covariance was then used as the basic statistical technique for analyzing the data.

After two years, then, there were two classes each (N=15 per class) of the B-E, K_1, and the K_2 programs and one class each of the Montessori and Community-Integrated. The Community-Integrated, Montessori, and Bereiter-Engelmann programs were directed by their own staffs. I directed the K_1 and K_2 programs. In each program, children attended daily sessions of approximately two hours and fifteen minutes, five days per week, for a period of no less than seven nor more than eight months.

The five programs of classroom intervention may be distinguished as follows:

1. The major goals of the **Traditional** nursery school program (K_2 were to promote the personal, social, motor, and general language development of the chilren. Karnes directed this program and instructed the teachers to capitalize on opportunities for incidental and informal learning, to encourage the children to talk and to ask questions, and to stimulate their interest in the world around them. Music and art activities were scheduled regularly. There was a daily story period. Outdoor play was a part of the daily routine; indoor play focused on centers of interest. Through inservice training, the teachers were made aware of the strengths and weaknesses of disadvantaged children. This preschool was modeled after the Child Development Laboratory program at the University of Illinois.

2. The **Community-Integrated** program, operated at four neighborhood centers, provided a traditional nursery school experience similar to the one above. These centers were licensed by the state and were sponsored by community groups. Classes were composed predominately of middle- and upper-class Caucasian children. Two to four disadvantaged children from the research pool attended sessions at one of these four centers. Socioeconomic integration was the pertinent variable, rather than racial integration, which was achieved in all programs. Central to the altered classroom dynamics in the Community-Integrated program was the presence of an advantaged-peer language model in addition to the teacher model provided in all programs. To the extent that all children in a traditional nursery school acquired language from each other, the Community-Integrated program provided the optimum setting for verbal development. Observational data, however, revealed that the disadvantaged were on the fringes and interacted little verbally with the other children.

3. The **Montessori** program was administered by the local society, and staff and classroom materials met Montessori standards. The daily schedule began with a routine health check and toileting. The group then met "on the line" for conversation, songs, fingerplays, and exercises. The next half hour was devoted to "spontaneous choice" of approved materials and was followed by a second period on the line devoted to musical activities, stories, and games. A "practical life" demonstration, juice time, toileting, the silence. exercise, and tidying the classroom occupied the next half hour. The final ten or twenty minutes of the session were given over to playground activities or supervised short walks.

The specific nature of the "prepared environment" raised the level of structure within the Montessori classroom beyond that of the two traditional programs. The Montessori teacher did not, however, maintain the high level of specific control over the actions of the children provided by the teachers in the two highly structured programs. Structure in the Montessori program did not usually derive from direct teacher-child interaction, but rather from the prescribed manner in which the child learned from the materials. Observational data revealed that there was very little verbal interaction among the children and between children and adults as compared to the two highly structured programs of Bereiter-Engelmann and Karnes (K_1), and to a more limited extent the K_2 (Traditional) program.

4. In the **Karnes structured cognitive** program (K_1), a psycholinguistic model derived from the clinical model of the Illinois Test of Psycholinguistic Abilities was used to guide instruction. Since inadequate language represented one of the greatest problem areas for the low-income child, verbalizations in conjunction with the manipulation of concrete materials were considered to be the most effective means of establishing new language responses. Initially each class was divided into three groups of five children, on the basis of IQ and teacher evaluation. A game format (card packs, lotto games, models and miniatures, sorting, matching, and classifying games) created situations where verbal responses could be made repeatedly in a productive, meaningful context without resorting to rote repetition. If the child was unable to make a verbal response, the teacher supplied an appropriate model. When the child began to initiate such responses, the teacher had the opportunity to correct, modify, and expand his verbalizations. Particular prominence was given to helping the child acquire the effective information-processing skills needed to cope successfully with school tasks (Karnes et al. 1972). Each teacher taught three twenty-minute structured periods to the same group of five children. The remainder of the morning was given to music, art, directed play, snack time, and rest.

5. In the **Bereiter-Engelmann** (B-E) program (Bereiter & Engelmann 1966; Bereiter 1972), intensive oral drill in verbal and logical patterns was chosen as the mode for instruction, since disadvantaged children were considered adequate in perceptual and motoric skills but inadequate in verbal and abstract skills. Each B-E class was divided into small groups on the same basis as the K_1 group. Each of the three teachers conducted a twenty-minute learning period (language, arithmetic, or reading) for the three groups. The general instructional strategy was that of rule followed by application. A verbal formula was learned by rote and then applied to a series of analogous examples of increasing difficulty.

The children were taught to read with a modified Initial Teaching Alphabet. Innovations had to do with instruction in the formation of long-vowel sounds and the use of a convention for blending words. As early as possible, the children were introduced to controlled-vocabulary stories written by the reading staff. Songs were written especially for the music period and provided practice in language operations, as did the story period.

RESULTS AND CONCLUSIONS AT THE
END OF THE PRESCHOOL YEAR

Children were tested on Saturdays, rather than being taken from the classroom and possibly revealing classroom placement. Individual test data were obtained by experienced school psychologists who were assigned to test the children on a "blind basis." Thus, except for an occasional inadvertent disclosure, the results were essentially obtained without the knowledge of assignment to programs. Psychologists were encouraged and provided the time to establish rapport with the children. These psychologists had had previous experience working with this age and type of child.

The two highly structured programs (K_1 and B-E) demonstrated a substantial mean gain (14 points) in *intellectual functioning* (Binet IQ, see Fig. 1) at the end of the first year (7- to 8-month interval). No child in either of these two programs failed to make an IQ gain; 92 percent of the children in the K_1 program and 74 percent of the children in the B-E group fell into the above-average intelligence strata. The other three experimental groupings made more modest mean gains (5 to 8 points), and from 15 to 24 percent of these children regressed. Clearly, the test-two performance of the K_1 and B-E groups on the Stanford-Binet was superior to the performance of the other three groups. Although the K_2 group was not significantly lower than the K_1 or the B-E groups, neither was it significantly higher than the Community-Integrated or Montessori groups. (A discussion of the results of Battery 3 appears later.)

On the initial assessment of language development (ITPA), the children in this study were most deficient on the three subtests related to verbal expressive abilities: Vocal Encoding, Auditory-Vocal Automatic, and Auditory-Vocal Association. During the treatment period, children in the K_1 group eliminated their initial major deficiencies (six to fifteen months below CA) on each of these three subtests (Fig. 2), while the B-E group eliminated a major deficiency on two of these three subtests. The K_2 group made improvements in all three areas, but not to the extent of

Figure 1.
Stanford-Binet IQ
Five Groups for Two Years

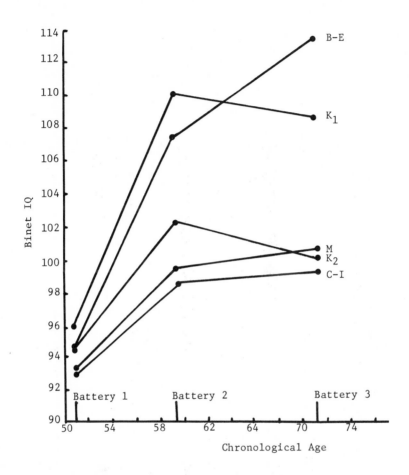

Note: The times of the three batteries are plotted at the mean Binet
chronological age of the three groups.

the B-E and K_1 groups. The performances of the Community-Integrated
and Montessori groups on these three subtests were, at most, static. On
the ITPA total, the K_1 group was significantly higher than the
Community-Integrated and Montessori groups, but did not differ
significantly from the B-E and K_2 groups. The B-E and K_2 groups were
significantly higher than the Montessori group only.

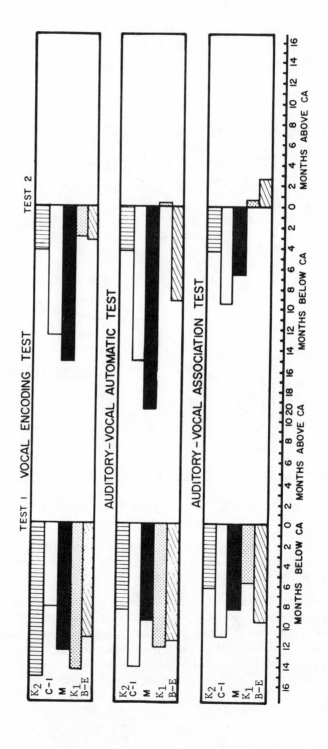

Figure 2.
Difference Score Means for the Three ITPA Subtests
in which the Five Groups Demonstrated the Greatest Initial Deficit

The magnitude of the gains of the K_1 group on the nine subtests of the ITPA and the consistency with which it made these gains resulted in an essentially nondeficit test-two performance. The K_2 group made consistent but more modest gains and had no major deficits (i.e., in excess of six months) at the time of test two. The B-E group made somewhat larger gains than the K_2 group, but made these gains somewhat less consistently and had major deficits on two subtests at test two. The Community-Integrated and Montessori groups generally made smaller and less consistent gains than the other three groups. The movement of the Montessori group was such that the children *decreased* their rate of development in language, while that of the Community-Integrated group was more nearly static.

The performance of the K_1 group in visual perception (Frostig 1964) at the end of the first year was significantly higher than those of the other four groups. Only 21 percent of the children in the K_1 group scored at a level that indicated need for remediation, while 43 percent of the children in the B-E group revealed such a need. Over 75 percent of the children in the K_2, Montessori, and Community-Integrated groups earned deficit scores.

Since the five intervention programs were chosen to represent points along a continuum of structure, one might assume that the results would order themselves along this continuum to the extent that structure is a valid dimension in effecting change. Such was not the case. The children in the K_1 and B-E programs (high on the structure continuum) generally showed the greatest gains. Those who participated in the K_2 program (low on the structure continuum) showed more modest gains. Children in the Community-Integrated program (also low on the structure continuum) and those who participated in the Montessori program (midway on the structure continuum) showed the least progress.

The failure of the Montessori children to demonstrate appreciable progress seems to invalidate the notion that the level of structure relates to the progress made by the disadvantaged child. The Montessori program provided a high degree of structure in terms of careful planning for the kinds of sensory-motor activity thought appropriate to the development of an adequate base from which language and cognitive skills arise, and these provisions may be considered comparable to the activities used to elicit verbal responses (the game format) in the K_1 program or to the pattern drill employed in the B-E program. The Montessori teacher provided a "prepared environment," but did not systematically engage the child in verbalizations or require such verbalizations as part of the definition of productive involvement. This failure of the Montessori program resulted, at least during the intervention interval, in somewhat regressive language behavior. Structured emphasis on sensory-motor development without similar concern for verbal development programmatically moves in the wrong direction for the disadvantaged child.*

The expectation that children in the Community-Integrated group would show progress equal to or greater than that of the children in the K_2 group was not substantiated. The disadvantaged children in the Community-Integrated program failed to incorporate the language model of their advantaged peers, because they did not reciprocate in verbal interactions at any significant level. The program of the K_2 group, on the other hand, ensured that the children responded verbally during certain activities. Their teachers necessarily accommodated these activities to the verbal level of the children and gradually developed more acceptable and extended responses. The progress in verbal expressive ability made by the children in the K_2 program reflects this accommodation.

The very real progress made by the children in the K_2 program must be viewed against the generally superior performance of the children in the two highly structured programs (B-E and K_1). The magnitude and consistency of the gains of the K_1 and B-E groups in intellectual functioning (Binet IQ) clearly endorse the importance of providing a setting in which the child is required to make appropriate and increasingly complex verbalizations. There is some evidence that obtaining these verbalizations in conjunction with productive, manipulative experiences (K_1 program) more effectively developed visual perceptual skills (Frostig), as well as the visual-motor skills involved in certain ITPA subtests (Visual Decoding, Visual-Motor Sequencing, and Motor Encoding). In addition, children who made verbal responses concurrent with meaningful, manipulative experiences more effectively incorporated syntactical constructs into their verbal repertoire (Auditory-Vocal Automatic subtest). On the other hand, verbal pattern drills (B-E program) provided unique opportunities to develop the auditory reception of structured aspects of language (Auditory-Vocal Association and Auditory Decoding subtests).

RESULTS AND CONCLUSIONS AT THE END
OF SECOND YEAR (KINDERGARTEN)

During their second year in the study, the children in the K_2, Community-Integrated, and Montessori programs attended a public kindergarten for a half day where no research intervention was made. In contrast, the children in the K_1 program attended public kindergarten in the morning and, in addition, participated in a one-hour supportive program at the

*Maria Montessori (1870-1952) seems to have based her method on a pre-Binet theory of intelligence similar to the views of the prominent psychologist J. McKeen Cattell in the 1890s, which were discredited in the early 1900s. [Ed.]

research center in the afternoon. According to the research design, children in the B-E program were not to attend public kindergarten and were to return to the research center for a half-day program.

The children in the K_1 program were divided into two classes of twelve children each. The one-hour session consisted of two periods: language development/reading readiness and mathematics concepts. An effort was made to avoid repeating activities which had already been provided in the morning public kindergarten and to emphasize activities directly related to first-grade academic success. Because the test-two performance of the K_1 group on all ITPA subtests had been essentially nondeficit, the major orientation of the supportive program was toward school readiness rather than language development. Since these children had demonstrated competence in visual perceptual skills (Frostig) and a mean Binet IQ substantially above 100 (only two children scored below 100), and because they were approaching an age appropriate to more specific academic endeavors, this shift in program emphasis seemed reasonable.

The B-E program in the second year of the study offered an extension of the first year's curriculum, and the children were again grouped by ability for 25-minute instructional periods in reading, arithmetic, and language. The language program included concepts of measure, the formal use of function words, and the vocabulary engendered by a study of part-whole relationships of over 100 objects. The B-E staff developed a highly systematized reading method which emphasized subskills such as blending, rhyming, visual discrimination, left-to-right orientation, and sequencing. The children were taught to recognize symbols as sounds and to combine these sounds, using the subskills, into words. In arithmetic the children received further work in the curriculum initiated the first year, and no significant alterations were made.

At the end of the second year of intervention, the performance of the B-E group in intellectual functioning (Binet IQ) was superior to that of the other four groups (see Fig. 1). Only the children in the B-E group made a substantial gain during the second year (6 points). The four groups that attended public kindergarten the second year basically maintained the gains in intellectual functioning made during the first year; typically, losses or gains did not exceed 3 points. Although the supportive program for the Karnes group (K_1) was unsuccessful in fostering further IQ gains, it did result in gains in other areas, as will be seen later.

Of the three groups who attended only public kindergarten the second year, the Community-Integrated and Montessori groups demonstrated the least change on verbal expressive abilities (Vocal Encoding, Auditory-Vocal Automatic, and Auditory-Vocal Association). To simplify the reporting of these findings, the combined means of these scores are presented graphically in Figure 3. The K_2 group, although it had shown relatively

Figure 3.
Combined ITPA Verbal Expressive
(Verbal Expression, Auditory Vocal Automatic, Auditory Association)
Difference Score Means—Five Groups for Two Years

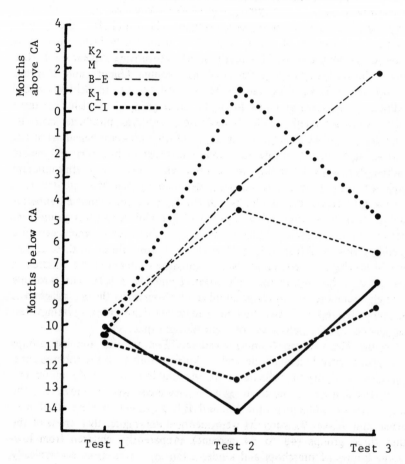

good progress on these three subtests during the preschool year, tended to regress during the kindergarten year. The Montessori group, on the other hand, which had demonstrated a regressive pattern the first year, made substantial gains during the kindergarten year. The regressive performance during the second year of the K_1 group is particularly distressing, since these children also attended a one-hour supportive program in reading and arithmetic readiness. Note, however, that language was not given primary emphasis the second year. The B-E group was the only group that showed continued and appreciable progress in language development over the two-year period and was at or above its chronological age on the three subtests related to verbal expressive abilities. As reported earlier, the B-E children were provided with two-and-a-half hours daily of an intensive program with major emphasis on language development. *These results, together with the results on intellectual functioning, provide information to endorse the need for continued special programming, especially in language.*

On the assessment of *school readiness* (Metropolitan), the reading readiness performance of the K_1 group was significantly higher than those of the other four groups. This result is rather surprising in view of the B-E group's higher scores in intellectual functioning (Binet) and language development (ITPA). The failure of the B-E group to achieve school readiness scores superior to those of the other groups, especially the three groups who attended public kindergarten only, is puzzling, since its curriculum included an intensive two-year reading program beginning at age four. A major intent of the K_1 supportive program had been to prepare children for formal reading instruction, and this focus appropriately developed reading readiness skills as measured by the Metropolitan test. Thirty-eight percent of the children in the K_1 program achieved a superior reading readiness status, and 67 percent of the children in this group were rated high normal and above. No child in the other four programs earned a superior rating, and from 15 to 31 percent of the children in these groups were in the high normal range. Nearly equal percentages of the children in these four groups fell in the high, average, and low ranges. The favorable reading prediction for the large number of children in the K_1 program is complemented by the few children who received low normal ratings, less than one-fourth the percentage of any other group.

On the Metropolitan Number Readiness Test the K_1 and B-E groups were significantly higher at the end of kindergarten than the other groups. A substantially higher percentage of the children in the K_1 group (83 percent) achieved a superior number readiness status; however, the percentages of children in the K_1 and B-E groups who were rated high normal and above (91 percent) were identical and higher than those of the other three groups (48 to 64 percent). Apparently, children from low-income homes of preschool and kindergarten age profit from academically oriented instruction in mathematical concepts, and both programs seemed appropriate and effective with these children.

The one-hour supportive K_1 program was successful in fostering further development of school readiness (Metropolitan) and visual perception (Frostig). Only the B-E group made consistent and continued progress in all areas over the two-year period. They were also the only one of the five groups that had two and one-half hours per day of special programming.

It seems clear that one year of preschool programming, no matter how immediately effective, did not equip disadvantaged children to maintain performance in the kindergarten setting. Regardless of the progress made in preschool by the four groups of children which attended public kinder-garten, their relative performances deteriorated during the second year, which supports the current belief that typical public school kindergarten programming for disadvantaged children is inappropriate. Since one of the principal findings of the first year was that intensive teacher-child inter-action is critical to maximum language development, and since this kind of interaction cannot occur with the teaching ratio of the public kindergarten, the deterioration in language development is not surprising. Only children in the B-E program, which maintained a low pupil-teacher ratio and intensive pupil-teacher interaction the second year, made continuing progress in language development.

During the first year of the study, the K_1 programming was appropriate and highly effective, and the children made remarkable progress in all areas, particularly those of initial inadequacy. This encouraging educational prognosis contributed to a shift in emphasis from language development to school readiness in the one-hour supportive program. The marked regression in verbal expressive abilities experienced by these children during the kindergarten year suggests that this shift in emphasis was ill advised or at least premature. The additional one-hour supportive program did indeed promote superior academic readiness, but failed to maintain the level of language functioning achieved in the K_1 preschool.

Only the children who attended the B-E preschool were provided low pupil-teacher ratios and intensive language programming over the two-year period, and only these children showed continued growth in all aspects of the test battery. The second-year IQ gain of this group is particularly encouraging, as are the remarkable two-year gains in verbal expressive abilities. Only in the area of reading readiness did these children fail to achieve superior performance. This study offers no direct evidence to support the early introduction of reading instruction to disadvantaged children.

RESULTS AND CONCLUSIONS OF
A FOLLOW-UP OF THREE OF THE FIVE PRESCHOOL
INTERVENTIONS OVER A THREE-YEAR PERIOD

Because not all of the interventions were initiated during the first year of the study, data at the end of first grade were not available for the Montessori and Community-Integrated groups or for the second Bereiter-Engelmann class at the times analyses were made. Thus, follow-up data over three years were gathered on the K_2 group (N=25), the K_1 group (N=24), and the first class of the B-E group (N=10). *Thus, the available N for the B-E group was reduced from 23 to 10, and therefore conclusions based on data obtained during the third year for this group must be especially tentative.*

School achievement at the end of the first grade was considered to be a critical criterion in assessing program effectiveness. The *reading achievement* of the K_1 and B-E groups, as measured by the California Achievement Tests, was significantly higher than that of the K_2 group. Two years of reading instruction in the B-E program prior to first grade seems to have been only as effective as the extensive readiness preparation in the K_1 program in producing accelerated reading development. This follow-up study provides little evidence to support the introduction of early reading programs for disadvantaged children.

The K_1 and B-E groups were significantly higher than the K_2 group on the California *arithmetic* test at the end of the first grade, confirming the prediction that the structured groups would better prepare the children for the more formal work of first-grade mathematics.

The Binet performances of the three groups were clearly differentiated over the three-year period (see Fig. 4). Although some of the large initial IQ gain might be consonant with learning test-taking behavior, such an explanation does not account for the differences among groups after a constant for learning test-taking behavior is removed. Thus, some of the differences can be probably attributed to the effects of differences in programs. The performance of the K_1 and B-E groups was significantly superior to that of the K_2 group at the end of the preschool year. At the end of the kindergarten year, the Binet performance of the B-E group was significantly superior to that of the other two groups. (The K_1 group was very nearly significantly higher at the 0.05 level than the K_2 group.) At the end of the third year of the study, when all children were completing the first grade, there were no significant differences among the three groups. The modest preschool gain (8 points) of the K_2 group remained relatively stable during the following two years (5 points at the end of the first grade). Although the one-hour supportive program was unsuccessful in fostering a further gain for the K_1 group, it may have been responsible for maintaining the relatively large preschool gain (14 points). The K_1 group did, however, lose 6 points of this gain during the kindergarten and first-grade years. Only the B-E group received sustained special programming during the preschool and kindergarten years, and only the B-E group made large and continuing gains (13 and 10 points) during the first two years of the study. When special programming terminated and these children entered the first grade of the public schools, they experienced a sizable loss (11 points).

There were no statistical differences among the ITPA total performance of the three groups at the end of the third year of the study. All groups regressed during the first-grade year. The extent of the losses of the K_1 and

Figure 4.
Stanford-Binet IQ

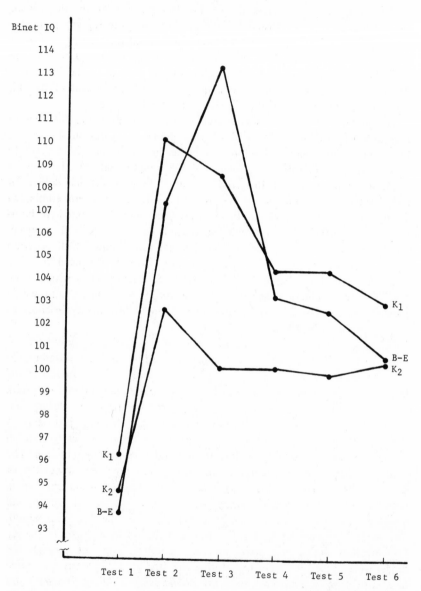

K_2 groups during the kindergarten and first-grade years exceeded the gains they had made in the preschool year. Although the B-E group was performing at its chronological age, the loss experienced by this group during the first grade exceeded its gain of the kindergarten year and does not support an encouraging language prognosis.

All groups made progress during the first-grade year on the Frostig Developmental Test of Visual Perception; however, the K_2 group made a substantial gain, and there were no longer significant differences among the groups. Initially, nearly all of the children fell in the lowest quartile on this instrument. At the end of the first grade, only 8 percent of the children in the K_1 group scored in the lowest quartile, while 20 percent of the B-E children and 48 percent of the K_2 children earned such scores.

No intervention program was entirely successful in providing the impetus necessary to sustain at the end of first grade the gains in intellectual functioning and language development made during the preschool years. In spite of the disappointments of some of the longitudinal data, however, a major accomplishment of this study remains: Serious learning deficits of the disadvantaged children in the K_1 and B-E groups were eliminated during the preschool year. In the B-E program, where an extensive intervention was sustained over a two-year period, continued growth occurred. The deterioration in language and intellectual functioning which occurred at the termination of intensive programming suggests the need for continued intervention, characterized by low pupil-teacher ratios which make possible the interaction necessary for language development and which provide the opportunity to design and implement learning experiences to achieve specific objectives.

Although these three short-term interventions (even a two-year classroom intervention is essentially a short-term effort) did not differentially alter intellectual functioning in any permanent fashion, two aspects of the Binet data have important implications. The sizable gain of the low-strata children in the K_1 group remained stable, most pertinently, during first grade when no research intervention was provided. It seems justifiable to conclude that the K_1 program offered particular opportunities to develop the intellectual functioning of low-normal and slow-learning children. The small number in each stratum of the B-E group precludes discussion of gains by strata. The IQ losses experienced by the high-strata children in both the K_1 and K_2 groups during the first grade are of real concern and resulted in an IQ change in a negative direction over the three-year period. The modest gain of the K_2 high stratum and the substantial gain of the K_1 high stratum during the preschool year remained constant through the kindergarten year, but were lost during the first grade. *It seems reasonable to assume that in important ways the public schools during first grade did not meet the needs of disadvantaged children with demonstrated potential. This assumption is further supported by the substantial regression during first grade of twenty-four of the twenty-six children from the three intervention groups who had scored 110 and above at the end of kindergarten.*

Since the intent of preschool intervention for disadvantaged children is to alter in positive ways later school performance, both structured programs (B-E and K_1) must be judged successful. Virtually all of the children in the two structured programs were making at least adequate academic progress. In spite of two years of traditional preschool programming, nearly half of the children in the K_2 group obtained California Achievement Test scores which indicated sharply limited school achievement. This differential achievement level demonstrates the potential for school success among disadvantaged children which can be developed through structured preschool experiences. Functioning effectively in the public school setting is a critical first step in altering the life circumstances of the disadvantaged child to the end that he may participate more fully in the educational and economic opportunities of a democratic culture.

DISCUSSIONS AND CONCLUSIONS
ON FOLLOW-UP THROUGH THE THIRD GRADE
OF THREE OF THE FIVE PROGRAMS

The results and analyses of follow-up data on intellectual functioning and reading achievement of K_1, B-E, and K_2 are contained in Figures 4 and 5. The differences among the group in intellectual functioning as measured by the Stanford-Binet Individual Intelligence Scale had disappeared by the end of the first grade (test four). The K_2 group had stabilized at test three at an IQ of 100, an overall gain of 6 IQ points. The B-E group lost 10 points in IQ from test three (when they entered the public schools) to test four. They continue to decline steadily over the next two years and at test six had an overall IQ gain of 7 points. The K_1 group took somewhat smaller losses through grade three and maintained an overall gain of 7 points.

The reading achievement of the three groups, as measured by the California Achievement Test, reveals significant differences among the groups through the third grade. At the end of the first and second grades, the K_1 and B-E groups were significantly higher than the K_2 group and were reading above or at grade level. At the end of the third grade, the situation had changed. The K_1 group was significantly higher than the K_2 and B-E groups, and the K_1 group was at grade level. The B-E and K_2 groups were about one-fifth year below grade level and the K_1 group.

Generally, one can say from the longitudinal comparison of the three programs that the two programs that were initially most successful had a high level of verbal interactive behavior. These two programs (K_1 and B-E) were highly structured and characterized by careful planning toward academic-cognitive goals. At the end of the third grade, however, the one

Figure 5.
California Achievement Test:
Total Reading Grade
Placement Scores

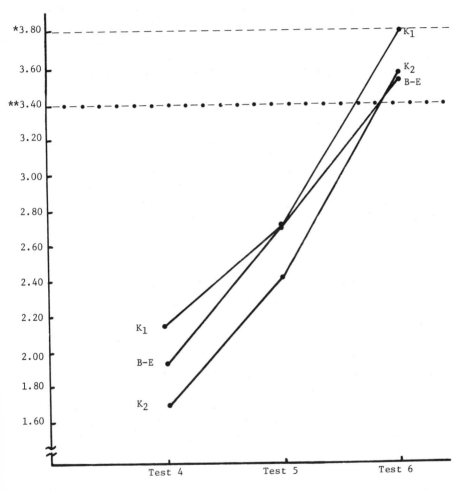

* _ _ _ _ represents grade expectancy based on month of testing and Test
6 mean IQ of K_1.

** _●_●_● represents grade expectancy based on month of testing and
initial mean IQ of K_1

program that remained significantly higher than the other two in academic achievement was the K_1 program. The difference between the two initially more effective programs (B-E and K_1) at the end of the third grade may well be attributed to the greater emphasis on divergent responses and teaching for transfer associated with the K_1 program.

Based on *initial* IQ scores, the children might have been expected to achieve a grade placement score of 3.4, when tested the seventh month of the third grade. Thus, they would be three-tenths of a year behind expectancy at that point. The cumulative effects of such mild retardation at this point might well increase as the child progresses through school. Such a pattern is characteristic of the disadvantaged child.

Further, there is some evidence to suggest that such children may well be expected to make much poorer progress without intervention. In contrast to the projected negatively accelerating rate of academic progress, the children in the K_1 program are almost a half year ahead of expected grade placement, based on their initial IQ scores and consistent with academic expectations based on their test six IQ scores. It can be noted that the B-E and K_2 children are slightly below their test six IQ-based expectancy scores, although they are both above expectations derived from test one IQ scores.

A COMPARISON OF TWO APPROACHES (K_1 AND K_2) ON SOCIAL AND AFFECTIVE BEHAVIOR

One concern has been the differential effect of the programs on the social and affective behavior of children. Thus, in February 1971, a report comparing the Karnes prescriptive cognitive program (K_1) with the Karnes Traditional program (K_2) (Karnes et al. 1971b) was submitted to the Office of Child Development for inclusion in their publication on successful projects. In addition to a report on the findings in the cognitive area, which appears earlier in this paper, findings on the social and affective data were included and will be summarized here.

Social Area

Social development has been an area of concern in preschool education, since some educators feel that emphasis on cognitive development means neglect of social and emotional development. Because of the questions that have been raised, it seemed important to demonstrate, if possible, that the social and emotional behavior of a child can develop along with, rather than separate from, his cognitive growth. This would provide support for the entire rationale for the K_1 structured program, which is concerned with social, emotional, and cognitive development.

Since one of the goals of the K_1 program was to enhance the social development of children so that they might better function in the classroom, it was deemed appropriate to obtain the teacher's perception of the children's social behavior. As a result, a brief follow-up questionnaire was administered to each child's public-school teacher at the time of the follow-up testing at the end of the children's kindergarten year. Neither the teachers nor the interviewers knew which of the preschool programs the child had attended.

Inspection of the scores on the items relating to social development revealed that the two groups did not differ significantly on six of the eight items. On two of the items, one relating to the child's confidence in approaching new tasks and the other to the child's self-concept, the teachers rated the children who had attended the K_1 preschool significantly higher than the children who had attended the K_2 preschool. This finding is of special interest, since the goals of the K_2 program express substantial concern for the social and emotional development of the child, yet the children who attended that program seem to have done somewhat less well than the children who attended the K_1 program. Although the evidence presented here should not be considered conclusive, it does support Weikart's (1967; 1972, p. 28) point that programs directed at language and intellectual development are effective not only in achieving that goal but also in promoting social and emotional development.

A second concern, expressed by some, lies in the area of possible negative effects on work habits that might be fostered by a highly structured program. These critics feel that since the teacher maintains a high degree of control in a structured program, the children will not internalize good work habits and will subsequently demonstrate poor work habits in the less structured public school setting with its higher pupil-teacher ratio. Since one goal of the K_1 program is to develop the child's confidence and enjoyment of the learning situation, the findings on the six items of the questionnaire relating to work habits are most interesting. Substantial and significant differences in favor of the children who attended the K_1 program are found on all six of the "work habit" items in the questionnaire. In these aspects of behavior, so critical to the effective functioning in the public school classroom, the children from the K_1 program are functioning at the "Usually" and "Always" levels, while the children from the K_2 program are functioning at the "Sometimes" level. From the foregoing data, it appears that the K_1 program resulted in social gains that were equal to or greater than those made by children in a K_2 program, in spite of the fact that the goals of the K_2 program expressly state that the acquisition of social skills is of prime importance.

Affective Area

One of the basic questions raised about programs in early education is: "What effect does the program have on the affective development of the child?" This question is raised most often when highly structured programs are being evaluated, because the traditional belief about preschool is that children should be able to select, freely, the activities in which they will engage, rather than being provided with teacher-selected activities designed to be interesting and appropriate yet stimulating in the cognitive and language areas.

One of the goals of the K_1 program is to enhance the affective, as well as the cognitive, development of the child. It is believed that structuring helps the child more readily discriminate that which needs to be learned from the less relevant aspects of the world about him, so that he can learn more quickly and easily. Further, it is believed that children who learn in a setting where they receive positive reinforcement frequently, and who are helped to believe that they can learn something, will be positively oriented toward school and work and thus feel more positive toward themselves. Data were gathered on an incomplete sentence test to determine the effects of a structured program on the affective development of children and, if possible, to ascertain whether or not the K_1 curriculum did, in fact, enhance affective development.

Information pertinent to the affective development of children was gathered on subjects who had been previously enrolled in either the K_1 or K_2 programs (N=24 in each group). At the time these data were collected, the subjects were at the mid-fourth-grade level.

Evaluation of these findings reveals that, contrary to popular belief, the children in the highly structured, cognitively-based K_1 preschool curriculum were no more conflicted in their attitudes toward school than children in the K_2 program. Further, if any trend might be evidenced it is that the children in the K_1 program had fewer conflicts in their attitudes toward school and therefore would be assumed to be better adjusted. For example, children in the K_1 program are likely to give responses such as "School *is fun*; *is good for learning*; *does many things for you*" rather than "School *makes me sick*; *gives me a headache*" or "Reading *is my favorite subject*; *is fun*" rather than "Reading *is OK*; *is horrible.*"

One interesting question raised by a post hoc review of the completions is "What effect does a structured program have on a child's perception of his peers?" To the stem "My classmates _____," children might answer "*are my friends*; *play*; *are fun.*" They might, on the other hand, answer "*are smart*; *beat me in my work*; *are very good at math.*" A post hoc study of responses to this stem suggested that they might be scored along two dimensions: One, with regard to social acceptance, and two, with regard to the extent to which the responses suggested that the child might be aware of the behavior of peers, especially achieving behavior. Comparison of the K_1 group with the K_2 children on the social acceptance subscale revealed almost identical means. This suggests no probable difference in the amount of positive social acceptance felt by the subjects.

In spite of dire predictions of negative effects of a structured program on the social and affective growth of children, these beliefs were not only refuted but the data also suggest that the structured program significantly enhanced children's functioning, at least in the social area. Thus, the data support the contention that the K_1 program significantly enhances the functioning of children in the cognitive, social, and probably the affective area. Serious consideration must, therefore, be given to the further study and implementation of structured programs.

HOW LONG MUST INTERVENTION BE CONTINUED TO STABILIZE EFFECTIVE FUNCTIONING?

Only a partial response can be given to this question. It would seem clear that a single year of intervention, no matter how immediately effective, is not sufficient to stabilize acceleration in functioning (Karnes 1969). As noted in the previous discussion, the children in the B-E program made continuing gains in the second year of this program; however, they experienced substantial losses the following year when special intervention was discontinued and when the children attended first grade in the public schools. Thus, it would seem that even two years is not sufficient.

WHAT IS THE MOST STRATEGIC AGE FOR INTERVENTION?

Presented below are the results of the four studies that were initiated to answer the question regarding the most strategic age for intervention.

K_1 Program Initiated at Age Three

The K_1 program was implemented with a group of three-year-old children and was continued for a two-year period (Karnes et al. 1968a). The results at the end of the first year of the study generally support the earlier initiation of the K_1 program. The first-year gains (16.9 IQ points for the younger group) essentially matched the remarkable gains made previously by the four-year-old children in the K_1 program (14 IQ points). After one year of intervention only one three-year-old child had a Binet IQ below 105 (it was 95). On seven of the nine ITPA subtests this group was performing at or above its chronological age; on three of these seven tests this group was performing substantially (six to eight months) above its chronological age. Apparently the K_1 program as modified for three-year-old children was appropriate and highly effective.

This rate of acceleration did not continue during the second year, but the gains made during the first year were essentially maintained. The acceleration achieved in one year represented a movement from deficit to nondeficit levels of functioning, and it may have been unrealistic to assume that such acceleration could be continued. Maintaining an essentially non-deficit performance may in itself represent a major achievement, particularly in view of the tendency of disadvantaged children in this and other projects to fail to maintain very promising first-year gains. The accelerated rate of growth achieved during the first year and the demonstrated stability of these gains the second year suggest an optimistic school prognosis for these children.

Effects of the K_1 Program with a Class of Low-IQ Children

Typically, mentally retarded children are not admitted to an organized program until age six or even later. A deliberate effort was made to identify and intervene with young (age four) mentally handicapped children. Children from low-income families who obtained IQs ranging from 37 to 74 (mean IQ 66.4) were provided with the Karnes cognitive program. After one year in the program the mean IQ of the group was 87.5, representing a 21 IQ point gain. The child with an original IQ of 37 obtained an IQ of 57 at the end of that year. He was kept in the K_1 preschool for two years, and at the termination of the year his IQ had increased to 84. He was discussed with personnel in the school system where he resided and was placed in a regular first grade with supportive help from a teacher of learning disabilities. When he completed first grade, he had achieved a reading grade placement of 3.3 on the California Achievement Test. A follow-up at the third-grade level revealed that he was making good progress in a regular class.

After the subjects in this study had been three years in the public schools, a follow-up revealed that none of the children had been referred to a special class for the mentally retarded and that they were making good progress in regular classes. This finding is especially interesting since the community has comprehensive services for the retarded, and since 70 to 80 percent of children in special classes for the educable mentally retarded are usually from low-income homes. Thus, preschool programs can well prevent many of such children from needing special class placement when they enter elementary school.

Tutorial Infant Program

A tutorial study with infants was conducted under the direction of Samuel Kirk. Infants were tutored in the home by professional personnel for one hour a day, five days a week, for a period of two years. Mothers were involved little if any in this training program. At the end of the two-year period, Kirk reported that this experimental group scored 7 IQ points higher than the control group, a difference statistically significant at the .05 level. Then, to test the hypothesis that tutoring in the home at the ages of one to two was more beneficial than intervention at ages three, four, and five, his home tutoring group was provided with a K_1 preschool program. At the age of four, children who had received the Kirk home tutoring plus the K_1 preschool program at age three were compared with children who received only the K_1 program at age three. The results reveal no differences between these two experimental conditions. Kirk states that the hypothesis that home tutoring at an earlier age is beneficial appears to be negated, since equivalent results were obtained by placing children at age three for one-half day in a specialized preschool with a ratio of one teacher to five children.

Although the superiority of early intervention was not demonstrated, it may be that gains obtained by intervention through the mother would affect the child's total environment on a sustained basis and prove more stable and be reflected in later school progress. Kirk says: "It should be pointed out, however, that this experiment does not exclude the possibility of obtaining marked improvement in children when intervention is initiated in the home at the age of one and two, if the intervention consists of a program in the home that includes more than one hour of tutoring plus a program of parent training and parent participation. The present writer is convinced that a little intervention is not significantly beneficial, and that if results are to be achieved, the program must be a 'total push' program throughout the waking hours of a child over a four- or five-year period" (Kirk 1969, p. 248).

Karnes Mothers' Training Program

Another study investigating strategic age for intervention (Karnes et al. 1968b) involved the training of mothers to teach their infants at home. This program was based on the assumption that the mother might serve as the primary agent in preventing deficits commonly associated with being a member of a low-income family. Over a two-year period, during weekly meetings, mothers from low-income homes were provided with a sequential educational program to use at home in stimulating the cognitive and verbal development of their children. They were given specific help in acquiring principles of teaching which stressed positive reinforcement. A toy and a book lending library provided instructional materials for the mothers to use. In addition to these child-centered activities, each meeting devoted a portion of the time to mother-centered goals related to promoting a sense of dignity and worth as the mother demonstrated capabilities in self-help not only in the family setting but also in the community at large.

The mean Binet IQ of the children whose mothers had worked with them at home was 16 points above that of children who had received no intervention. The ITPA performance of the experimental group closely approximated its chronological age, while that of the control group was nearly six months below its chronological age. Although the experimental and control groups were originally constituted on a random basis, this original control group was contaminated when ADC involved the mothers in a training program. Consequently, the above findings are based on a reconstituted control group. To provide another contrast group, the IQs of six of the experimental children were compared with that of older siblings who were tested at a comparable age, before the mother had the benefits of a Mothers' Training Program. Comparability of rapport was sought by using the same psychologist for all of the children. A 28 IQ point difference in favor of the experimental subjects was obtained.

Although difficulties were encountered in constituting a comparable contrast group, the results of this study appear to support the effectiveness of the Mothers' Training Program in altering in positive ways the development of disadvantaged children before the age of three. The 16-point Binet IQ difference between the experimental and control subjects of the Karnes study is equivalent to the 17-point Binet IQ difference between experimental and control groups of the Schaefer (1969) research. In his project, graduate students tutored the infants one hour a day, five days a week, a design comparable to that of the Kirk study. While the results of the Karnes Mothers' Training Program, as reflected in the accelerated growth of the infants, appear promising, similar results were obtained in less time using a structured classroom approach (K_1) started at age three. It could be that gains made by children through the mother had a better chance of being sustained; however, data to test this hypothesis are not available for analyses. Greater differences were found between the experimental subjects and their siblings (the 28 points mentioned above) than between the infant groups in the short-term study.

CAN A STRUCTURED PROGRAM BE IMPLEMENTED BY PARAPROFESSIONALS, CLASSROOM TEACHERS, AND MOTHERS AT HOME?

Training of Mothers of Three- and Four-year-old Children

The first attempt to answer this question was a pilot study conducted with mothers of three- and four-year-olds from low-income families in which the children were not enrolled in a preschool program (Karnes et al. 1968b). The mothers of the experimental children attended eleven weekly two-hour meetings. At the beginning of each session the mothers made educational materials to use during the following week in teaching their children at home. Inexpensive materials or items commonly found in the home were incorporated into these activities. The teachers taught the mothers appropriate songs and fingerplays and distributed copies of the words as a teaching aid at home. In addition, books and toys were available on a lending-library basis. Generally, materials were chosen to stress useful vocabulary, basic manipulative skills, and mathematics readiness concepts. Language development was the major emphasis of all activities, which were designed to teach the child the words he needs to label the objects in his immediate environment, to make more precise verbal observations, to generalize, to use grammatically correct forms, to understand and to ask questions, and to formulate answers.

When a mother was absent, the other mothers made the materials for her and the teacher delivered these and the instructions for their use to the home the following week. In addition, the teacher visited each home at two-week intervals to become acquainted with the child, to demonstrate teaching techniques, to evaluate the appropriateness of the activities by observing mother and child at work, and to assess the extent to which mothers were working with their children.

Experimental subjects evidenced significant gains in intellectual functioning as measured by the Stanford-Binet Intelligence Scale. The mean gain of the experimental group was 7 points, while the control group remained unchanged. The ITPA gains of the experimental group exceeded those of the control group by two to eight months on seven of the nine subtests. On eight of the nine subtests the gains of the experimental group were at least twice the program interval of approximately three months.

The results of the previously discussed study on training mothers of infants also confirms the hypothesis that mothers can be trained to implement a preschool program effectively at home.

Paraprofessionals as Classroom Teachers

Another study directed by Karnes (Karnes et al. 1970a) was designed to determine whether a paraprofessional teaching staff indigenous to the poverty area could, through sustained inservice training and daily supervision, implement the highly specific instructional program developed in the K_1 preschool. Intervention effectiveness was evaluated by comparing the performance of a standardized test battery on children taught by paraprofessionals with that of children taught by professional staff implementing the same instructional program. One class was staffed by three young Negro mothers who had no previous teaching experience and no formal education beyond high school. Another was taught by sixteen- and seventeen-year-old girls enrolled in a high school work-study program. In addition, a qualified preschool teacher served as the paraprofessional trainer in each of the latter two classes. This study, then, goes beyond the feasibility of employing paraprofessional staff in peripheral positions and addresses itself to the question of whether such staff can be trained to assume the major responsibilities for implementing a preschool instructional program.

The staff variables explored in this study (professional, adult paraprofessional, and teenage paraprofessional) did not produce significantly differential performances on any component of the evaluation battery. The results of this study clearly endorse the feasibility of alleviating preschool staffing problems through employing paraprofessional teachers who receive sustained inservice training and daily supervision. The paraprofessionals, adult and teenage, who participated in this study did indeed demonstrate the ability to implement the highly specific instructional program developed in the K_1 preschool as effectively as professionally trained teachers.

It might have been assumed that implementing a highly structured instructional program would make the training of paraprofessional staff even more arduous. This did not prove to be the case. The supervisor of the adult paraprofessionals felt that the choice of the K_1 curriculum may have been critical to the success of the program. Structured programming proved to be a rather ideal vehicle for training paraprofessionals: (1) The paraprofessional teacher approached her teaching with confidence, since she knew precisely what she was to do. (2) She was able to evaluate immediately her effectiveness as a teacher by observing the child's performance on defined tasks. (3) She could see the specific results of her efforts in the day-to-day development of the children. Although these observations were required to implement the structured curriculum, they also served to reward teaching efforts by emphasizing child growth.

Summer Sibling Training Projects

For three successive summers, young teenagers (twelve to sixteen years of age) from low socioeconomic homes were trained to tutor their younger brothers and sisters. The programs were conducted by experienced teachers who selected activities from the Karnes (K_1) curriculum and trained the teenagers to use these activities to teach their three- to four-year-old siblings. Each summer the program for training the siblings varied in some important respects (Karnes et al. 1970a). While these programs were of short duration, research data did indicate that experimental children taught by the teenagers in at least two of the three programs made significant IQ gains during the six-to-eight-week tutoring period (10 and 7 Binet IQ points gain). Several positive effects were noted during the course of these training programs. The teenagers enjoyed working in the program and seemed to gain self-confidence as they acquired effective teaching skills. One girl who initially had low esteem and who was having difficulty in school said, "No one ever expected me to do anything. I found out I could do something." Another said, "It is hard to be a teacher. I didn't know it was so much work." Apparently this experience affected the teenagers' attitudes toward school positively. This program has important implications as a potential source of manpower for day care and Head Start programs. These teenagers are often in frequent contact with their younger siblings and are a resource for positively influencing the development of younger children.

As a result of the studies using paraprofessionals as teachers in the classroom and at home, and the inclusion of the teenager as a tutor for younger siblings, my associates and I have developed a theoretical "Paraprofessional Educator Manager (PEM) Model" (Karnes et al. 1971a). The role of the PEM is to supervise and coordinate activities of the paraprofessional teachers and home visitors. As the individual responsible for both the paraprofessional teacher and home visitor, a PEM is able to ensure that the activities for the child in the home and school are integrated.

CURRENT RESEARCH EFFORTS

A Material Development and Evaluation Project with Four-Year-Olds with Higher IQs from Low-Income Families

Concern for what happens to the higher IQ children from low-income families in subsequent years was accentuated when it was discovered, as pointed out earlier in this paper, that the children with the highest IQs who had been in the K_1 program failed to achieve at a rate consistent with their first grade entering IQ status. In an effort to better prepare four- and five-year-old children from target areas for subsequent schooling, a curriculum is being developed based on Guilford's (1967) Structure of the Intellect. Two approaches are being used to evaluate the program. One focuses on the assessment of the curricula in the form of lesson plans and the other on the development of the children. The effect of the program on the child is being assessed, using both formative and summative data, an improvement over the earlier studies that used only summative evaluation. It is too early to determine the worth of this approach; however, formative data suggest that the lesson plans drawn from a pool of 340 that have been developed using the SI model are effective with these young children. This program is being supported by the Illinois Gifted Program, Office of the Superintendent of Public Instruction.

A Model Program for the Early Education
of Handicapped Children (Precise Early Education
of Children with Handicaps [PEECH])

As an outgrowth of the work with young disadvantaged children, a program for the multihandicapped (ages three through five) was initiated in the fall of 1970 with supporting funds from the Bureau of Education for the Handicapped (Karnes et al. 1970*b*). Typically, the children served were excluded or dropped from existing programs in the community because of the seriousness and complexity of their handicaps. The children were drawn from a wide range of socioeconomic levels and had two or more handicapping conditions, one of which was functional mental retardation.

Visitors to the program (administrators, supervisors, consultants, teachers, ancillary personnel, paraprofessionals, parents) will be able to observe the following:

1. The implementation of curricula which apply developmental guidelines to the special needs of individuals with severely handicapping conditions. Behaviorally described objectives are one unique feature of the curriculum. Embedded (concurrent) evaluation is another.

2. A model process for involving family members in the direct evaluation of their handicapped child.

3. A model training program (pre- and inservice) for (a) staff members and (b) paraprofessionals, including teachers in the classroom.

In addition, the following will be provided to the visitors who plan to implement the program:

1. Model lesson plans in the following areas: Fine motor, social, cognitive, self-help, language, directed play, art, gross motor, and music.

2. An evaluation plan which can be implemented in a local site using paraprofessional evaluators.

3. A blueprint for a model playground for the handicapped.

4. A plan for inservice training of paraprofessionals.

5. Videotapes of various facts of the program.

The assumptions underlying this educational program for young handicapped children are:

1. An effective educational program must be developmentally based and its implementation must be structured and individualized.

2. The earlier the handicapped child and his family are involved in an intervention program, the greater the potential for enhancement of their subsequent development.

3. Gains (intellectual, social, and emotional) made during the early years can have a cumulatively beneficial effect in subsequent years.

4. Increasing the child's level of cognitive functioning will enhance his ability to perceive and cope with his environment, thus maximizing his social and emotional growth.

5. A high teacher-pupil ratio is a requisite of an early educational program.

6. The services of the limited number of competent professionals can be extended through the use of paraprofessionals as teachers.

7. Effective programs for the handicapped child require on-going staff development activities.

In contrast with earlier research efforts, this program is carefully evaluated on a formative level as well as on a summative level. The major components being evaluated are: (1) classroom, (2) parent involvement, (3) inservice training, (4) administration, and (5) dissemination. An outside evaluator evaluates the evaluation of the project. The major goal of the project is to have the program replicated in ten sites during the 1971–72 school year and in fifteen additional sites during the 1972–73 school year.

The dissemination component of this project has great promise for bridging the gap between research and practice. A well-developed plan for delivery of the program to the field entails a full-time disseminator on the staff who interprets the program to visitors, a training program to provide staff for implementing the program, and a follow-up plan to help directors interpret the program in their own community and replicate it. Coordination with the Department of Mental Health ensures complementary support for delivery to the field. The fact that Illinois now has mandatory legislation which requires providing for handicapped children as young as three years of age helps ensure the success of the delivery plan.

While the program has been in progress for only a year and a half, a number of the children in the demonstration center have progressed to the extent that they no longer function in the retarded range. The behavior of the children has markedly improved, to the extent that several have been able to leave the project and enter a public school or a preschool for normal children.

IMPLICATIONS OF FINDINGS ON COMPARATIVE STUDIES

A careful survey of the findings of these various studies suggests the following implication for early education of young children, especially those from low-income homes:

1. One year of intervention during the preschool years is not sufficient to ensure sustained gains in subsequent years.

2. Parents from low-income families can acquire improved skills in teaching their children in the home. Thus, various delivery systems should be open to parents, some of which may very well be home-based.

3. Since parents can learn to enhance their child's rate of development, preschool programs should have a strong parent-involvement component.

4. While the age for most effective intervention has not been conclusively determined, there is evidence that early intervention (as early as infancy) can significantly accelerate the development of children from low-income homes.

5. Paraprofessionals from target areas, if supervised by professionals, can serve as teachers in the classroom and promote as great a development in the children as an all-professional staff can.

6. A structured program such as Karnes's does not impede social, emotional, and affective development; in fact, the contrary can be anticipated.

7. Early intervention can ameliorate learning deficits in children and prevent the need for putting many children from low-income homes into special classes.

8. Persons attempting to accelerate the development of infants should give careful consideration to working through the mother by enhancing her skills, rather than providing professionals to work directly with the infants, for two reasons: (a) training the mother has greater promise not only for accelerating the infant's development but also for helping her sustain his gains; (b) tutoring infants is not feasibly practical.

9. Generally, structured, cognitively based programs with a high level of verbal interactive behavior seem to have the greatest impact on the intellectual functioning and academic progress of children from low-income homes.

10. Curricula which stress acquisition of information-processing skills seem to ensure transfer of learning to a greater extent than those which have as a primary goal the acquisition of content.

11. To determine the differential effects of various program models, formative evaluation must be undertaken.

12. Training young teenagers to teach their younger brothers and sisters can be successfully accomplished and is an important resource that should be tapped in day care programs, Head Start, and public-school-based preschool programs. An exploration of the effect of such activities on the teenagers themselves may show positive results.

13. Teacher-training institutions must prepare teachers to work effectively with paraprofessionals who teach in the classroom and work in the home.

14. Attention to individual differences, precise planning, inservice education, parental involvement, and on-going evaluation appear to be important components of any preschool program, especially for the disadvantaged and handicapped.

15. Children with higher IQ from the low-income strata will need special early programming if they are to attain their potential.

REFERENCES

Bereiter, C. 1972. An academic preschool for disadvantaged children: Conclusions from evaluation studies. Ch. I (pp. 1–21), in J. C. Stanley (ed.), *Preschool programs for the disadvantaged*. Baltimore: The Johns Hopkins University Press.

Bereiter, C., and Engelmann, S. 1966. *Teaching disadvantaged children in the preschool*. Englewood Cliffs, N.J.: Prentice-Hall.

Bereiter, C., and Washington, E. D. 1969. *Curriculum development and evaluation*. Vol II. *Research and development program on preschool disadvantaged children* Final report to U.S. Office of Education, Bureau of Research. Bethesda, Md.: ERIC Document Reproduction Service (ED 036 664).

Farber, B., Harvey, D. L., and Lewis, M. 1969. *Community, kinship, and competence*. Vol. III. *Research and development program on preschool disadvantaged children*. Final report to U.S. Office of Education, Bureau of Research. Bethesda, Md.: ERIC Document Reproduction Service (ED 036 665).

Frostig, M. 1964. *Administration and scoring manual for the Marianne Frostig Developmental Test of Visual Perception*. Palo Alto, Cal.: Consulting Psychologists Press.

Guilford, J. P. 1967. *The nature of human intelligence*. New York: Holt, Rinehart and Winston.

Hunt, J. McV. 1961. *Intelligence and experience*. New York: Ronald.

Karnes, M. B. 1969. *Investigations of classroom and at-home interventions*. Vol I. *Research and development program on preschool disadvantaged children*. Final report to U.S. Office of Education, Bureau of Research. Bethesda, Md.: ERIC Document Reproduction Service (ED 036 663).

Karnes, M. B., Hodgins, A. S., Stoneburner, R. L., Studley, W. M., and Teska, J. A. 1968*a*. Effects of a highly structured program of language development on intellectual functioning and psycholinguistic development of culturally disadvantaged three-year-olds. *Journal of Special Education* 2: 405–12.

Karnes, M. B., Studley, W. M., Wright, W. R., and Hodgins, A. S. 1968*b*. An approach for working with mothers of disadvantaged preschool children. *Merrill-Palmer Quarterly* 14: 174–84.

Karnes, M. B., Teska, J. A., and Hodgins, A. S. 1970*a*. The successful implementation of a highly specific preschool instructional program by paraprofessional teachers. *Journal of Special Education* 4: 69–80.

Karnes, M. B., Zerbach, R. R., and Teska, J. A. 1970*b*. *A model program for the early education of handicapped children—Precise Early Education of Children with Handicaps (PEECH)*. Research proposal submitted to Bureau of Education for the Handicapped, U.S. Office of Education.

—— · 1971*a*. A new professional role in early childhood education. *Interchange* 2(2): 89–105.

—— · 1971*b*. *The Karnes Preschool Program: Rationale, curricular offerings, and follow-up data*. Washington, D.C.: U.S. Office of Child Development, in press.

—— · 1972. The conceptualization of the ameliorative curriculum. In R. K. Parker (ed.) *The preschool in action: Exploring early childhood programs*. Boston: Allyn and Bacon.

Kirk, S. A. 1958. *Early education of the mentally retarded*. Urbana: University of Illinois Press.

—— · 1969. The effects of early education with disadvantaged infants. Pp. 233–48, in M₄ B. Karnes (ed.), *Investigations of classroom and at-home interventions. Vol. I. Research and development program on preschool disadvantaged children*. Final report to U.S. Office of Education, Bureau of Research. Bethesda, Md.: ERIC Document Reproduction Service (ED 036 663).

Schaefer, E. S. 1969. A home tutoring program. *Children* 16: 59–61.

Scriven, M. 1967. The methodology of evaluation. Pp. 39–83, in R. E. Stake (ed.), Perspectives of curriculum evaluation. *AERA Monograph Series on Curriculum Evaluation*, No. 1.

Skodak, M., and Skeels, H. M. 1945. A follow-up study of children in adoptive homes. *Journal of General Psychology* 66: 21–58.

Weikart, D. P. 1967. Preschool programs: Preliminary findings. *Journal of Special Education* 1: 163–81.

—— · 1972. Relationship of curriculum, teaching, and learning in preschool education. Ch. II (pp. 22–66), in J. C. Stanley (ed.), *Preschool programs for the disadvantaged*. Baltimore: The Johns Hopkins University Press.

VIRGINIA C. SHIPMAN
Educational Testing Service, Princeton, N.J. 08540

VI. DISADVANTAGED CHILDREN AND THEIR FIRST SCHOOL EXPERIENCES, ETS-HEAD START LONGITUDINAL STUDY[1]

This report concerns what is perhaps the most complex study yet undertaken by the Head Start Research Office. It is a summary statement intending to: (1) raise some basic questions about the nature of education, human learning, and research; (2) explain the potential value of the study in terms of its design; (3) describe the type of information being collected—and how it is being collected; (4) describe the children, families, and communities involved in the study; and (5) discuss some preliminary findings and their implications.

EDUCATION, HUMAN LEARNING, AND RESEARCH

"Education is the reaction of society to the facts of development" (Bernfeld 1925). It would be difficult to construct a more universal definition of the educational process than this, or to dispute Ekstein's (1969) recent observation that the adult community often reacts to children in terms of national concerns rather than developmental needs. One has only to look at the last ten years of shifting educational priorities in this country for confirming evidence of the above observation—from the "excellence"-dominated concern that focused on science and mathematics curricula following the threat of Sputnik, to the advent of massive social action programs which have been responses to domestic pressure. This is not to imply that "reaction in terms of society's need" is necessarily misguided, but only that it may involve hazard. When such reaction

[1] Preliminary description of the initial sample prior to school enrollment. The research reported herein was supported by the Office of Child Development, U.S. Department of Health, Education and Welfare, under Contract OEO-4206 and Grants H-8256 and CG-8256.

145

becomes the dominant stance of a nation's educational system, then the dangers of short-sighted planning, premature evaluation, bitter disappointment and ineffective use of resources are prominent.

There are probably many reasons why society reacts to the young primarily in terms of its own needs. A major reason would appear to be that the needs of the child are either insufficiently understood, poorly formulated for public dissemination, or obscured by other issues and therefore not available to society for decisionmaking purposes. This is essentially a problem of the effective pursuit and communication of knowledge more than anything else; fortunately, this can be substantially resolved by concerted research efforts. To contribute toward a better understanding of the "facts of development"—and how educational institutions and the larger community might rationally react to those "facts"—is what this longitudinal study represents in essence.

Of the knowledge we do possess about human development, certain things have not been sufficiently communicated to either professional teachers or the public at large. The complexity of intellectual development is a case in point. For example, a useful distinction can be made between the notions of *construction* and *instruction*, which many Americans (including teachers and those engaged in educational research) have failed to appreciate until quite recently. The physical world in which we move so easily is one that adults rarely think about—a world of time, space, number, cause and effect, and object permanency. This world is not innately "given" to the child, however, nor can he possibly "learn" it by being told or "instructed" as to its characteristics. The child literally constructs (or reconstructs) the world of physical reality by his own vigorous interactions with it. In a similar manner, he constructs a basic understanding of language from the natural flow of speech that surrounds him. The implications of this distinction for education would seem to be that instruction is most powerfully used in the service of construction; that instruction should complement—not stifle or compete with—the child's own constructive mental activity by helping him differentiate, synthesize, consolidate, and generalize. While these appear well-warranted implications on the basis of present knowledge, we need more definitive information about the course of children's intellectual constructions over time and the nature of instruction which best facilitates overall cognitive development.

Although the complexity of what might be called "intellective processes" has been mentioned thus far, it is necessary to emphasize that these processes do not develop in isolation. They are shaped by, mutually reinforce, and merge with other facets of human personality, such as imagination, social and emotional characteristics, temperament, and stylistic traits. All of these, in turn, are influenced to a large extent by the nature of the child's interaction with his environment. Education's task does not consist merely in providing the right "mix" of instruction and construction; it extends to a broad concern for the quality of child life. And it is at this juncture that our knowledge is probably most hazy. How does the institutional nature of the school affect the community and vice versa, and what is the impact of these influences upon the child? What are the components of a "good" educational environment which foster creative abilities and emotional maturity as well as basic skills? Do these components remain relatively stable or change as the child grows older?

The acquisition of skills is often discussed as if it were an ultimate *end* of primary education, and great significance is attached to evidence (usually of the standardized test variety) that children have indeed mastered the basic skills. Acquisition of a skill such as reading, however, is in many respects the starting point of education—it is a *means* whereby the child may now further his own experience, knowledge, and esthetic appreciation. Sheer skill in being able to read may meet some minimum definition of a "literate" population, but it does not define an informed, cultured, critical thinking, or broadly concerned population. On the other hand, the process of education itself—the act of going to school—is frequently regarded almost as a necessary means to some futuristic goal. Until the important "means" and "ends" of education are better understood, educators will tend to regard their primary responsibility as a rather simplistic charge— that of making the child into the man as quickly as possible. What such an attitude precludes is the possibility that a rich childhood is the surest foundation for a mature adulthood.

What do these assertions about the complexity of learning imply for educational research? Above all else, they imply that research must be broadly conceived. It must be multivariable; that is, it must be directed not only to several aspects of intellectual functioning (the child's individual constructions, his acquisition of skills, his use of skills) but also to other facets of his development—style characteristics, social and emotional development, attitudes toward self and others. It must take into account the quality of classroom life and of the larger family and community environment that surrounds the classroom. And it must look at all of these elements over time, if we are to untangle and identify those factors which can undermine even the best-intentioned efforts of an educational institution and cause it to fail to develop the rich potential of most children. One can reasonably speculate that lack of money *alone* does not constitute that poverty which truly impoverishes.

Such concerns are certainly commensurate with the broad objectives of a massive social action program such as Head Start, but they have thus far received relatively little concerted research effort. Much as we might desire it, there is no easy "short-cut" route to understanding the complex process of human growth and the influences of the environments in which it takes place. Broadly based longitudinal research seems an essential step in providing concrete answers about the failure to develop human resources and a better understanding of the complex process of human development—knowledge which should enable us to react with clearer vision to the "facts of development."

DESIGN OF THE STUDY

Rationale

While the general nature of the study was anticipated in the preceding section, specific features of its design will be discussed here. Officially entitled "The Longitudinal Study of Disadvantaged Children and Their First School Experiences," this research effort was initiated in the spring of 1967 as a cooperative venture of the Head Start Research Office (Office of Economic Opportunity) and Educational Testing Service. The study brings together the concerns of the psychologist, sociologist, and educator as it seeks answers to two questions: What are the components of early education that are associated with the cognitive, personal, and social development of disadvantaged children? What are the environmental and background variables that moderate these associations? More specifically, what are the processes underlying these influences?

The specific age range chosen for study was the developmental span of approximately four through eight years of age—or from two years prior to entrance into first grade through completion of third grade. This period is thought to be particularly important because it is a time during which many abilities consolidate, and the child makes the social transition from familiar home surroundings to the world of school, peers, and unfamiliar adults. The first data were collected during the spring and summer of 1969 on over 1,800 children, the majority falling between the ages of three years nine months (3-9) and four years eight months (4-8). All were scheduled to be enrolled in first grade in the fall of 1971. Data collection on these children and their families, communities, and schools is planned to continue through spring of 1974. Of particular interest as the study progresses is identification of differential growth patterns that may be associated with certain characteristics of Head Start and Follow Through programs and their interaction with characteristics of the child and his family.

The study population was identified and information was gathered *prior* to the time when the target children were eligible to enter a Head Start program. Decisions about sending or not sending children to Head Start or kindergarten were therefore made without our intervention by the parents involved, after the study was underway. Thus, given a lack of control in assigning children to "treatments" or programs, the prior information (baseline data) is used to assess the comparability of children receiving different treatments. By following the same children over a number of years, one can also assess the comparability of beginning grade school experiences for both Head Start and non-Head Start youngsters—e.g., the degree to which primary grade curricula are congruent with and capitalize on what the child has learned in preschool. Finally, a longitudinal design affords the opportunity to study variables which might be expected to have long-term rather than short-term effects. Such a strategy has potential value for educational and social planning, theories of child development, and development of techniques for assessing young children and their environments. It offers the possibility to:

a. determine the cognitive, personal, social, and physical characteristics of "disadvantaged" children prior to any formal preschool experience and to relate these characteristics to home and community variables;
b. determine the differential characteristics of families that do and do not send their children to Head Start;
c. identify the characteristics of preschool and primary grade programs in the study sites and determine the relationships among these characteristics within and between the educational levels involved;
d. determine the cognitive, social, and personal outcomes in children that seem to be associated with various aspects of compensatory preschool experience and study the permanence of such effects through the first three primary grades;
e. determine the relationship of Head Start to family and community characteristics and attitudes;
f. relate particular characteristics of children and their growth patterns to particular characteristics of families and educational programs;
g. determine relationships among physical, personal, social, and cognitive characteristics of children in each of the years of the study;
h. describe changes in the structures of cognitive abilities and personal-social characteristics of these children over the crucial developmental period of the study; and
i. develop much-needed and, it is hoped, generally useful techniques for the assessment of some of the individual and environmental characteristics under consideration.

A longitudinal design thus enables better understanding of the interaction of variables over time—and this, in turn, promises greater insight into those critical conditions and processes which constitute truly "disadvantaged" and "facilitating" environments. It should be noted, however, that no single research design is *the* answer to the complex questions being posed. For example, by choosing to allocate resources to assess in depth the several domains of potential influence upon the child's development, the present study is restricted in degree of representative variation in Head Start programs. We have described some of the advantages of a longitudinal design and of a strategy that capitalizes on "natural" rather than randomly assigned groupings; these advantages are complemented by the information obtained from other research designs.

Aside from attempting to answer the several questions listed above, another potential contribution of the study is its provision of a unique data bank. Most knowledge of child development is based on data from middle-class children; the ETS—Head Start Longitudinal Study affords an opportunity to obtain basic knowledge for more informed program planning for children from low-income families. The study is thus both basic research on human development and social research on the pressing domestic problems of poverty and alienation from the mainstream of society. It is also a practicum on how to do research in the real world and how to put the knowledge gained from such research to practical use as quickly as possible.

A detailed description of the study, including theoretical rationale and measurement considerations, appears in Educational Testing Service (1968) Project Report 68-4. Some of the critical design and logistic problems are also elaborated in Anderson and Doppelt (1969) and Educational Testing Service (1969) Project Report 69-12.

Selection of Study Sites

Other aspects of the research design concern the selection of study sites, the selection of a sample population within sites, and the cross-sectional comparison groups. The selection of study sites was a major staff task during the first two years of planning. Since sites had to offer an opportunity for children to attend Head Start, the areas considered were necessarily those with a substantial proportion of the population below the poverty level. Considerations of cost and feasibility of the study determined that four communities could participate; these were selected according to the following major criteria: (a) *Program*. To be considered, a school system had to serve children who had an opportunity to attend a year-long Head Start program. To increase the variety of preschool-primary grade experiences, we preferred school systems with Follow Through programs and tried for at least one without a kindergarten. (b) *National spread*. Urban-rural variation, population stability, and representation from different sections of the country were all considered vital criteria. (c) *Sufficient number of students*. A community was considered eligible if it had a sufficient number of children in school and in the Head Start program. We attempted to obtain a reasonable racial mix and also took into account factors that might significantly change the area's characteristics during the life of the study. (d) *Opportunity to follow*. Bussing of children to schools outside their home districts and high mobility reduced the chance of a city's being selected. (e) *Cooperation*. The study would, of course, be impossible without the cooperation of the community, including its school officials and community leaders. Areas whose continued support was doubted were disqualified. As an added condition, we decided that one participating community should be relatively near Princeton, thus making possible a close interaction between ETS staff and a local site.

We began the selection procedure by examining a list of the thirty school systems having Follow Through programs at the time. The list was scrutinized carefully in terms of the other criteria, and several systems were selected for further investigation. Members of the ETS staff visited the respective sites for additional information, including evidence of willingness to engage in a relatively long-term study. Since the Follow Through program was nonexistent in any Southern rural school system which met all our criteria, additional lists of Southern communities had to be reviewed as well. After an extensive period of information-gathering and the preparation of a list of eligible pairs of cities to guide our selection, the following study sites were finally chosen:

a. **Lee County, Alabama.** Lee County is mainly a Southern rural area. There are two small cities, Auburn and Opelika, within the county, but outside the city limits the area is distinctly rural and poor. Auburn is dominated by its university, which is the major employer in that city. Opelika has a few small factories and serves as the county seat. The population of the county (61,268) is approximately 33 percent Black (Office of Economic Opportunity 1970).

b. **Portland, Oregon.**[2] Portland is a medium-size city on the West coast. Its population is quite stable, having risen from 373,000 in 1960 to 375,000 in 1970. About 6 percent are Black. Unlike the populations of other large cities which have greater Black populations, Portland Whites have not fled to suburbia. The population is better educated than in many other parts of the country, and poverty in Portland is not as intense as in our other sites.

c. **St. Louis, Missouri.**[3] St. Louis is a central city, with declining population amid quickly growing suburbs. The city's population dropped from 750,000 in 1960 to 607,000 in 1970. As the White

[2]The statistics reported are based on 1970 U.S. Bureau of Census figures supplied by Opinion Research Corporation, Princeton, N.J.

[3]The statistics reported are based on 1970 U.S. Bureau of Census figures supplied by local city officials.

population moved out of the city, the non-White population increased from approximately 29 percent in 1960 to 43 percent in 1965; it is believed to have been nearly 50 percent in 1970. Largely industrial, the city is also a trading center.

d. **Trenton, New Jersey.**[4] Trenton is a small city on the Eastern seaboard. The city's population dropped from 114,000 in 1960 to 102,000 in 1970. The non-White population was estimated to be 35 percent to 38 percent of the total population in 1968. The city is industrial and also serves as the state capital.

Within these communities, elementary school districts with a substantial proportion of the population eligible for Head Start were selected for participation. For the most part, the schools in the target districts are located near Head Start centers. It is in these school districts that the longitudinal sample is expected to be enrolled when they reach third grade in the fall of 1973. In each school district, an attempt was made to include all children of approximately three and one-half to four and one-half years of age in the initial testing and data collection of 1969, although some children were excluded from the sample (e.g., children from families whose primary language was not English and those with severe physical handicaps). The 1969 sample was identified through a canvass of each school district neighborhood and an enumeration of the resident children. Of this sample of over 1,800 children, some will move and, due to the costs and logistics involved, be lost to the study, but the design allows us to add children who move into the preschool and school classes of children in the original sample. Although these children will lack some antecedent data, they provide valuable information concerning the school environment of the original sample children as well as clues to the effects of repeated testing on test scores.

Cross-sectional Comparison Groups

A word should be said about the cross-sectional testing of comparison groups during the spring of 1970. Children in kindergarten through grade three attending the target schools were tested and various characteristics of their school programs were described. We plan to readminister these measures to the same grades in 1973–74. These cross-sectional comparison groups are viewed as an important design feature, because they provide a source of baseline data against which to interpret longitudinal results. Comparisons should be especially relevant in communities experiencing major social changes or upheavals during the course of the study and with respect to the cumulative effects of compensatory education.

[4] See footnote 3.

MAJOR STUDY VARIABLES AND DATA-COLLECTION PROCEDURES

Overview

So far, the three years of research with the longitudinal study sample have included a total of about thirteen hours of testing for each child, three hours of interviews with each of their mothers, one and one-half hours of observing each mother-child pair working together on tasks, and a physical examination for each child. In addition, there have been eighteen days of observing what happened in Head Start classes, three days of observing kindergarten classes, two half-hour periods of watching each child during "free play" in preschool, about four hours of each Head Start and kindergarten teacher's time to supply information about herself and the children in her classes, an hour from each Head Start aide, more than an hour of each Head Start Center director's and principal's time to describe the preschool centers and schools in general, and many consultations with community agencies to obtain information about the environments in which the children live. As mentioned previously with respect to the cross-sectional testing, data were also collected during the spring of 1970 from all children and teachers in kindergarten through third grade, as well as from administrators in the elementary schools which the study children will be attending.

The major variables toward which these information-gathering efforts have been directed include: (a) *The Family*: both status and process variables, that is, those variables describing what the family is (e.g., ethnic membership, occupational level) and what it does (e.g., the mother's teaching styles with her child and her attitudes toward the schools and the learning process); (b) *The Teacher*: including such things as background characteristics, attitudes, abilities, and teaching goals; (c) *The Classroom*: both program components and child-child and teacher-child relationships; (d) *The School*: both physical characteristics and organization, as well as relationships between teachers and administrative staff; and (e) *The Community*. The largest percentage of measures included, however, were those designed to tap several aspects of (f) *The Child*—e.g., health information, perceptual-motor development, cognitive development, personal-social development. While a detailed description of these measures is not appropriate here, it does seem important to mention something about their general nature. Testing is usually thought of as "serious business," a procedure in which grim-faced individuals determinedly put pencil to paper. Four-year-olds are not apt to see it that way, however—nor would they subject themselves to such an experience if they did. If it is to be successful, the testing of young children must involve attractive, game-like materials and be conducted in a pleasurable social context. Thus our "child measures" included such things as blocks, toy cars, dolls, picture story books—and the children "took their tests" sitting at a table, standing up, sprawled on the floor, or sitting on an examiner's lap. Indeed, many casual outside observers would have found it difficult to distinguish a play area from a testing room at the test centers. Detailed administration manuals were provided, and adherence to standard instructions and probes and detailed recording of responses was emphasized, however, to preserve comparability across children.

This admittedly cryptic summary of study content will have to suffice as an overview, since elaboration of the many variables and constructs within each of the above categories is clearly beyond the scope of the present report. A thorough explication of the study rationale, variables, and measurement strategy is contained in a 279-page document submitted to the Office of Economic Opportunity in December of 1968 (see Educational Testing Service 1968). Some variables, however, will be described in greater detail in the last section of this report under "Preliminary Findings."

Research Logistics

Having shelved further discussion of content for the time being, we move next to a consideration of the study's logistics, or the day-by-day progression of data collection. The research procedures used with any given population should reflect sensitive recognition of the conditions existing within that population. While the point seems obvious enough, it has been more often ignored than honored in actual practice, particularly with "disadvantaged" populations.

The way things "really are," of course, is as complex and varied as the people who live in a community—disadvantaged or otherwise. Still, few would quarrel with the statement made by one Black psychologist discussing research in the ghetto: "These times are potentially explosive in the black community. A complex subject, highly charged emotionally, mixed with countless fears and anxieties, requires experts to handle the special problems." As another ghetto resident and activist succinctly put it: "We're sick and tired of graduate students with clipboards." With an increasing number of research studies focusing on the ghetto, there are good reasons for these expressions of concern. Among the most compelling reasons for discontent and disenchantment are the stark, undeniable facts that the people living in the ghetto—the "subjects" of so much recent investigation—have rarely received any visible benefits from all the research flurry, or had any control over what research was to be done or how it was to be done. To the extent possible, we have tried to alleviate both of these conditions in the present study.

As the first step in what we hope will be a better direction, we immediately initiated communication with leaders of the poor community in each of the study cities. Formal leaders, represented by the community action agency officials and leaders of established organizations, were informed about the study at the time their city became a serious candidate as a site. Other people who did not occupy formal leadership positions but who were influential in the community also were consulted. At the same time, cooperation and understanding of the study were sought from school administrators and boards. Because we felt it was of utmost importance, we asked that written intents (not merely consents) to participate in the study be sent to ETS by both community agencies and local school boards.

We also recognized that there are feelings of frustration in a community when outsiders appear to be the only ones qualified to manage research operations, give tests, conduct interviews, etc. Communities in which research is conducted must be actively involved *on both sides* of a study. Thus, after final site selection, we placed on our staff a full-time person from each of the communities to work as the local study coordinator. This person was responsible for the initial screening of all local (part-time) project personnel, the day-by-day management of project operations, and public relations within the community and city. In addition, the local coordinator was an active participant in joint decisions with ETS Princeton staff regarding the final hiring (and occasional firing) of local personnel. All coordinators received intensive briefings about the study and continuing support whenever necessary from our professional staff. Major briefing sessions were held at the Princeton office, but discussions and the working through of problems more frequently took place at the local sites during periodic visits by Princeton and regional office staff. For all involved, however, the telephone turned out to be the mainstay of ongoing communications.

From the beginning of the study it had been argued that the use of local people as testers, interviewers, observers, etc. would facilitate community cooperation, increase the validity of the data obtained, and provide training which would contribute to future employment possibilities for community residents. This belief was put into practice by ETS during the testing phase of the study and by Audits and Surveys during the initial enumeration and interview phase.

Enumeration and Parent Interviews[5]

The first phase of data collection, household canvassing and parent interviews, was subcontracted to Audits and Surveys (A & S) by ETS. The task of A & S was first to locate all eligible children within the geographic

[5] See Educational Testing Service (1969), "From Theory to Operations," for a more detailed accounting of Year 1 data-collection procedures.

areas being studied and then to complete a ninety-minute interview with each child's mother or mother surrogate. An eligible child was one who, on the basis of his birthdate, was expected to enter first grade in the fall of 1971.

Since previous experience with similar surveys had demonstrated the importance of community support, cooperation through the use of local media and through contact with key community leaders was effectively sought. Interviewers were recruited from the community, with A & S staff responsible for both training and supervision. Interview supervisors and our local coordinators worked in close cooperation and, where feasible, shared the same field office.

During the enumeration phase, several problems were encountered. One of the most difficult involved development of individual location maps to monitor interviewer assignments. This was particularly difficult in rural areas of Lee County because frequently there were no named streets or official county roads. The problem was finally resolved by hiring several local long-term residents who traveled through the county making detailed maps of each school district. The problem of locating the expected number of households was not unique to the rural areas of Lee County. In St. Louis, for example, it was found that many of the neighborhoods in the study have houses with entrances in alleyways that do not appear on official maps. Here, too, the solution involved reliance on the knowledge and cooperation of local residents. As a cross-check, to ensure that as few eligible households as possible were missed during prelisting, a question about first-grade enrollment was used. However, unexpected variations in local enrollment practices did cause problems, several of which are discussed in ETS Progress Report 70-20 (1970).

Following initial piloting in the metropolitan New York area, a full-scale pilot test of about ten completed interviews was conducted in each of the four study sites. The interviewing procedures paralleled the final design and execution to as great an extent as possible. Three interviewers in each city underwent an extensive briefing in order to conduct the pilot test. All three completed practice interviews and later had the opportunity to discuss their reactions and opinions at a group debriefing session. The debriefing report, supported by tape recordings of the discussions and independent analysis of the pilot-test questionnaires, proved to be extremely useful in the final revision of both questionnaire and training procedures.

Since changes in the interview involved only deleting or rewording a few ambiguously worded questions, or modifying format rather than the nature of an item, another pilot testing proved unnecessary. The actual interviewing of eligible mothers or mother substitutes went relatively smoothly, and each interview protocol was reviewed on a question-by-question basis for consistency, clarity, and completeness.

Individual Testing

General training and testing procedures were the same in each site. Prior to the arrival of the ETS training team, the local coordinator preselected the tester trainees, all of whom were female, choosing approximately 30 percent more than the number who eventually would be hired. Depending on a variety of factors (such as resources in the community, the local coordinator's preferences, publicity concerning the project, and intra-community relations), trainee characteristics varied both within and between sites. The usual educational credentials were not required, but experience in working with young children was considered highly desirable, as was the ability to read well and speak with ease. The adequacy of the tester's affective reactions to children and her ability to learn the tasks were the two focal criteria for final selection. Most of the trainees were housewives who had limited work experience, and most were Black.

On-site training was undertaken at staggered two-week intervals, beginning in March, 1969. Several trainers were sent to each site from the Princeton office. After receiving a general orientation in the local coordinator's office, trainees broke into smaller groups and began practice on one of the simpler tasks with a trainer. It was felt that facility in handling the variety of problems a tester was likely to encounter could best be developed in the context of a particular test. These general procedures were then repeated more meaningfully in the context of other tasks. As in training trainers, the tasks were first demonstrated (live and by videotape), and then the trainees practiced by administering them to each other and later to children volunteered by other trainees and their friends. The first tasks demonstrated were those in the Day 1 battery. To reduce the number of tasks that she would be required to learn, each trainee was assigned to learn one of the three remaining batteries. Observations and brief written tests were used to assess the trainee's knowledge of the tasks.

During the third week trainees moved to the actual testing centers. An ETS staff trainer was assigned to each center to ensure adequacy of physical arrangements and testing supplies and to function temporarily as a center supervisor, so that trainees could concentrate on improving their testing skills. The local coordinators arranged for practice subjects who would be comparable to sample subjects and provided for their transportation to and from the center. During the fourth (and sometimes fifth) week of testing practice, the trainees were observed by ETS staff—in all cases this included the project director and a senior member of the professional research team—in order to evaluate performance and to select those women who seemed best prepared to be center supervisors, testers, or play-area supervisors. In those cases where an individual was not selected, every attempt was made to structure the situation as a growth experience instead of a failure and to maintain the person's interest and involvement in the study.

Once evaluations were completed, each center operated one or two weeks more for a dry run. A trainer from ETS's Princeton office remained at each center to provide general assistance and additional instruction in testing, while the center staff practiced their new roles. Once actual testing began, monitoring of center operations (except at Trenton) was assumed by ETS regional office personnel with the assistance of the Princeton office staff; the Princeton office staff itself monitored Trenton operations.

As in training interviewers, piloting of procedures was an essential part of the training process. Prior to initial selection, each measure had been administered to children similar in age and socioeconomic level. However, since most instruments were not off-the-shelf tasks and also had never been given by paraprofessional testers, it was important to allow for the flexibility of refining test manuals, formats, and procedures to facilitate actual field operations. The first two sites (Lee County and Portland) were therefore used during training for continued simplification and clarification of testing and scoring procedures based on trainer and trainee experience and suggestions.

Similarly, the grouping of tasks into batteries had been arranged to take into consideration the need to balance type of response (active vs. passive, verbal vs. nonverbal), to maintain constancy of certain sequencing (e.g., Johns Hopkins Perceptual Test before Matching Familiar Figures, since the former involves practice on the responses demanded in the latter, i.e., looking at each figure before matching to sample), to offer a variety of stimuli, and to provide the child with something to take home each day (a photograph, bag of toys, coloring book, Tootsie Roll). In addition, the batteries also had to be representative of the various domains. The first week of dry-run cases in each site piloted the adequacy of the sequencing. After experiences in the first two sites, minor adjustments were made to permit more equivalent testing time and level of test administration difficulty across batteries. Trainees and trainers were encouraged to discuss the merits of the various modifications, and not until it was time to test actual sample children were procedures stabilized for final production of manuals and answer sheets. From such cooperative efforts were derived not only more adequate measurement techniques but also valuable community-based feedback on research procedures. (Table 1 shows the final order of the tests in the Year 1 batteries.)

Testing centers were located in churches or community recreation facilities in or near the districts where the children lived. Each center provided at least six individual testing rooms or partitioned spaces and a larger play and rest area; most also included kitchen facilities. Each center, operating five days a week, was staffed by nine persons—a center supervisor, a play area supervisor, a driver, and six testers—with each child being scheduled for a four-day testing sequence, usually of one and one-half hours duration daily, and the fifth day scheduled for makeups. A rigid

Table 1. The Measures and Testing Sequence Used in the
Initial Assessments

Day 1	Average Time in Minutes
First-Day-of-School Question (mother) (Hess et al. 1968)	2
Mother-Child Interaction Tasks (Hess et al. 1968)	
Hess & Shipman Toy Sorting Task	15
Hess & Shipman Eight-Block Sorting Task	30
Hess & Shipman Etch-a-Sketch Interaction Task	15
Motor Inhibition Test (Maccoby et al. 1965)	10
*ETS Matched Pictures Language Comprehension Task I	5
Battery A	
Preschool Inventory (Caldwell, Cooperative Tests and Services 1970)	20
*Vigor I (Running)	3
*Spontaneous Numerical Correspondence	10
*Massad Mimicry Test I	12
*TAMA General Knowledge I	5
*Risk Taking 1 and 2	20
Picture Completion (WPPSI) (Wechsler 1962)	5
Battery B	
Sigel Object Categorizing Test (Sigel & Olmsted 1968)	20
Mischel Technique (Mischel 1958)	2
Johns Hopkins Perceptual Test (Rosenberg et al. 1966)	10
*Open Field Test	10
*ETS Story Sequence Task, Part 1	10
Seguin Form Board Test (Stutsman 1931)	10
Matching Familiar Figures Test (Kagan et al. 1964)	15

Table 1. (Continued)

Battery C	Average Time in Minutes
Fixation Time (Kagan & Lewis 1965)	16
*Vigor 2 (Crank-turning)	2
Brown IDS Self-Concept Referents Test (Brown 1966)	10
Preschool Embedded Figures Test (Coates 1969)	15
Children's Auditory Discrimination Inventory (Stern 1966)	10
Peabody Picture Vocabulary Test, Forms A & B (Dunn 1965)	15
*Boy-Girl Identity Task	5
*ETS Enumeration I	7

*Tests developed for ETS–Head Start Longitudinal Study. For a description of these tasks the reader is referred to Structure and Development of Cognitive Competencies and Styles Prior to School Entry, PR-71-19 (Shipman 1971).

schedule was not always possible or desirable, however. For example, centers sometimes operated in the early evenings and on Saturdays for the convenience of working mothers; if necessary, staffs were transferred to new locations to accommodate the children in other sample school districts within a community; and in the testing situations, testers were instructed to wait until the children were ready, with breaks taken whenever necessary.

The first longitudinal sample children were tested seven to eight weeks after the beginning of tester training. During the actual testing, the center staffs worked independently except for periodic visits by monitors, who were responsible for providing general advice on both testing and administrative problems to the center staff and to the local coordinator and for observations to determine whether standard testing procedures were being followed.

Medical Histories and Examinations

The third phase of data collection involved medical histories and examinations. As is true for other aspects of the study, there were regional variations in the procedures for conducting the medical examination. In St. Louis, a neighborhood health center was contracted to do the examinations. In Portland and Trenton, a single physician examined all the study children. Distances in Lee County made it impossible to concentrate the medical examinations in one location, so three physicians examined the children in their respective areas. Examinations were scheduled routinely following completion of the testing cycle.

Field Operations

Considering the scope and innovative nature of the study, data collection during the first year went surprisingly well. Problems arose, of course. While they loomed as potential crises at the time, coping and dealing with these problems provided valuable learning experiences for everyone and generated the kind of pride and esprit de corps which comes from cooperative group effort. In retrospect, some of the "crises" now occasion laughter—as when the shipment of test materials to Portland was lost, finally tracked down to some obscure corner of the Portland airport, and eventually delivered at the local coordinator's office in a 200-pound crate! Even had we been able to lift this, it would have been impossible to manipulate the crate through the narrow doorway and up the stairs to our second floor office. The solution was simple: we opened the crate with the aid of a few crowbars donated by neighboring storekeepers, and then tester trainees, ETS staff, the driver of the air express van, and several nearby residents proceeded to unload a cargo of dolls, wooden cranks, small umbrellas, tow trucks, and other assorted oddities onto the sidewalk and carry them up the stairs. The local coordinator was somewhat embarrassed, but undaunted.

Despite initial predictions that all testing would be completed by early July, centers continued in operation throughout the summer in an attempt to test the desired number of children. Several factors contributed to delays: difficulty in locating all of the families who were interviewed, longer training periods than anticipated, and some reluctance on the part of parents. Increased project publicity and personal visits by the local coordinator and testing staff helped to combat the latter problem. Also, there was greater turnover in testing staff than had been anticipated, because of the temporary nature of the job, because of previous summer or other family commitments, and also due to various private emergencies which arose frequently, since many of our testers lacked personal support and back-up resources. The high turnover rate made it necessary to introduce training activities again in the summer, although actual training time was shortened, since the trainee could obtain more individual attention and the trainer could share his duties with regional office and local center staff.

Frequently the staff also faced emergencies of a community nature, such as rent strikes, incidents of dope peddling, and in one site a local riot, which were especially debilitating and reflected the conditions of social turmoil that often characterize life in disadvantaged areas. Considerable time and attention from ETS as well as local study personnel was devoted to allaying the fears and distrust many ghetto residents display toward being interviewed—coupled with a hostility and boredom engendered by their having been overinterviewed in the recent past.

Despite the many difficulties encountered, however, the study continued operating and data were collected. We believe they are "good" data. The only substantial change in procedure made during the second year of data collection was to appoint a local professional person as monitor in each study site—someone intimately acquainted with the community, who could be readily available to answer questions concerning the various data-collection procedures. Assistant trainers, who in some instances were testers the year before, were also recruited locally. Princeton staff instructed trainers and made periodic visits, but the study became increasingly community based.

DESCRIPTION OF THE STUDY POPULATION

As already indicated, the attempt to gather data on children in the four selected sites was, in general, successful. At least partial data were obtained for a total of 1,875 children, 99.6 percent of the 1,882 children originally expected from these four communities (Educational Testing Service 1968). However, the distribution of children from site to site was different from our expectations, since we had expected St. Louis and Trenton to be our largest sites (and we were least successful in enrolling subjects there), but found more children than we had anticipated in Lee County and Portland (and we were most successful in enrolling subjects there). The other problems were the slightly older ages at testing time of the St. Louis sample, because we had extended their test period (although the ages of the children are actually in the appropriate range), and the impossibility of collecting full data on all subjects.

Table 2 presents the percentages of boys and girls classified by race and sex on whom information has been collected. The percentages add up horizontally, and the number of cases on which the percentage is based is shown in the right-hand margin. These are the children who fulfilled initial qualifications for inclusion in the study and about whom at least one unit of information had been collected during the first period of data collection in 1969. In some cases data available for included children are incomplete.

There are some fairly substantial differences in sample size by site; Lee County and Portland have over five hundred cases, whereas Trenton and St. Louis have under four hundred. Consequently, there is a need for caution in interpreting statistics computed over all subjects, since any factors associated with site (such as region of the country, city size, and socio-economic status) are disproportionately represented.

Table 2. Percentages of Children in Each Site, Classified by Race and Sex
(Spring 1969: Year 1)

		Boys	Girls	N
Lee County	Black	57.7	42.3	279
	White	51.9	48.1	312
	Other	0.0	100.0	2
	Total	54.5	45.5	593
Portland	Black	58.0	42.0	350
	White	46.1	53.9	180
	Other	50.0	50.0	12
	Total	53.9	46.1	542
St. Louis	Black	50.2	49.8	243
	White	52.3	47.7	109
	Other	100.0	0.0	1
	Total	51.0	49.0	353
Trenton	Black	50.8	49.2	301
	White	52.4	47.6	82
	Other	75.0	25.0	4
	Total	51.4	48.6	387
Total	Black	54.5	45.5	1173
	White	50.5	49.5	683
	Other	52.6	47.4	19
	Total	53.0	47.0	1875

Racial composition: Racial composition varies strikingly from site to site. The basic numbers are shown in the last column of Table 2. The total sample is 62.5 percent Black and 36.4 percent White, with a few (1 percent) classified as "Other" (i.e., Puerto Rican, American Indian). The proportion of Blacks varies sharply from site to site, with nearly 78 percent of the Trenton sample being Black, but only 47 percent in Lee County. Therefore, general comparisons from site to site will inevitably require consideration of racial differences.

Sex differences: There are some appreciable differences in the number of boys and girls from site to site. The percentage of boys and of girls is about equal in Trenton and St. Louis, but there is a disproportionately large percentage of boys (54 percent) in both Lee County and Portland. The composition of the total sample is 53 percent boys and 47 percent girls. This difference is sufficient to warrant care in making general comparisons of Lee County and Portland with Trenton and St. Louis, but it does not appear as serious as the confounding on some of the other variables.

Preschool attendance: Table 3 presents a percentage summary of attendance in Head Start and other preschool programs, classified by race and site. The three percentages in each of the five "Total" rows add up to 100 horizontally, and the number of cases on which the percentage is based is shown in the right-hand margin, N column. It should be noted that Head Start was not available to Lee County children until their kindergarten year.

The children are divided into three groups. The first group consists of children who attended Head Start during 1969–70 in Portland, Trenton, and St. Louis and during 1970–71 in Lee County. Information specifying attendance was obtained from community Head Start registers. The second group, other preschool (OP), consists of children who are known to have attended other preschool or nursery programs during 1969–70 in Portland, Trenton, and St. Louis, and during 1970–71 in Lee County. Children who were not on Head Start or other preschool lists are in the "no known" category. It is likely that most of these children attended neither Head Start nor other preschool programs, but this category also includes children who may have moved out of the community and were enrolled in Head Start elsewhere or those who were enrolled in Head Start outside the general area. As the children in the "no known" category are followed up, some of them may be reassigned to the Head Start or other preschool categories; therefore, numbers for the latter categories should be considered minimal estimates.

Across the three urban sites 37 percent of the children attended Head Start. In Lee County 42 percent attended Head Start. However, the percent of children in the Head Start category at the individual site ranged from 33 to 42, and the percent in the other preschool category from 3 to 19. As can be seen, there are substantial interactions between race and Head Start attendance which vary from site to site; this may, perhaps, make Head Start children incomparable to other children at the different sites.

Table 3. Percentage of Children Who Attended Head Start (HS) and Other Preschool (OP) Programs, Classified by Race and Site

		Black	White	Other	N
Lee County	HS	39.1	2.5	0.0	247
	OP	1.3	17.4	0.3	113
	No Known	6.6	32.7	0.0	233
	Total	47.0	52.6	0.3	593
Portland	HS	33.2	6.5	0.7	219
	OP	7.9	5.7	0.0	74
	No Known	23.4	21.0	1.5	249
	Total	64.6	33.2	2.2	542
St. Louis	HS	26.1	11.3	0.3	133
	OP	3.1	0.3	0.0	12
	No Known	39.7	19.3	0.0	208
	Total	68.8	30.9	0.3	353
Trenton	HS	30.7	1.6	0.0	125
	OP	11.9	2.3	0.0	55
	No Known	35.1	17.3	1.0	207
	Total	77.8	21.2	1.0	387
Total	HS	33.2	5.1	0.3	724
	OP	5.8	7.7	0.1	254
	No Known	23.6	23.6	0.6	897
	Total	62.6	36.4	1.0	1875

Eligibility by preschool attendance classification: The sample was classified according to family economic eligibility under the 1969 Head Start poverty guidelines for varying size households ($3,000 for a family of three, with increments of $600 per additional person). Eligibility data were obtained as part of the interview with the mother or the maternal surrogate at the testing center the spring of the Head Start year (Year 2 for Portland, St. Louis and Trenton; Year 3 for Lee County). When the respondent was unable or unwilling to provide income information, eligibility was coded as indeterminate. Missing from these results are those initial study families who were not able to be interviewed during the Head Start year.

Seventy-five percent of the families who were eligible did send their children to Head Start. The percent attending varied from 58 percent in Trenton to nearly 89 percent in Lee County. This estimate is reduced to the extent that children in the no-known-preschool attendance category also attended Head Start, and those in the indeterminate eligibility category were actually eligible. A review of the interviews revealed that many of the household heads in Head Start families in which income information was not obtained held jobs that appeared unlikely to provide wages above the guidelines. About one-third of the children from families at higher income levels also attended Head Start. The proportion of those ineligible who attended varied from 25 percent in Trenton to 61 percent in St. Louis. Thus there was socioeconomic diversity in the programs sampled in the study, and low-income children were not completely segregated from their more advantaged neighbors. In looking at these percentages the reader is cautioned to remember that the families were in many different Head Start programs, and families economically ineligible may, therefore, be a smaller percentage of a particular program's enrollment. Moreover, income data were obtained in the spring of the Head Start year, whereas enrollment was in the fall. Given the greater instability of job opportunities for the poor, and the very low income defining eligibility, the line between "eligible" and "ineligible" for many of the families in this study may be fine indeed.

The basic information discussed so far concerning site, race, sex, and preschool attendance differences may be summarized as follows:

1. The number of subjects at different sites varies, with Lee County and Portland together constituting 60 percent of the sample.
2. The sample is 62 percent Black.
3. Boys make up 53 percent of the sample, girls 47 percent.
4. For the three sites in which children had the opportunity to attend Head Start in Year 2 of the study, 37 percent of the sample attended Head Start, 11 percent attended other preschool programs, and 52 percent had no known attendance in Head Start or other preschool programs. In Lee County, where Head Start is a kindergarten level program, 42 percent of the initial sample attended Head Start, 19 percent attended other preschool programs, and 39 percent had no known attendance in Head Start or other preschool programs.

While the above facts are useful for summary descriptive purposes, they represent a simplistic generalization about the sample. That is, there are substantial interactions between certain classification variables—as well as between classification variables and socioeconomic status—which must be kept in mind in interpreting any findings. The first confounding interaction is between race and Head Start attendance. In this sample, a substantially greater percentage of black children than of white children attended Head Start. While this varies from site to site, in the combined sample 86 percent of the children who attended Head Start were Black. It should be noted that our sample thus differs from Head Start population statistics. According to the Bureau of Census sampling of 5 percent of the children attending a full-year Head Start program in 1969, 52.6 percent were Black. Socioeconomic status is also confounded with race. Thus, although the fathers of both Blacks and Whites tend to be in blue-collar positions, a disproportionately large number of Blacks are so classified (7 blue-collar to 1 not-blue-collar for Blacks, vs. 10 to 9 for Whites). The parents of white children, in general, have also had more schooling than the parents of black children (by about a half to five full years more)—except in St. Louis, where the reverse is true. The average highest school level attained by both mothers and fathers across all sites was ten and one-half grades. Finally, it should be noted that educational and occupational data were obtained for substantially fewer fathers than mothers—and this difference was greater for Blacks than for Whites and for children who attended Head Start than for others. This actually reflects the fact that there are more father-absent families within the black sample.

There are, thus, a number of important disproportionalities in the various classifications. There are almost one and three-quarters times as many Blacks as Whites, more boys than girls, more children who did attend Head Start or other preschool programs, and various interactional differences—such as different proportions of Blacks and Whites attending Head Start.

Such differences in the numbers of children in various classifications is a necessary and in some ways desirable part of the type of design used in the study. It would inevitably be impossible in such a study to identify and select equal or proportional cell sizes, because of the very large number of correlated classification variables, but even if the number of classification variables were to be kept small, the differential attrition over the life of the study would still result in an unbalanced sample. As recompense for the disproportionality, however, we have a measure, albeit crude, of the naturally occurring interrelationship among the classificatory variables at various sites. Such disproportionalities, however, complicate interpretation of general means, for one must be concerned that an apparent effect is not due to important differences among other variables that are not cancelled out in computing a general mean. Consequently, there is a need for caution in the interpretation of analyses, since any factors associated with demographic characteristics are disproportionately represented.

PRELIMINARY FINDINGS AND IMPLICATIONS

So far, we have developed only the barest statistical picture of our sample—how many fall into certain classification categories (site, sex, race, preschool attendance) and how they may be described with respect to such standard indices as level of education and family structure (father present/absent). In this section of the report we will attempt to put some flesh onto the statistical skeleton.

General Considerations

The initial study report (Educational Testing Service 1968) specified a wide variety of measures that we felt would help us describe more adequately the complex interrelationships and structure of children's abilities and characteristics over time and enable us to tease out their interaction effects with particular preschool and primary school programs. Selection of these measures followed certain inherent assumptions about what we felt was necessary to accomplish the goals of the study. Whenever possible, multiple sources of information about a particular phenomenon were proposed (e.g., verbal behavior was seen as a function of the stimulus materials, the communicator-communicant relationship, and the purpose of the act—to inform, seek help, express emotion). We emphasized process rather than static variables, especially those process variables involving parent-child and teacher-child interactions, such as modes of information processing, influence techniques, and reinforcement strategies. Implicit throughout was our belief that only for the intermediate purpose of structural analysis and derivation of measures within domains could one separate cognitive-perceptual and social-personal domains or study the child without taking his environment into account.

The present report is a description of the interrelationships among certain cognitive, perceptual, and personal-social behaviors of the children in the first year of the study, as assessed by the initial test battery. The questions asked of the data were: To what extent are these indices of the functioning of the four-year-old describable in terms of differentiated processes? How do cognitive styles and competencies interact? Within the particular age period represented, are differential results obtained by age, sex, social status, or general ability level of the child, and/or by their interactions? In addition to contributing to our understanding of the young child, answers to such questions have obvious implications for interpretation of particular test findings obtained in various assessment situations.

It must be emphasized, however, that the data presented here provide only some beginning answers to the questions to which the study is addressed. Further analyses are planned which, it is hoped, will provide a more comprehensive picture of the children in our sample and which will help delineate important sociocultural determinants. As noted earlier, the project's focus is on *interactions* as well as main effects; moreover, the questions being asked must be answered within a framework of *repeated* measures and observations of the same children (and their parents) over a period of time.

What should be clearly stated now (if not already apparent) is that this type of research is both time-consuming and costly. Not only is data collection costly in the utilization and training of local personnel but also in the nature of the measures and procedures used. Because there are few standard "off-the-shelf" measures suitable for the purposes of this research with very young children, we have relied almost exclusively on experimental measures and, where necessary, have devised new instruments. Thus, careful analysis of each measure is of primary importance. Similarly, we have stressed procedures for collecting information about human beings—not just "subjects." No mother responded to an interview by answering on a multiple-choice IBM answer sheet, though such a procedure would have been vastly more economical, nor was any child shunted through testing with little individual attention paid to him or his unique responses. To do so would have been to obtain poorer cooperation and less valuable data for a basic understanding of child development. For some of the assessment procedures, the child's responses were fully taped and then analyzed at ETS. In all cases, on-the-spot scoring and coding procedures were simplified so that testers could concentrate their maximum attention on gaining the child's cooperation and involving him in the task. When procedures such as these are used, data do not come back from the field in computer-ready form. Each answer sheet is individually checked, and additional scoring and coding operations are performed at ETS before the information is ever keypunched onto cards for machine processing. Thus, given the inevitable limitations of finite staff resources and funds, the priorities of this research dictate that data analysis can best proceed in a series of steps. This report reflects only the first in that series.

With this by way of introduction, let us try to depict something of the children's cognitive, affective, perceptual, and physical characteristics as they appeared initially in the study. These are set against a background of information obtained from their mothers. (See Educational Testing Service 1970 and Shipman 1971 for a detailed presentation of these findings.)

The Families in the Study

In measuring aspects of the family environment that influence a child's development, it is important to distinguish between *status* and *process* variables. Simply stated, this is the distinction between what parents *are* (e.g., ethnic membership, occupational-educational level) and what they *do* (e.g., styles of interaction with the child, aspirations and expectations communicated to him, and behaviors reflecting attitudes of optimism, alienation, and hopelessness). Previous research (e.g., Hess et al. 1968) suggests that it is the process variables which have the greater impact on a child's life, and they certainly have greater theoretical utility than demographic indices for explaining how the environment mediates experience in critical ways. A corollary assumption is that the mother is particularly influential in transmitting to the young child behaviors and adaptations shaped by the environment. In later years other aspects of the environment may exert relatively greater influence upon the child, but during the preschool years the exchange between mother and child is perhaps the most critical focus of attention. For these reasons, then, greater priority has been given to process variables in the study—particularly process variables related to the mother's perceptions and styles of interaction. Information about situational and status characteristics have been obtained only insofar as these either define important aspects of the child's psychological as well as physical environment, or identify subpopulations which should be analyzed separately.

To study these various family influences, we administered both a home interview (approximately ninety minutes) and three structured mother-child situations in which the mother is taught a relatively simple task which she, in turn, teaches to her child. For this report, however, only data from the closed-ended questions of the interview are included—with resulting limited information on such process variables as the mother's teaching techniques or language codes.

As expected, the sample is predominantly a lower socioeconomic one, with many of the concomitants of low status: feelings of powerlessness and alienation from society, with limited confidence in one's ability to change schools and other institutions for the better, discrepancies between aspirations and actual expectancies, limited knowledge of community resources, limited home resources, less adult availability to the children, more physical crowding and material deprivation, greater reliance on kinship contacts, and substantially fewer fathers present in the home. To elaborate on some of these generalizations, a substantial number of mothers (ranging from 8 percent to 35 percent at different sites) revealed that they did not know what local nursery schools, clinics, summer day camps, or after-hour school programs were available to their community. A majority of mothers (61 percent) felt that political candidates run more for personal advancement than for accomplishing campaign promises, and 32 percent of the mothers had never voted. Although 61 percent reported willingness to join their neighbors to solve local problems, the majority of them felt that their combined efforts would be ineffective. Similarly, although the majority (56 percent) were able to describe a concrete problem in the

community that needed attention, they also repo⌐
improvement did not occur. In the opinion of
mothers, there was no local person presently su⌐
munity problems. Twenty-two percent reported
their child to play outside. Probably as a conse⌐
complaints, the majority of mothers (59 percent) w⌐
that anyone move into their area.

As previously found with groups of similar status level, most ⌐
reported belonging to no clubs or groups. Memberships that did occur were
primarily in school-related and religious groups. Most of the study families
(83 percent) had relatives living within twenty miles whom they visited,
but other types of social interaction were less common. Twenty-eight
percent of the mothers said they had no friends *at all* in the general area;
32 percent said they did not go out for entertainment.

Although nearly all families had a TV set or radio, a substantial number
had no car, phonograph, telephone, encyclopedia, or dictionary. One-fourth
to over two-fifths of the children (depending on site) did not have their
own bed or place to keep clothes, toys, and other possessions. Only 17
percent of the children slept alone.

Some of the data suggest that many mothers lack differentiated criteria
for evaluating their child's achievements and/or lack of knowledge about
those achievements. For example, when asked about the child's ability to
name the primary colors and various body parts, to give his own full name,
and to count to five, from 56 percent to 95 percent of the mothers said
their child could do each of the above tasks "now"—a statement markedly
contradicted by their child's performance on those same items in the
testing situation.

Although a majority of parents responded positively when questioned
about their neighborhood schools, a sizable minority indicated discontent.
Thirty-one percent felt that teachers in their district schools did not
understand local problems, and an equal number indicated they felt
teachers make children doubt what they are taught at home. Fifty-three
percent reported overcrowding in their schools, and 43 percent felt that
teachers neglect some children in their classes. (Present coding of the
open-ended interview responses is concerned with the more important
question of the perceived reasons for teacher neglect.) Although 74 percent
stated they felt they could disagree with the school principal, almost 30
percent said they could not improve their neighborhood schools—with an
additional 20 percent not knowing whether they could or could not. While
no national norms for the general population are available, these data
suggest that the mothers in our sample have only a moderate level of
confidence in their ability to change schools for the better and have rather
strong feelings of alienation.

these were the *general* findings, considerable variation was also ced. The occurrence of this variability agrees with Zigler's (1968) clusion that there are greater differences in child-rearing practices within cial status levels than between levels, and with Caldwell's (1970) recent discussion of the much greater range (than had previously been reported) in level of stimulation and support offered a child in lower-class homes. It is inappropriate, therefore, to speak in terms of a single homogeneous "culture of poverty." There are many such subcultures, reflecting a variety of life styles.

Variation was notable between the preschool attendance categories. Those families who enrolled the study child in Head Start were, on the average, characterized by greater deprivation than those families who sent their child to another preschool program or who were not known to have enrolled their child in any program. Thus, for this sample, participation in Head Start was generally by those who would appear to need it most. They lived in older, more run-down homes and under more crowded conditions. Fathers were absent in 50 percent of the "Head Start" homes. In contrast to families not known to have sent their child to any preschool program, mothers in "Head Start" families, although having completed less schooling, expressed somewhat more favorable attitudes toward local schools, participated somewhat more in the community, and expressed more active responsibility for their child's school performance. Since the Head Start group had a higher percentage of siblings who attended Head Start, this prior exposure may account for their greater involvement with the schools and community. Of course, it is equally possible that involvement in community concerns had led them in the first place to enroll their children in Head Start. It is hoped that more sophisticated analyses and longitudinal data will enable us to untangle such questions.

Future investigations will be directed toward analyzing the relationship of the various status and process variables with each other and with the several child measures. By isolating more exact indicators of home environment (and of parental characteristics, including cognitive ones) rather than just demographic characteristics, we should be in a better position to explain why, within homes of similar socioeconomic status, so much variation in process is found, and why there are so many notable exceptions to the "low status–low achievement" maxim.

The Children in the Study

In considering the children, we will first turn attention to the vitally important concern of health. Following completion of the testing cycle, physical examinations were scheduled for all study children. Unfortunately, the information obtained is limited in both extent and interpretability. This stems in part from the necessity for relatively brief individual appointments and from the fact that administration of some measures must be considered only crudely standardized. While a comprehensive medical examination was not given, attention was focused on those physical variables considered especially relevant to intellectual/social development. In addition, two tasks were administered at the testing centers aimed at assessing the child's vigor—one was speed of running a given distance; the other, the number of turns the child could make on a large wooden crank within a given time limit.

On both of the latter tasks (running time and crank turning) the data showed practice and age effects, suggesting that differences in coordination and muscle strength were also being tapped. Notwithstanding the many cautions which must be considered in interpreting the Child Health Record, physical examination results do suggest differential exposure to conditions of health risk, permitting us to delineate subgroups of children whose health-related conditions potentially handicap them for school adjustment. Consistent with previous research findings, we found a higher frequency of health-related problems among our predominantly low socioeconomic sample than is found with the upper socioeconomic groups—e.g., more prenatal, birth, and postnatal complications, more abnormal findings on the visual and auditory screening tests, higher suggested incidence of neurological problems, below average hemoglobin values, and fewer immunizations. It is interesting to note that site differences in average hemoglobin values, which may reflect iron-deficiency anemia, paralleled the site differences in vigor scores.. The St. Louis data, as a whole, suggest the pervasive physical and emotional consequences of living under deprived conditions, since there was a higher incidence of a variety of health-related problems at that site.

Other findings from the Child Health Record with immediate relevance to the testing results are the mothers' reporting of significantly more developmental problems for boys, the already mentioned high incidence of problems in St. Louis, and the significantly fewer problems reported for children who later attended "other preschool" programs.

To describe the child's functioning in other areas, we included measures to encompass objectives claimed by many preschool and primary programs and aspects of development that social science theory holds as important. That is, we included measures of more academic "school-related" skills (behaviors and skills which are "expected" of the child enrolling in kindergarten or first grade in most public schools) as well as measures which would help us delineate basic perceptual, cognitive, and personal-social processes and their course of development. As Bereiter (1972) pointed out, there is very little evidence that learning one thing does more good than learning another. We need to determine the transfer value of such learning and assess what can be built upon in later years.

In the first project report, Messick (1968) proposed a tentative outline for mapping the perceptual-cognitive-intellectual domain in a cross-classification scheme organized into hierarchical levels reflecting breadth of function and different orders of complexity. Basically an extension of Guilford's (1967) theory for the structure of the intellect, this outline combined features of dimensional, hierarchical, morphological, and sequential models of intellect and incorporated variables derived both from the child development literature and from studies of adult performance. It also provided a guide for selecting instruments to represent the different types of contents, products, and operations delineated by Guilford.

Attention also was given to assessing those personality dimensions, referred to as controlling mechanisms, that cut across affective, personal-social, and cognitive domains and thereby serve to interlace the cognitive system with other subsystems of personality organization. In that same report Emmerich (1968) delineated three other distinct but interrelated areas of personality investigation—social motives, attitudes, and interests—and suggested measurement strategies across the years of the study.

On the basis of this and other reviews of domains to be represented, variables considered salient for the study population were selected. Given the state of the art in the development of measures, tasks were selected which would allow (a) continuity of measurement across age periods by using the same or vertically equivalent forms and (b) multiple measurement of the same variable (within a context) across several age periods, so that possible developmental shifts in expression could be monitored. Other factors affecting task selection were constraints related to available testing time, balance among areas and modes of response, sufficient knowledge of the appropriateness of the task for the intended population, and ease of administration.

Prior to statistical analysis, the Year 1 child test measures were grouped according to the above classifications (i.e., cognitive, perceptual, affective, and physical), with certain subdomains also suggested (e.g., within the cognitive domain, both Piagetian-derived measures and "academic" skills represented by verbal, quantitative, and general information measures). Included in subdomains were measures clustered according to contents, products, or operations. Thus, verbal skill measures included comprehension of syntax, sequence, and vocabulary; classification ability; and the ability to discriminate and mimic phonemes. In addition, cognitive styles (e.g., reflection-impulsivity, analytic functioning) and other controlling mechanisms such as risk-taking, curiosity, and attention deployment were delineated. A logical series of analyses were planned to study data within and across domains by mode and time of data collection. This report presents the results of the first "within-method" (i.e., individual testing) analyses, both within and across domains.

OVERVIEW OF STRUCTURAL FINDINGS

Following reduction to logically distinct scores for each task, principal components factor analyses using both unity and Tucker adjusted communalities on the diagonal were obtained. These analyses were performed for the composite sample and for major subject classifications; i.e., by age, sex, SES level, later preschool attendance controlled for Head Start eligibility, and Preschool Inventory score with age partialled out. To facilitate interpretation, varimax and promax rotations of the first 2, 3, 4, and 5 principal components were performed successively. Six and seven factor varimax and promax rotations were also obtained for the composite sample. The same series of analyses were performed for a reduced set of variables posited to be in the cognitive domain. For these various analyses, five to ten additional scores were included in extension analyses to study their relationships with factors derived from the main set of variables. In addition to the factor analyses, Guttman-Lingoes smallest space analyses (Lingoes 1965) for 1, 2, and 3-dimensional solutions were performed on the same set of subject classifications and set of variables to insure that conclusions would not be based on results which were dependent on the method of analysis.

The main findings of the factor and smallest space analyses of the data for the total group can be summarized as follows. (1) There was clear evidence of a general dimension accounting for most of the *common* variance among cognitive tasks. (2) A second orthogonal dimension relating to the child's speed of responding to a multiple-choice task was obtained. (3) Additional factors that appeared were apparently tapping task-specific styles and behaviors (e.g., a factor principally defined by measures from the Open Field Task; a factor defined by two scores on the Fixation Task; a Spontaneous Numerical Correspondence factor; a Boy-Girl Identity Task factor). (4) Subclusters of tasks were not obtained; instead, considerable nonerror specific variance was revealed for the many tasks used in the study. These findings were strikingly consistent across statistical methods and across subject classifications.[6]

Table 4 presents the Tucker communality estimates for each score, along with the estimated reliability where available. The estimates in Table 4 are based on the composite sample. Score abbreviations are included; task descriptions and a more detailed explanation of the scores used are presented in Project Report 71-19 (Shipman 1971). For all scores, coefficient alpha (Cronbach 1951) was the index of reliability. With few exceptions,

[6]Among the six preschool attendance by eligibility categories, two groups, those Head Start eligible who attended a different preschool program and those who were not known to have attended preschool, had Ns too small to permit adequate comparisons of the factor structures.

estimated communalities were moderate to low, with considerable reliable but unique variance remaining. Table 5 presents the 6-factor promax solution for the composite sample using communalities in the diagonal, with intercorrelations among factors reported in Table 6. The task-specific nature of the 3rd through 6th rotated factors may be seen quite clearly in Table 5.

Table 4. Estimated Communalities* and Reliabilities for Selected Scores

Score		Communality	Reliability (Coefficient α)
1	Hess and Shipman Toy Sorting Task: Total Score	.32	
2	Hess and Shipman Eight-Block Sorting Task: Total Score	.35	
3	Interaction Ratings: Mean Cooperation Rating (for 2 or 3 tasks)	.23	.81
4	Motor Inhibition Test: Average Time, Trial 2, for the Walking and Drawing Subtests	.26	.67
5	ETS Matched Pictures: Total Score	.21	.57
6	Preschool Inventory (Caldwell): Adjusted Total Score (minus items 52–55)	.68	.92
7	Form Reproduction: Total Score	.40	.65
8	Vigor 2 (Crank Turning): Average Number of Turns	.14	.86
9	Spontaneous Numerical Correspondence Task: Total Deviation Score	.35	.74
10	Spontaneous Numerical Correspondence Task: Configuration Matching	.54	.57
11	Massad Mimicry: Nonsense Words, Total Sounds (standardized)	.58	.91
12	Massad Mimicry: Meaningful Word Phrases, Final Sounds (standardized)	.53	.63
13	Risk Taking 2: Derived Score (0=toy only; 1=bag, trial 2; 2=bag, trial 1)	.03	
14	Picture Completion Subtest: Total Correct	.47	.89
15	Sigel Object Categorization: Total Grouping Responses	.33	.91
16	Sigel Object Categorization: Average Time to Response (Log 10)	.55	.77
17	Sigel Object Categorization: Total Correct Object Labels	.19	.62
18	Mischel Technique: Choice (0=smaller now; 1=larger later)	.02	
19	Johns Hopkins Perceptual Test: Total Correct	.46	.74
20	Open Field Test: Mean Play Complexity	.35	.61
21	Open Field Test: Number of Periods Child Talks to Himself	.09	.73
22	Open Field Test: Number of Periods Child Talks to Tester (1=if any)	.66	.81
23	Open Field Test: Number of Periods Child Approaches Tester (1=if any)	.07	

Table 4. (Continued)

Score		Communality	Reliability (Coefficient α)
24	Open Field Test: Number of Periods Child Attempts to Leave Task (1=if any)	.18	
25	Open Field Test: Longest Simple Sequence	.28	.64
26	ETS Story Sequence Task: Total Score	.31	.50
27	Seguin Form Board: Fastest Time for Correct Placement	1.00	
28	Seguin Form Board: Number of Errors (for Trial with Fastest Time)	.35	
29	Matching Familiar Figures: Mean Log (X+1) of Response Times	.40	.90
30	Matching Familiar Figures: Mean Errors per Valid Item	.58	.70
31	Fixation: Mean Recovery Time	.71	
32	Fixation: Mean Habituation	.40	
33	Brown Self-Concept Task: Number of Items Omitted	.16	.91
34	Brown Self-Concept Task: Self-Concept Score (No. positive (1)/No. Coded 0 or 1)	.11	
35	Brown Self-Concept Task: Smiling (1) or not smiling (0)	.04	
36	Preschool Embedded Figures Test: Total Correct	.20	.85
37	Preschool Embedded Figures Test: Average Time for First Response	.17	.77
38	Children's Auditory Discrimination Inventory: Total Correct	.52	.81
39	Peabody Picture Vocabulary Test, Form A: Total Correct to Criterion	.71	.96
40	Peabody Picture Vocabulary Test, Form B: Total Correct	.65	.93
41	Boy-Girl Identity Task: Task 1 (Girl), Item 1 Score	.67	
42	Boy-Girl Identity Task: Task 2 (Boy), Item 1 Score	.30	
43	Boy-Girl Identity Task: Sum of Task 1 Items 2, 3, 4, & 5	.01	.59
44	Boy-Girl Identity Task: Sum of Task 2 Items 2, 3, 4, & 5	.02	.64
45	Enumeration Task 1: Total Correct (Items 1–12)	.26	.85
46	Enumeration Task 1: Correct on Item 13 (counting)	.20	

*Communalities were obtained using Tucker's adjusted highest off-diagonal element.

Thus, structural analyses of the Year 1 child test data yielded (a) a general ability dimension (i.e., information-processing skills) cutting across contents and operations sampled in the cognitive test battery and (b) a stylistic response tempo dimension. Additional factors apparently tapped task-specific styles and behaviors. Although previous research has reported

Table 5. Promax Correlations with Reference Factors[a]

Score	1	2	3	4	5	6
1	0.42 [b]	-0.09	0.08	0.15	0.08	0.02
2	0.47	-0.02	0.01	0.12	0.07	0.05
3	-0.36	-0.08	0.03	-0.16	0.02	0.04
4	0.44	0.07	0.02	0.03	-0.04	0.04
5	0.41	0.05	-0.02	0.03	0.03	0.01
6	0.70	-0.01	-0.02	0.13	0.06	0.02
7	0.56	0.02	-0.02	0.18	-0.06	-0.02
8	0.34	0.09	0.02	0.01	-0.05	0.01
9	-0.07	0.19	0.03	-0.50	-0.03	-0.04
10	0.14	-0.16	-0.04	0.60	0.11	-0.01
11	0.46	-0.04	-0.16	-0.20	0.11	-0.07
12	0.41	-0.05	-0.10	-0.25	0.13	0.02
13	-0.01	-0.10	-0.01	0.06	0.00	-0.01
14	0.63	0.12	0.01	0.04	-0.04	-0.02
15	0.46	-0.09	0.10	-0.01	0.08	0.05
16	0.03	0.66	0.02	0.01	0.01	-0.04
17	0.34	-0.18	0.03	-0.10	-0.04	-0.05
18	-0.03	-0.03	0.00	-0.09	-0.03	0.04
19	0.42	-0.28	0.10	-0.04	0.01	0.04
20	0.01	0.23	0.06	-0.16	-0.36	0.09
21	0.02	0.19	0.06	-0.12	0.00	0.12
22	0.09	0.23	0.06	0.02	0.47	0.14
23	-0.01	0.13	0.02	0.03	0.21	0.02
24	-0.06	0.02	0.06	0.02	0.35	0.00
25	0.12	0.05	-0.04	-0.08	-0.48	0.08
26	0.44	-0.26	0.03	0.03	0.03	0.02
27	-0.65	0.12	-0.03	-0.03	0.29	-0.04
28	-0.43	-0.02	-0.01	0.06	0.16	0.02
29	0.06	0.56	0.02	-0.05	0.07	-0.07
30	-0.56	0.13	-0.09	0.07	0.02	0.03
31	0.06	0.05	0.79	-0.05	0.06	-0.03
32	0.04	0.01	0.60	-0.02	0.04	0.00
33	-0.35	-0.10	0.01	-0.02	0.03	0.01
34	0.28	0.05	0.08	0.00	-0.01	-0.05
35	0.14	0.09	-0.02	-0.02	0.10	0.08
36	0.38	0.16	0.06	0.13	-0.08	0.00
37	0.14	0.31	-0.03	-0.15	0.01	0.03
38	0.60	0.20	-0.03	-0.05	0.07	-0.01
39	0.73	0.18	-0.02	-0.06	0.04	-0.02
40	0.68	-0.06	-0.04	-0.09	0.00	-0.02
41	-0.01	0.02	-0.05	0.01	0.00	0.74
42	-0.04	-0.04	0.02	-0.03	-0.03	0.52
43	0.00	-0.01	-0.02	-0.03	-0.04	-0.03
44	-0.10	-0.04	-0.03	0.01	0.00	0.08
45	0.42	0.07	-0.04	0.18	-0.07	-0.04
46	0.40	0.08	-0.06	0.10	-0.01	-0.02

[a]Using communalities in the diagonal.
[b]Loadings equal to or greater than 0.30 in absolute value are underlined.

Table 6. Intercorrelations among Promax Primary Factors
for Six-Factor Solution*

	1	2	3	4	5	6
1		-0.16	0.06	0.08	0.18	0.36
2	-0.16		0.18	0.14	-0.03	-0.02
3	0.06	0.18		0.08	-0.09	0.08
4	0.08	0.14	0.08		-0.27	-0.02
5	0.18	-0.03	-0.09	-0.27		0.12
6	0.36	-0.02	0.08	-0.02	-0.02	

*Using communalities in the diagonal.

differentiated abilities in very young children ranging down to ages two and three (Hurst 1960; Meyers et al. 1964; Meyers et al. 1962; McCartin & Meyers 1966), and several cognitive dimensions have been delineated in analyses of infants' and preschool children's performance on standard preschool scales (Stott & Ball 1965; Ramsey & Vane 1970), primary factors differentiated by content, operations, and/or products did not emerge in the present data. Given the generally high internal consistency of the various scores and their moderate to low communalities, considerable nonerror specific variance remained. These findings were strikingly consistent across a variety of statistical methods and across major subject classifications (i.e., by sex, age, SES, preschool attendance controlled for eligibility, and Preschool Inventory score).

Many theorists, including Piaget and Guilford, emphasize the importance of interactions with the environment for intellectual development. Although the child may start with certain innate mechanisms, such as predispositions for Guilford's five operations or Piaget's invariant functions of assimilation and accommodation, the rate of progression and the variety of dimensions in cognitive functioning appear to depend upon the extent to which these mechanisms are exercised in interaction with a varied environment (Hunt 1961). Ferguson (1954, 1956) has suggested that cognitive factors represent behavioral domains that happen to have been learned together, along with those similar behaviors that become associated through generalization of learning and transfer. As Messick (1968) has pointed out, some of the determinants of these shared learnings are developmental, in the sense that certain things are experienced together because they are appropriate to particular ages, but most of the determinants appear to be more directly sociocultural (Lesser et al. 1965; Stodolsky & Lesser 1967). It would be expected from a transfer theory of abilities that factor structures would be more clearly defined for subjects having had the benefit of more varied experience. Thus, the absence of differentiated factors in the present data may reflect a relatively narrow range of environmental variations experienced by this sample as compared to subjects assessed in previous studies. For example, Meyers et al. (1964), Stott and Ball (1965), and Ramsey and Vane (1970), all of whom tested children from primarily middle-class and upper-class socioeconomic backgrounds, found greater evidence for differentiation at this age or even earlier.

INFORMATION-PROCESSING FACTOR

The first factor seemed to be best defined as "g" or information-processing skills which contribute to level of performance on all of these tasks. For this sample, it was best represented by performance on the Preschool Inventory and Peabody Picture Vocabulary Test (PPVT), which correlated 0.62. The Preschool Inventory was developed to measure achievement in areas regarded as critical for successful kindergarten performance. To some extent performance on this task is an index of the child's ability to process general information from the environment. Millham, Jacobson, and Berger (1971) recently described scores on a vocabulary test as measuring associative information-processing ability. Both tests have been found to be highly sensitive to environmental impoverishment. As might be expected, the most general task in the test battery, the Preschool Inventory, had the highest loading (0.70) but the following all had loadings of 0.42 or higher: certain verbal measures, i.e., receptive and productive vocabulary (Peabody A and B), classification skill (Sigel Object Categorization Test Grouping responses, Toy Sorting, and Eight-Block Sorting Task scores); certain perceptual measures, i.e., auditory discrimination (Children's Auditory Discrimination Inventory), form discrimination and matching (Johns Hopkins Perceptual Test score and Matching Familiar Figures Test errors); and the perceptual-motor measures, i.e., visual-motor coordination (Seguin Form Board) and form reproduction (Form Reproduction Test). Included in measures of "g," of course, are such "noncognitive" aspects as ease and willingness to relate and assert oneself in the testing situation, attention, persistence, and task orientation. A common cognitive component is the ability to understand and follow directions. These aspects of "g" may, however, be somewhat age-specific.

There was a substantial amount of variance in the present data, however, that was not part of the general ability dimension. The lack of clustering prevents us from knowing at this time if such specific variance is related to special abilities limited to one task, incomplete sampling of the processes represented by tasks, or particular situational determinants. The fact that a general ability dimension or "g" was somewhat less evident in less mature subjects (i.e., in younger children and those performing below their age-group mean on the Preschool Inventory) suggests that for this sample at this age behaviors were being tapped at the beginning of a period of integration rather than during a period of differentiation. Subsequent measurement might be expected to reveal increasing common variance on "g," followed later by increasing differentiation in terms of contents, operations, and/or products. Discontinuity in cognitive structure would thus be indicated by changes in the number or size of dimensions over time and/or by changes in the meanings of dimensions as revealed in new patterns of correlates or factor loadings.

The tentative finding of a battery-defined clustering of cognitive measures suggested the role of situational determinants (i.e., day and tester) as a secondary structuring variable. Perhaps children from more restricted environments are less familiar with test-like settings and, therefore, show greater variation in performance across days. Some children may increasingly adapt to testing and generalize skills learned in the testing situation, while others, especially those who find the tasks or the testing center situation more difficult and frustrating, may become increasingly alienated from the situation. This interpretation suggests the possibility of analyzing the data by categorizing groups of children by the extent of their consistency over the four testing days. This battery effect, however, was least for those measures with highest loadings on the general ability factor. The child who appeared particularly able in one assessment was generally able in another.

The less clearly defined general ability dimension which was found for the younger, less "academically" prepared, economically poorer children in the sample may reflect both greater susceptibility to situational determinants and less generalizable information-processing skills. That is, they may have been less able to apply what they know, or, in Piagetian terms, to "decenter." These data reflect in part the greater instability and reduced variability of measurement for the less mature subjects, but they also suggest that the least able children don't yet have "g" well enough developed so they can integrate their behavior. As noted earlier, considerable differentiated behavior was reflected in the large amount of unaccounted-for nonerror variance. The above findings suggest that such differentiated behavior may reflect fragmented behaviors which have not yet been organized or integrated. The difference in generalization of these skills would seem to reflect differential training and practice in the various task components as well as in the transfer of skills from one task to another. These data would suggest that the differentiation seen in the present data is task-specific and may not be under the control of generalized cognitive mechanisms. With continued practice and experience, cognitive mechanisms may come into play that will give order and consistency to these behaviors. It may be that only after such integration and generalization of the specifics occur can differentiation into stable cognitive factors take place. Longitudinal data will enable us to chart such developmental patterns and assess the differential utility of various theories, such as Garrett's (1946) hypothesis of a single general ability that differentiates over time, or the more general notion that cognitive structure tends to become increasingly differentiated (and hierarchically integrated) during the course of development, as propounded by Werner (1957) and Lewin (1951).

RESPONSE TEMPO DIMENSION

A major question posed in the study was the relationship between cognitive style and skill. The concept of ability implies measurement of capacities in terms of maximal performance, whereas the concept of style implies measurement of preferred modes of operation. Both are necessary for a full understanding of cognitive functioning (Cronbach 1970). Some controlling mechanisms represent dimensions of individual differences in the structural characteristics of the cognitive system itself. Other controlling mechanisms appear in the form of preferences or information-processing habits, which determine a person's typical modes of perceiving, remembering, thinking, and problem-solving. In the Year 1 test battery an attempt was made to assess the cognitive styles of reflection-impulsivity and analytical functioning.

A general dimension defined by the three latency measures did emerge. Thus, response tempo, frequently used to measure the cognitive style of reflection-impulsivity (Kagan et al. 1964), appeared as a consistent individual difference variable; however, for this sample during this age period response tempo was not related to performance level on the first factor. Similarly, latency and adequacy of response were not correlated within tasks (r = -.07 with grouping responses on the Sigel and .02 with errors on the Matching Familiar Figures Test). Response latency, therefore, did not have the same implication for performance as has been found with older and/or more advantaged subjects (Messer 1970; Eska & Black 1971), since it did not reflect individual differences in the degree to which the child considers the adequacy of his response. Perhaps, prior to school experience, there is a lack of anxiety or concern over error and/or fewer internalized standards of performance. These findings suggest that temperamental components have not yet become integrated into the cognitive domain.

The orthogonal relationship between cognitive competency and tempo factors was paralleled by an apparent lack of similarity in the relationships of scores to age, sex, and SES. Moreover, other possible indices of the impulsivity dimension—the ability to inhibit a response when appropriate and the ability to delay gratification—were not related to the latency scores or to one another, which suggests that impulsivity is not a unitary trait or generalized dimension in this population at this age.

Other cognitive-stylistic factors, such as analytic functioning, did not appear. There were too few scorable sorting rationales given on the Sigel Object Categorization Test to assess differences in preferred categorization style at this age. Data from the Sigel in future years of the study should enable us to assess not only the child's classificatory ability over time but mode and stability of response style.

DIFFERENCES AMONG GROUPS

In accord with recent findings (McGaw & Jöreskog 1970; Wasik & Wasik 1970), the factor pattern was relatively constant over a range of socio-economic and ability levels. Inspection of standard errors of the means and patterns of correlates of the measures in the Year 1 battery indicated no major differences in construct validity of the tasks for the major classifications used in these analyses. Similar results were reported by Stevenson et al. (1971), who found the pattern of interrelationships among learning tasks for four- and five-year-old low-income children to be similar to that reported for middle-class preschoolers.

Mean performance levels did show significant group differences, however. Performance on those tasks defining the general ability dimension was shown to be a function of developmental level (age) and experience (socioeconomic status), despite the relatively restricted ranges of both variables. Thus, general information-processing skills, conceptual understandings, and favorable responses to the testing situation were greater for older children and for those from families of higher socioeconomic status. Given the diversity of tasks represented on the first factor, age and SES were shown to be associated with a wide variety of behaviors. Differences were manifest on verbal, quantitative, and perceptual tasks. Nonverbal as well as verbal performances were involved, although for this sample at this age a verbal-nonverbal distinction may be difficult to make, since the verbal component of any task performance might be substantial. For example, the child could not point to the picture that matched the stimulus without understanding the meaning of the instruction. Those tasks which appear to require more active environmental interchange showed larger SES and age differences. Thus, tasks requiring knowledge of specific information (e.g.,

Preschool Inventory) and communication skills (Peabody B) showed larger differences than those requiring form discrimination and matching or comprehension of syntax.

Age and SES may be viewed, however, as differentially producing these effects. Given the relatively short age span, only three measures showed larger age than SES effects—Child Cooperation, Vigor, and number correct on the Enumeration Task. These are all among the few measures which showed significant sex differences; in accord with our later discussion of such differences, these results may indicate greater compliance and task persistence, along with superior motor coordination in older subjects. On the other hand, those measures that showed the largest SES effects relative to age differences were the Eight-Block Sorting Task, the Motor Inhibition Test scores, Sigel grouping responses, and Story Sequence. All these appear to require not only careful attention to verbal instructions but also the demonstration through another modality of a verbally based understanding of the task, or, conversely, verbal explanation of the child's own nonverbal performance. This difference suggests that higher SES is associated not only with a greater number of experiences—as age would be—but also with differences in the cognitive organization of these experiences.

Seventy-five percent of the study children who were eligible for Head Start did attend Head Start subsequent to our initial testing. According to the present results these children generally were performing significantly less well than those children who attended other preschool programs or no known preschool program on a variety of cognitive-perceptual tasks *prior* to their enrollment. Such effects were particularly evident on tasks highly saturated with "g," including those tapping acquisition of information considered necessary for success in school (Preschool Inventory and Peabody) and use of language as a cognitive tool (e.g., classificatory skills). Piaget has argued that classificatory structures which emerge during the preschool years are an essential foundation for later concrete operations (Flavell 1963). Longitudinal data may enable us to assess the extent to which retardation in the development of logical operations in socio-economically disadvantaged children may be due to inadequate foundations for such processes.

Those children who later attended other preschool programs were found to be more advanced *prior* to entering any preschool program. As pointed out earlier in this volume, however, the variables defining the several groups are confounded and thus no simple main effect comparisons for classificatory variables such as Head Start vs. non-Head Start can be made without careful consideration of their interactions with other variables. For example, preschool attendance is confounded with site, race, and the four indicators of socioeconomic status (mother's and father's educational and occupational levels). Thus, to interpret simple mean differences for Head Start vs. non-Head Start groups would be quite unwarranted.

Assignment of tasks to the "cognitive domain" does not imply they are independent of motivation. For the young child especially, one cannot readily separate intellective and nonintellective factors. Specifically, motivational factors cannot be separated from the learning process. As was found, measures of persistence and cooperation loaded on the general ability dimension (cf. Zigler & Butterfield 1968). Although there was probably insufficient sampling of such behaviors in the test battery to produce factors in the affective domain, the affective domain may nct be highly differentiated at this age. However, there was rather strong evidence for differentiated personal-social characteristics of these children when seen later in the classroom setting (Emmerich 1971).

For this sample at this age "noncognitive" measures did not show the same SES differences found on the measures of cognitive competence. The majority of children were willing to choose the uncertain outcome, to accept the delayed reward (which also might be seen as an uncertain outcome), and to express positive statements about themselves. Consistent with the findings of other investigators (Brown 1966; Clark et al. 1967), self-concept scores were predominantly high. This may reflect the fact that "significant others" at this age are primarily family members and particularly the mother, whom we might expect the child to perceive in a supportive role. (In subsequent analyses we will look at the child's self-concept score in relation to the mother's supportiveness in the interaction tasks.) As the child grows older, with increasing opportunity for interaction with others in a variety of situations, we would expect a more differentiated concept of self to emerge, resulting in greater variance of scores. For many low-income children, especially those of minority status, such interactions may lead to negative self-evaluations and markedly lower scores (Katz 1969; Tannenbaum 1967).

There were few significant sex differences; those that were obtained showed girls performing better when sustained attention was required, whereas boys gave the preferred response when assertiveness seemed a more critical component. It should be noted that the usual finding of superior performance by girls on verbal measures was not evidenced in these data. Girls generally obtained slightly higher scores on the verbal tasks, but for this sample at this age these differences were not significant. No such trends were present for the perceptual tasks. Whether such sex differences in performance on verbal and perceptual tasks will emerge in subsequent years remains to be determined. With one exception, a Sex by Age by SES effect for Seguin time to quickest solution, there were no significant interaction effects. Age and SES did not show different effects for boys and girls, nor did SES have different effects for younger and older children.

Also, new clusterings of tasks according to patterns of effects were not obtained.

The above discussion should not lead us to overlook the most striking finding of all, namely, the wide range of variation in performance exhibited. Although group differences were statistically significant, many mean differences in task performance were small relative to within-group variability. Low-income youngsters are *not* a homogeneous group. Children from low-income families span a wide range of cognitive, personal-social, and perceptual functioning. The fact that the same factor pattern was found within the low SES group as within the high SES group reflects this finding also (cf. Lesser et al. 1965; Stodolsky & Lesser 1967).

In general, tasks in the Year 1 battery proved to be appropriate for this age group. They were sensitive to individual differences, were enjoyed by most children, and were relatively easy to administer. Of particular importance for this age group was the fact that the tests were not speeded and the administration procedures allowed for great flexibility. Because of the young child's greater susceptibility to situational variables in testing (Sattler & Theye 1967), the total testing climate was geared toward making the child more comfortable. Time (in some cases, several days) was taken to establish rapport, relatively familiar testing rooms in church schools were used, and the tasks were administered by local testers whose dialect and race (wherever possible) were similar to the child's. Future analyses will investigate influences of tester characteristics on child performance. All of these factors contributed to a congenial and supportive atmosphere. In addition, we attempted to schedule so that each mother could accompany her child on the first testing day. These test conditions, differing as they do from the rigidities of nonessential components of standardized practice, may have contributed substantially to the level of competency observed—as well as to the validity and reliability of measurement.

The present analyses were based primarily on total scores which might mask differences in patterning or level of response; data reduction entails a risk of losing critical information. There is the possibility that individuals pass through a developmental sequence of qualitatively different structural organizations, usually held to be in an invariant order, which is the more classical developmental view of stage progression. The emphasis in measurement would then be upon the assessment of qualitative features that are characteristic of particular stages of cognitive functioning and upon ordered sequences of tasks capable of gauging the transition from one stage to another. Few "markers" of stage level, however, are represented in the Year 1 battery. An exception is the Sigel Object Categorization Test; analyzing the performance of children differentiated into three groups that may represent different developmental stages—e.g., above the median on nonscorables, on color responses, or on form responses—might give clues as to developmental stage.

Those tasks that might have yielded scores representing different levels on a developmental scale (e.g., Boy-Girl Identity and Spontaneous Numerical Correspondence) did not do so at this time. The Boy-Girl Identity Task did not tap a cognitively based reality judgment of gender identity constancy in this population at this age, but instead yielded four almost orthogonal scores; children's performance on the Spontaneous Numerical Correspondence Task indicated that understanding of number at this preoperational stage was essentially perceptual in character, reflecting global rather than articulated intuition processes. Thus, the study children were generally preoperational. Measurement in subsequent years on these tasks might provide such scaled scores. Also, additional tasks amenable to such differentiated scoring have been included in later test batteries. The later use of conservation items with the Spontaneous Numerical Correspondence Task will enable assessment of changes associated with shifts from preoperational thinking to concrete logical operations.

Efforts will continue in deriving other, more sensitive, indices of level of performance and of task sequences. The generally quick test responses of this sample suggest that at this age most subjects could not inhibit long enough to enable cognitive processes to operate optimally in contexts where greater reflection would be functional. As suggested recently by Eska and Black (1971), future analyses may fruitfully separate children into "reflective" (long latency, low errors), "impulsive" (short latency, high errors), "quick" (short latency, low errors), and "slow" (long latency, high errors) groups in order to obtain a better understanding of the factors which influence and/or determine a particular response style. Moreover, given the likelihood that response sets are particularly important in the responses of young children (Damarin & Cattell 1968), further internal analyses of tasks will be directed toward investigating such effects. For example, it was noted in describing the findings from the Children's Auditory Discrimination Inventory that children showed a differential preference for pointing to the real as contrasted to the nonsense picture.

Further understanding of the present data will be provided by mapping out similarities and differences in sociocultural determinants. Tasks loading on the first factor range from general to specific, and common dimensions may be defined where shifts in determinants occur. Moreover, the variety of measures included in the study enables one to examine the components of related but not identical constructs—e.g., cognitive styles as defined by Witkin et al. (1967) and by Kagan et al. (1964).

The findings of McGaw and Jöreskog (1970) in studying the factorial invariance of ability measures in high school students differing in intelligence and socioeconomic status suggest the value of looking at SES differences within ability level. They found the gap in mean factor scores between low and high SES groups to be much wider for low IQ than for high IQ; the facilitative effect of high SES thus appeared greater for low IQ subjects. Similar findings have been reported by Willerman et al. (1970) for infants and preschool children.

The above discussion illustrates some analyses presently planned to help study complex interrelationships among variables that must be investigated before one can understand the complexity of the child's functioning in the test situation. Present analyses used occupation of head of household and income as gross proxies for assessing the child's environment. These indices inappropriately assume constancies of meaning within and across groups, and they tell us little about the type of stimulation the child is being exposed to in the home environment. Within a given SES level, as defined by the usual demographic indices, the range of home environments can be so great as to make any generalizations about SES level and development extremely tenuous (Pavenstedt 1965; Tulkin 1968; Zigler 1968). More fine-grained analyses will become possible using indices from the parent interview and mother-child interaction sessions. As static group categories are thus replaced by delineation of those behavioral and attitudinal variables reflecting processes which link social and cultural environments to the emerging capabilities of young children, meaningful SES relationships may be determined. For example, we will look at the effect of variation in experience on the child's ability to use language as a tool for symbolic or representational thinking. The present data as well as those recently reported by Golden et al. (1971) suggest that the effects of variety of experience are particularly salient for those behaviors reflecting the cognitive use of language. In the first project report (Educational Testing Service 1968), Shipman and Bussis delineated other process variables in the child's environment that appear to be particularly influential in the child's cognitive development, especially the role of the mother in selecting, structuring, and transmitting information about the environment to her child and in regulating his behavior in relation to both the environment and the information transmitted. Such information should provide more direct evidence on the environmental interactions accounting for differences in these test performances.

Data in subsequent years will enable us to evaluate hypotheses generated by the present structural findings, especially whether there is increasing integration of cognitive behaviors followed by differentiation into clusters, as those found in previous research. We will also be able to assess the effects of differential experiences provided by Head Start and other preschool programs. Such experiences would be expected to show differential effects, depending on the nature of the processes involved and the level of the child's functioning. Thus, despite the size and extensiveness of the data base, the present findings must nevertheless be considered tentative; important clues to interpretability await relating these data to sociocultural determinants, developmental trends, and interrelationships that may become increasingly apparent with measurements in subsequent years.

Implications: Immediate and Future

What implications, or value, has the Longitudinal Study had so far, and what does it promise for the future? Within the realm of the more immediate, it is possible to single out at least three contributions worthy of comment. First, there has been immediate payoff in the communities involved in terms of dollars spent in hiring local employees and purchasing necessary testing supplies. More importantly, the job training provided has increased the skills and the confidence of some of the local residents.

A second immediate implication of our results to date concerns the fallacy of assuming that Head Start children and families are comparable to non-Head Start groups—regardless of how similar they may look on certain surface characteristics. As mentioned earlier in the discussion on research design, the "comparable group" assumption is questionable at best for naturally selected or post hoc groups; and results of studies on such an assumption must be regarded as "suspect" until proven otherwise (see Campbell & Erlebacher 1970). Our initial results indicate that Head Start families and children constitute a group which differs in many significant respects from other low-income groups.

A final immediate implication concerns Head Start program planning. If the data obtained from Year 2 of the study continue to support previous findings that rules governing the logical distinctions of negation and location (in, on, under, behind, etc.) are acquired or constructed very early by both disadvantaged and advantaged youngsters, then modification of certain aspects of some experimental language curricula would seem called for. These results would concur with Cazden's (1968) statement that basic grammatical structures seem to be learned despite differences in the child's linguistic environment; the manner in which children use language to express ideas, however, may be more sensitive to environmental manipulation. In her discussion of the previous symposium papers, Cazden (1972) cites several examples of differences in teacher-child interaction associated with differences in effects on various measures of the child's language development. Thus, although most children were able to label the objects correctly on the Sigel Object Categorization Test, few were able to give appropriate verbal rationales for their sorts; on the Eight-Block and Toy Sorting tasks, although the majority of children were able to categorize, that is, to sort the objects correctly, few were able to verbalize their reasons for doing so. Admittedly, it is anticipated that many more substantial and far-ranging recommendations for program planning will emerge in future years—but at least this one modification may be justified in the very near future. Moreover, a number of tasks have been developed that have proven themselves to be appropriate in their range of difficulty and sensitivity to individual differences, enjoyed by most children, and relatively easy to administer. There is immediate need for such measures in the many evaluation studies of preschool programs currently under way.

With respect to long-range implications of the study, we have already pointed out the variation which exists within our relatively restricted sample—restricted, at least, in terms of socioeconomic level. As the study progresses, we will have an opportunity to identify important distinctions among subpopulations who live in relative poverty. That is, we will be able to define more clearly those environmental influences and features which are simply "different" from middle-class standards—and those which act as genuinely impoverishing forces on the human mind and spirit.

There is another type of variation in the study which also has potential implications. By using such a wide variety of tasks, one becomes more aware of intraindividual differences in the patterning of skills and abilities. Knowledge of such patterning of strengths and weaknesses is, of course, a necessary and powerful diagnostic tool for the effective planning of educational programs. As indicated earlier, most preschool program planning has had to rely on research done with middle-class children; this study should provide a unique data bank, enabling more informed educational decisions to be made.

Most important of all, perhaps, is the opportunity this study provides for investigating the interactions between complex sets of variables over time. Among other things, this means an opportunity to pinpoint variables that are critical for understanding the interrelationship between affective and intellectual domains in child development and the differential effectiveness of various educational environments and programs. The overall picture of complex interaction between community-family-child-school influences should become clearer. A major thrust of Head Start is to help the low-income family resist alienation, i.e., resist the tendency to turn away from the community. Both formal and informal contacts with others are valuable sources of information, attitudes, and values; they bring perspective on community norms. Previous research suggests that as the mother interacts more, she feels less powerless, more optimistic, and less likely to resort to status and authoritarian appeals for controlling her child (Hess et al. 1968). Thus, programs reducing alienation may in turn increase the child's developmental progress. We would also expect that as a result of Head Start participation the family would become less alienated from the educational system and would come to define the school not only in a more positive way but also in a more differentiated fashion. This, in turn, should provide the child with more adequate and useful images of the school, of the teacher, and of the role of active student. As the recently completed report about the impact of Head Start centers upon community institutions (Kirschner Associates 1970) suggests, Head Start's *latent functions* in the educational and health areas may well equal the manifest ones. The diffusion of latent effects in the schools and local community over time would logically be expected to minimize differences between

Head Start and non-Head Start families—as these initially appeared in our sample. Since we have an opportunity to study families and communities over time, we have an opportunity to see. Additional examples of interactive processes that this study will enable us to investigate concern the match between teacher and maternal teaching styles and the effects on the child's behavior; the relationship between mother-child and teacher-child interaction; and maternal powerlessness and the extent of the child's involvement in the classroom.

It is impossible to conclude this report without one final comment about the data reported so far. They show that research can be done in low-income areas. It is accomplished by making measures as relevant as possible, getting advice from community residents, and recruiting and training local personnel to carry out most of the operations required. Further, they show that administering individual tests in educational research is not the exclusive prerogative of the graduate student and other educational elite. We have been strengthened in our belief that traditional training models must be questioned: effective training must involve mutual learning and cross-socialization. The local women in our study learned effectively to perform a wide variety of demanding tasks. They managed well under many difficult local conditions—often quite difficult ones. Clearly, we have joined many others in discovering a large pool of as yet untapped human resources. Through our continuing joint efforts, we hope to provide information that will contribute significantly to the policy-making decisions which affect the well-being of our nation's children and their families.

REFERENCES

Anderson, S. B., and Doppelt, J. (Jt. Chm.). 1969. *Untangling the tangled web of education.* Symposium sponsored by the National Council on Measurement in Education. Princeton, N.J.: Educational Testing Service, RM-69-6.

Beery, H. C. 1967. Developmental Test of Visual-Motor Integration: Administration and Scoring Manual. Chicago: Follett Education Corporation.

Bereiter, C. 1972. An academic preschool for disadvantaged children: Conclusions from evaluation studies. Ch. I (pp. 1-21), in J. C. Stanley (ed.), *Preschool programs for the disadvantaged.* Baltimore: The Johns Hopkins University Press.

Bernfeld, S. 1925. *Sisyphus or the boundaries of education.* Vienna: International Psychoanalytic Press.

Brown, B. 1966. The assessment of self-concept among four-year-old Negro and white children: A comparative study using the Brown IDS Self-Concept Referents Test. Paper presented at annual meeting of the Eastern Psychological Association, New York City.

Caldwell, B. M. 1970. The effects of psychosocial deprivation on human development in infancy. *Merrill-Palmer Quarterly* 16 (3): 260–77.

Campbell, D. T., and Erlebacher, A. 1970. Evaluations can mistakenly make compensatory education look harmful. Pp. 185–210, in J. Hellmuth (ed.), *Compensatory education: A national debate, Vol. 3, Disadvantaged child*. New York: Brunner/Mazel.

Cazden, C. 1968. Some implications of research on language development for preschool education. Pp. 131–42, in R. D. Hess and R. M. Bear (eds.), *Early education: Current theory, research, and practice*. Chicago: Aldine.

——— · 1972. Some questions for research in early childhood education. Pp. 188–99, in J. C. Stanley (ed.), *Preschool programs for the disadvantaged*. Baltimore: The Johns Hopkins University Press.

Clark, E. T., Ozenhosky, R. J., Barz, A. I., and O'Leary, J. V. 1967. Self-concept and vocabulary development in Negro and white preschool children. Paper presented at annual meeting of the Eastern Psychological Association, Boston.

Coates, S. W. 1969. Preschool Embedded Figures Test. Brooklyn: State University of New York, Downstate Medical Center.

Cooperative Tests and Service. 1970. Preschool Inventory, Revised Edition–1970 Handbook. Princeton, N.J.: Educational Testing Service.

Cronbach, L. J. 1951. Coefficient alpha and the internal structure of tests. *Psychometrika* 16: 297–334.

——— · 1970. *Essentials of psychological testing* (3rd ed.). New York: Harper.

Damarin, F. L., Jr., and Cattell, R. B. 1968. Personality factors in early childhood and their relation to intelligence. *Monographs of the Society for Research in Child Development* 33(6): Serial No. 122.

Dunn, L. M. 1965. Expanded Manual for the Peabody Picture Vocabulary Test. Circle Pines, Minn.: American Guidance Service.

Educational Testing Service. 1968. *Disadvantaged children and their first school experiences: Theoretical considerations and measurement strategies*. Princeton, N.J.: PR-68-4 (2 vols.). Prepared under Contract OEO 4206 and Grant CG-8256, Office of Economic Opportunity. (ED 037 486).

——— · 1969. *Disadvantaged children and their first school experiences: From theory to operations*. Princeton, N.J.: PR-69-12. Prepared under Grant H-8256, Department of Health, Education and Welfare. (ED 043 397).

——— · 1970. *Disadvantaged children and their first school experiences: Preliminary description of the initial sample prior to school enrollment*. Princeton, N.J.: PR-70-20 (2 vols.). Prepared under Grant CG-8256, Department of Health, Education and Welfare. (Vol. 1, ED 047 797; Vol. 2, ED 047 798.)

Ekstein, R. 1969. The child, the teacher and learning. In R. Ekstein and R. Motto (eds.), *From learning for love to love of learning.* New York: Brunner/Mazel.

Emmerich, W. 1968. Children's personal and social development. Pp. D2–D22, in *Disadvantaged children and their first school experiences: Theoretical considerations and measurement strategies.* Princeton, N.J.: Educational Testing Service, PR-68-4.

——. 1971. *Disadvantaged children and their first school experiences: Structure and development of personal-social behaviors in preschool settings.* Princeton, N.J.: Educational Testing Service, PR-71-20. Prepared under Grant H-8256, Department of Health, Education and Welfare.

Eska, B., and Black, K. N. 1971. Conceptual tempo in young children. *Child Development* 42: 505–16.

Ferguson, G. A. 1954. On learning and human ability. *Canadian Journal of Psychology* 8: 95–112.

——. 1956. On transfer and the abilities of man. *Canadian Journal of Psychology* 10: 121–31.

Flavell, J. H. 1963. *Developmental psychology of Jean Piaget.* Princeton, N.J.: Van Nostrand.

Garrett, H. E. 1946. A developmental theory of intelligence. *American Psychologist* 1: 372–78.

Golden, M., Birns, B., Bridger, W., and Moss, A. 1971. Social-class and differentiation in cognitive development among black preschool children. *Child Development* 42: 37–45.

Guilford, J. P. 1967. *The nature of human intelligence.* New York: McGraw-Hill.

Hess, R. D., Shipman, V. C., Brophy, J. E., and Bear, R. M. 1968. *The cognitive environments of urban preschool children.* Chicago: University of Chicago.

Hunt, J. M. 1961. *Intelligence and experience.* New York: Ronald.

Hurst, J. G. 1960. A factor analysis of the Merrill-Palmer with reference to theory and test construction. *Educational and Psychological Measurement 20: 519–32.*

Kagan, J., and Lewis, M. 1965. Studies of attention in the human infant. *Merrill-Palmer Quarterly* 11: 95–127.

Kagan, J., Rosman, B. L., Day, D., Albert, J., and Phillips, W. 1964. Information processing in the child: Significance of analytic and reflection attitudes. *Psychological Monographs* 78(1): Whole No. 578.

Katz, I. 1969. A catalogue of personality approaches to Negro performance with research suggestions. *Journal of Social Issues* 30: 13–28.

Kirschner Associates, Inc. 1970. *A national survey of the impacts of Head Start centers on community institutions.* Contract No. B89-4638, prepared for the Office of Child Development, U.S. Department of Health, Education and Welfare.

Lesser, G. S., Fifer, G., and Clark, D. H. 1965. Mental abilities of children from different social-class and cultural groups. *Monographs of the Society for Research in Child Development* 30(4): Serial No. 102.

Lewin, K. 1951. *Field theory in social science.* New York: Harper and Row.

Lewis, M., Rausch, M., Goldberg, S., and Dodd, C. 1968. Error, response time and I.Q.: Sex differences in cognitive styles of preschool children. *Perceptual and Motor Skills* 26: 563–68.

Lingoes, J. C. 1965. An IBM 7090 program for Guttman-Lingoes small space analyses: 1. *Behavioral Science* 10: 183–84.

Maccoby, E. E., Dowley, E. M., Hagen, J. W., and Degerman, R. 1965. Activity level and intellectual functioning in normal preschool children. *Child Development* 36: 761–70.

McCartin, Sister Rose Amata, and Meyers, C. E. 1966. An exploration of six semantic factors at first grade. *Multivariate Behavioral Research* 1: 74–94.

McGaw, B., and Jöreskog, K. G. 1970. *Factorial invariance of ability measures in groups differing in intelligence and socioeconomic status.* Princeton, N.J.: Educational Testing Service, RB-70-63.

Messer, S. 1970. Reflection-impulsivity: Stability and school failure. *Journal of Educational Psychology* 61: 487–90.

Messick, S. 1968. Measurement of general intelligence. Pp. C72–C73, in *Disadvantaged children and their first school experiences: Theoretical considerations and measurement strategies.* Princeton, N.J.: Educational Testing Service, RB-68-4.

Meyers, C. E., Dingman, H. F., Orpet, R. E., Sitkei, E. G., and Watts, C. A. 1964. Four ability-factor hypotheses at three preliterate levels in normal and retarded children. *Monographs of the Society for Research in Child Development* 29(5).

Meyers, C. E., Orpet, R. E., Atwell, A. A., and Dingman, H. F. 1962. Primary abilities at mental age six. *Monographs of the Society for Research in Child Development* 27: Whole No. 82.

Millham, J., Jacobson, L., and Berger, S. 1971. Effects of intelligence, information processing, and mediation conditions on conceptual learning. *Journal of Educational Psychology* 62: 293–99.

Mischel, W. 1958. Preference for delayed reinforcement: An experimental study of cultural observation. *Journal of Abnormal and Social Psychology* 66: 57–61.

Office of Economic Opportunity. 1970. *Lee County community profile.* Figures based on 1966 U.S. census report. Washington, D.C.: Office of Economic Opportunity.

Pavenstedt, E. 1965. A comparison of the child-rearing environment of upper-lower and very low-lower class families. *American Journal of Orthopsychiatry* 35: 89–98.

Ramsey, P. H., and Vane, J. R. 1970. A factor analytic study of the Stanford-Binet with young children. *Journal of School Psychology* 8: 278–84.

Rosenberg, L. A., Rosenberg, A. M., and Stroud, M. 1966. The Johns Hopkins Perceptual Test: The development of a rapid intelligence test for the preschool child. Paper presented at the annual meeting of the Eastern Psychological Association, New York.

Sattler, J. M., and Theye, F. 1967. Procedural, situational, and interpersonal variables in individual intelligence testing. *Psychological Bulletin*
68: 347–60.

Shipman, V. C. 1971. *Disadvantaged children and their first school
experiences: Structure and development of cognitive competencies and
styles prior to school entry*. Princeton, N.J.: Educational Testing Service,
PR-71-19. Prepared under Grant H-8256, Department of Health,
Education and Welfare.

Sigel, I. E., and Olmsted, P. P. 1968. The development of classification and
representational competence. Paper presented at the annual meeting of
the American Educational Research Association, Chicago.

Stern, C. 1966. Language competencies of young children. *Young Children*
22: 44–50.

Stevenson, H. W., Williams, A. M., and Coleman, E. 1971. Interrelations
among learning and performance tasks in disadvantaged children. *Journal
of Educational Psychology* 62: 179–84.

Stodolsky, S., and Lesser, G. 1967. Learning patterns in the disadvantaged.
Harvard Educational Review 37: 546–93.

Stott, L. H., and Ball, R. S. 1965. Infant and preschool mental tests:
Review and evaluation. *Monographs of the Society for Research in Child
Development* 30(3): Serial No. 101.

Stutsman, R. 1931. *Guide for administering the Merrill-Palmer Scale of
Mental Tests*. Yonkers-on-Hudson: World Book.

Tannenbaum, A. J. 1967. Social and psychological considerations in the
study of the socially disadvantaged. Pp. 45–63, in P. A. Witty (ed.), *The
educationally retarded and disadvantaged*. Sixty-sixth yearbook, Part I.
Chicago, Ill.: National Society for the Study of Education.

Tulkin, S. 1968. Race, class, family, and social achievement. *Journal of
Personality and Social Psychology* 9: 31–37.

Wasik, J. L., and Wasik, B. H. 1970. A comparative study of the Wechsler
Preschool and Primary Scale of Intelligence (WPPSI) and the Wechsler
Intelligence Scale for Children (WISC) for culturally deprived children.
Durham (N.C.) Educational Improvement Program 3: 157.

Wechsler, D. 1962. *Manual for Wechsler Preschool and Primary Scale of
Intelligence*. New York: Psychological Corporation.

Werner, H. 1957. *Comparative psychology of mental development* (rev.
ed.). New York: International Universities Press.

Willerman, L., Broman, S. H., and Fiedler, M. 1970. Infant development,
preschool IQ, and social class. *Child Development* 41: 69–77.

Witkin, H. A., Goodenough, D. R., and Karp, S. A. 1967. Stability of
cognitive style from childhood to young adulthood. *Journal of
Personality and Social Psychology* 7: 291–300.

Zigler, E. F. 1968. Learning, development and social class in the socialization process. Pp. 195–207 in M. H. Marx (ed.), *Learning: Interaction.*
New York: Macmillan.

Zigler, E. F., and Butterfield, E. C. 1968. Motivational aspects of IQ test
performance of culturally deprived nursery school children. *Child
Development* 39: 1–14.

SCARVIA B. ANDERSON
Educational Testing Service
Princeton, N.J. 08540

VII. EDUCATIONAL COMPENSATION AND EVALUATION: A CRITIQUE

We have been brought up to date in preceding chapters (by Ball and Bogatz and by Bissell) on three massive attempts to influence the development of young, poor children—*Sesame Street*, Head Start, and Follow Through. We have also heard (from Karnes and Sigel) of some dedicated smaller efforts in the same direction. All of these programs are described as *compensatory* education. All of them have been accompanied by a great deal of data collection. Most of this data collection has been undertaken in the name of program *evaluation*.

Since the notions of compensation and evaluation are so fundamental to the papers presented here—and indeed to the professions we represent and the people they are designed to serve—I shall couch my critique in an exploration of the social and scientific implications of the two terms. I shall refer less frequently to the chapter by Shipman than to the others, because I have too many close associations with that study to comment about it very effectively in my present role. In addition, the ETS longitudinal study is not primarily evaluative; it is more an in-depth analysis of *un*planned variation.

COMPENSATION

Ball and Bogatz drew six useful implications about education of disadvantaged children—if one accepts that connotation of "compensatory"—from their *Sesame Street* investigations. Then they speculated that "many children need compensatory education, including a large proportion we fail to recognize when we conventionally think of the term" (p. 23). Sigel grants the ambiguity, double meanings, and overload of emotionality associated with the term "compensatory education" and concentrates on "intervention" to which he assigns a relatively precise meaning. Other related words are "remedial" and "special" (Karnes certainly associates "special" closely with "compensatory"), but these are "old" adjectives as

196

applied to education. Something different must have been meant or wanted, or the expression "compensatory education" would not have been invented. (One of its first uses seems to have occurred in the early sixties in connection with the McAteer Act in California,[1] and the frequency of its use expanded greatly with the implementation of the Elementary and Secondary Education Act of 1965.)

"Compensatory" seems to be closer to "special" than to "remedial" in several senses. Both kinds of education are prescriptive or preventive. Both assume that some condition beyond the student's control will depress his achievement unless some extraordinary treatment is applied. The unfortunate condition that requires special education is usually physical; the child is crippled, deaf, brain damaged, or impaired in some other way that makes his attendance in regular classrooms unprofitable for him—and sometimes obtrusive for others. The condition that occasions compensatory education programs is primarily socioeconomic. It is assumed that because the child comes from a poor home certain generalized supports for the kinds of development that are *deemed important in school* are probably missing or deficient. Thus it is important to provide for these supports through some means other than the family.[2]

The more children who are presumed to have an education-relevant deficiency or need, the more likely it is, of course, that action will be taken.[3] Consider, for example, that some children can read before they enter kindergarten; however, this number is quite small. If the majority of children were ever able to read before they entered kindergarten and thus the kindergarten and first grade programs no longer emphasized reading readiness and related activities, then compensatory education programs would probably be introduced to try to get all children to start reading before kindergarten.

Numbers are important, too, for remedial education; the more children who need remediation, the more likely it is that provision will be made for them. However, remedial education differs in at least three significant respects from compensatory education. First, the diagnostic decisions that would direct a student into a remedial program are made *after* the student is already in the school; they are based on observations that he or she has not learned a skill or grasped a subject matter *the first time around*.

---

[1] See *California Education* (1963).

[2] It is even possible to conceive of compensatory education as teaching children to use non-family supports available elsewhere in the community. However, such an approach would probably have to be limited to older students.

[3] This statement oversimplifies matters somewhat. Action is likely to be taken on the basis of the intensity or gravity of a problem as well as its frequency. Recent extraordinary concern with mental retardation is a case in point.

Second, the term "remedial" allows for the possibilities that the student may bear some responsibility for his failure to learn or the school program may have been inadequate. It does not assume, as compensatory education assumes, that the difficulty arises entirely from external sources. Third, remedial education focuses on a specific, well-defined area (such as reading or mathematics) where the student has not been achieving, while compensatory education is more global in nature.

However, even in government agencies (where these words are used most frequently) there is considerable and confusing overlap in usage. For example, the United States Office of Education has defined "compensatory reading programs" as "any special reading instruction provided to students because of the fact that they are reading below grade level."[4] This would conform better to my definition of "remedial."

On the surface, "intervention" seems to have fewer emotional overtones than any of the other terms in this set. In Sigel's words, ". . . intervention is considered as a conscious and purposeful set of actions intended to change or influence the anticipated course of development" (p. 26). Thus, all education might be considered intervention, but the predictions that the educators are trying to "undo" are seldom specified with any precision. Emotionality *can* be invoked in connection with "educational intervention" when one questions the basis for some of the assumptions on which particular interventions are based, including the intervener's right to intervene. Sigel says: "To deliberately set out to change someone immediately engages several crucial . . . value questions. Who has the right to change anyone? What or who gives him that right?" (p. 26). I question his use of the word "immediately" if it in any way suggests "ordinarily" or "routinely." Although we know that many families are not necessarily happier if moved to better housing in a strange district (Young & Willmott 1957) and that many youngsters are not necessarily happier for being in *any* kind of school, we seldom bother to document the basis for our right to move them or school them—or the justification for the particular techniques we have decided to employ. Chazan (1968) and others point out that such value decisions are not themselves within the scope of scientific research. However, it is becoming increasingly recognized that science can have a major role to play in clarifying the range of alternatives that underlie major value decisions (Messick 1972). Unfortunately, funds for such efforts do not seem to be in abundant supply.

To try to make some summary distinctions then: Compensatory education is a preventive and global (otherwise it would be *remedial*) intervention into the lives of people judged to have socioeconomic handi-

---

[4]This is the definition used in "A Description and Analytic Study of Compensatory Reading Programs" being carried out by Educational Testing Service.

caps (physical handicaps would require *special* education) assumed to be predictive of unnecessarily limited school achievement and life chances.

Birren and Hess (1968) point out that there are at least six models against which judgments about socioeconomic handicap are processed, with the "malnutrition" and "cultural-disparity" models being the most popular. In their excellent and basic delineation of the concepts of deprivation and disadvantage, they also distinguish between two standards of deprivation: "*objective* standards (defined by experts or by social norms) and *subjective* standards (those the subject himself defines)" (p. 91).

It is important to note that decisions about needs for compensatory education are generally made about groups, and assignment to compensatory education programs is based on carrier variables: family income, language spoken at home, etc. In other words, children do not qualify either as individuals or on educational criteria. [There is some confusion in my mind about the implications of assignment of children to educational programs on the basis of family background, in light of the general conclusion of Coleman et al. (1966, p. 325): ". . . schools bring little influence to bear on a child's achievement that is independent of his background and general social context."]

There are a number of specific issues we should raise now about compensatory education:

1. When should it start? Advocates of compensatory education seem to be especially enamored with beginning the process as early as possible. As Ausubel (1967) and others have observed, there is no conclusive evidence that if skills are not acquired early they are not acquirable later on—perhaps more efficiently. But it is an inconvenience for social institutions such as schools to handle children who are "behind" their peers; if a child stays "behind" very long he may develop a hard-to-change acceptance of failure. It is heartening to working mothers to have a reliable and respectable place to leave their young children, and there are special pressures to intervene with minority children as soon as possible. Not the least of these pressures includes the early opportunity afforded by compensatory education programs to "reach" mothers (see Karnes, p. 136). Early education has become such a badge of the war on poverty that in some circles it is considered almost undemocratic to raise the issue of the appropriate age to begin. "The earlier, the better" is the cry.

2. How long should compensatory education last? Bissell and others who speak for Head Start invariably point out that a year isn't long enough, that "continuation of compensatory education into kindergarten and the elementary grades" is required (p. 87). Campbell and Frey (1970) have cited good reasons why "fade out" in achievement occurs for children when compensatory programs are discontinued. They state that "the only condition not entailing a fade out is a situation in which the compensatory

input is maintained throughout the educational years" (p. 462). However, these arguments do not imply that there is no justification for relatively short-term programs nor do they reduce the public's expectation that in a period as short as eight weeks or a year *something* should be expected to happen and a *little* of it remain. Certainly we are used to some long-term benefit from rather short-term training in tasks with a large physical component (typing, driving an automobile, playing the piano, etc.) even though we may not practice them regularly. (On page 28 of this volume Sigel summarizes his position on these questions of "when" and "how long" for compensatory education.)

3. What is the difference between compensatory education and *non-compensatory* education? Implicit in any discussion of compensatory education, of course, is that there are other types of education that are *not* compensatory. But how, for example, could a visitor from a foreign country tell which was which *in actual practice*?

A look at the budgets—do compensatory programs cost more than noncompensatory programs for the same age group?

The goals—are they different? The nature of the program—what's happening in the classroom? In this connection, some confusion is generated by such information as this: Head Start and Follow Through programs couldn't accommodate Montessori as a planned variation, according to Bissell, while Karnes allowed Montessori to compensate. And, of course, *Sesame Street* was meant to be compensatory, but "noncompensatory" children were not precluded from watching it—or learning from it.

Or do compensatory and noncompensatory programs differ chiefly in the kinds of teachers who teach in them? Or children who go to them? Are there more teachers in the compensatory classroom? Are the teachers more dedicated, better trained, more tired—or what? Could a substantial difference be detected between children in some of the Follow Through classes—30 percent poverty children, 27 percent not poverty, and 43 percent "undetermined," according to Bissell (p. 97)—and the children in many "ordinary" first grades?

While we are carrying out the exercise of taking sound movies of the twenty Follow Through variations and seeing if skilled judges can sort them into twenty bins, we might take pictures of rich black and white children in compensatory education programs and poor black and white children in noncompensatory education programs (and other combinations) and see if our foreign visitor can tell the difference.

This concern with what is meant by "compensatory education" is, of course, not just a semantic exercise. It is crucial to decisions about establishing and maintaining educational programs. It is also central to any attempts to evaluate that which purports to be compensatory—or interventional in other senses.

EVALUATION

If one is to evaluate compensatory education, one's first obligation is to show whether the program does in fact compensate. It would not be sufficient simply to show that something happened—for example, that children gained. If the program is also described as an "intervention," then it would also be important for the evaluator to show whether or how the status of the children at the end of the intervention differed from that unhappy state predicted for them without intervention. These two concepts imply two different kinds of comparison groups:

1. To determine if a program is truly compensatory, an appropriate comparison group would be similar in age and as many respects as possible to the "treatment" group, but judged "advantaged" or *not* needing compensation (see Cohen 1970).

2. To determine if an intervention was successful, an appropriate comparison group would be from the same subpopulation as the group involved in the intervention, but would be *un*treated.

Ball and Bogatz, without the option of denying *Sesame Street* to middle-class children, at least compared the performance of their lower-class group with that of an advantaged group who, presumably, did not need the compensation. However, such comparisons are not very frequent. As Shipman can tell you, at budget time one of the first things to "go" in the ETS Longitudinal Study was the prospect of a middle-class comparison group. Generally, only the second kind of comparison group is used—that is, those who are judged as needing compensation, but either receive no specific educational treatment or experience a "traditional" (or noncompensatory) treatment. That is the case in the Head Start and Follow Through evaluations reported by Bissell, and also in most of the studies described by Karnes. Sigel's comparison group is a variation on these: it consists of children in other day care programs in order to evaluate the effectiveness of his particular intervention program.

Beyond identifying an appropriate kind of comparison group, the evaluator has to justify through the design of the evaluation the particular comparison cases used. From the beginning of the compensatory era in education, there has been much talk in the literature about the difficulties of achieving sound experimental designs in the real world (see, for example, Dyer 1966; Messick 1969; Stanley 1969; Anderson 1970; and Sigel's paper in this volume). Some have even adopted postures of near contempt for the application of research methodology and experimental design to evaluation (Guba 1969). Campbell, among others, has argued both that researchers may be prone to accept inferior designs when they don't need to (1957) and that policy positions are possible that *could* increase the use of randomization in field studies (1969). However, Campbell and Stanley (1966) have also provided us with treatments of the logic of quasi-experimental design, so that, as Messick (1969, p. 24) has said: "Important as randomization is for experimental inference, its absence in a given study is no cause for despair."

This is not to say, however, that any data-collection effort that does not meet the requirements of random assignment qualifies as a quasi-experiment. Nor does it suggest that, because the design is more "casual" than might be desired, the evaluator is relieved of describing his subjects, treatments, and data-collection procedures and measures in as much detail as possible. On the contrary, since there are more potential threats to the validity of the conclusions that might be drawn from the data, he is obligated to include in his reports *more* information, enough to help the reader judge for himself what the data might mean.

Some of the kinds of information I am talking about, illustrated by omissions from some of the previous reports, include:

- Thorough descriptions of teachers as key parts of a compensatory treatment. (I would suspect in the Planned Variation efforts, for example, that variance attributable to teachers is greater than that attributable to program names.)

- What a noted difference in test scores corresponds to in such meaningful terms as the number and kinds of items it represents.

- Rationales for the selection and application of all measuring instruments. (I continue to deplore the use of an IQ score as a major criterion of success of any educational program, and greatly admire Sigel's preference for less refined but relevant measures over "the true and the tried" if the latter offer only global assessments.)

- Provision of data on dropouts in groups of subjects. (Failure to take account of differences in the number and kinds of dropouts in groups that are to be compared represents a major source of error in conclusions about the effects of educational treatments.)

- How the analysis allows for any lack of independence of subgroups of children within a treatment or comparison group (for example, the children in a class).

- Detailed information that would allow judgment about the comparability not only of experimental and control groups but also of the several treatment groups in such enterprises as Follow Through

Planned Variation; the investigator's own best interpretation of the effects of such apparent lacks of comparability as residence by the experimental and comparison groups in *different* communities, or a *smaller* percentage of a control than of an experimental group with previous compensatory education experience.

- Careful consideration of the multiple circularities implied by such statements as "Follow Through parents were more aware of their children's school programs, more likely to visit schools and work in classrooms . . ., and more convinced of their ability to influence school programs than parents of non-Follow Through children" (Bissell, p. 100).

At least two of the papers in this symposium have stressed the importance of considering the effects of educational programs on individuals as well as groups. Karnes cited Kirk's statement: "These results, though affirmative, do not tell the whole story. They do not tell us what kinds of children, and under what circumstances . . ., made the most progress" (p. 110). Ball and Bogatz remind us: ". . . in a worthwhile evaluation we must discover not only if an educational intervention . . . works . . . . For the long run we should also try to discover which children it works best for, which children it does not seem to work for, and the conditions under which it operates most efficiently. Too often evaluations have concluded that a new program is of little consequence, when in fact it is a boon to some children, a ruin to other children, but when averaged over all children, there seems little difference from the old program" (p. 12).

There is a good, straightforward example of this phenomenon in the first *Sesame Street* evaluation (Ball & Bogatz 1970). In terms of knowledge of body parts, there was no significant difference—on the average—between frequent and infrequent viewers on pretest or posttest. On pretest, however, the range was larger for both groups—and the distributions somewhat skewed. But some children *did* learn the body parts from *Sesame Street* and, in spite of averages, it probably makes a lot of difference to those children to know the difference between their elbows and their foreheads.

The consequences of failing to take account of the data for all subjects in an evaluation could lead to a decision completely to reject a program that worked very well for, say, a fourth of the group; similarly, on the basis of averages alone, a program might be retained for all students when it actually had a very negative effect on a fourth of the group. In other words, effects must be judged in terms of changes in *distributions* of scores, not just in terms of changes in average performance.

Another aspect of the program that evaluators frequently neglect because they do not have the techniques to deal with it, or do not consider it a fitting object of study, is cost. Yet it cannot be ignored. It would have to figure, for example, in decisions about direct (pupil) vs. indirect (parent) training costs, as described by Karnes; with whether to start preschool at age two or age three; and with almost every "innovation" described in this symposium. Related to an analysis of program costs in relationship to purposes and results is a weighing of estimated costs of carrying out evaluation studies—in terms of the possible utility or importance of the results. Put bluntly, is it likely that an evaluation will cost more than it is worth? Everything doesn't have to be evaluated—especially in situations where no end of careful reporting of results can really influence the continuance, abolition, or even revision of the program.

Plans for evaluation studies that don't take seriously such issues as comparison groups, design, specifications and rationales, and consideration of person-treatment interactions should be relabeled, appropriately, "plans for *data collection*." And such plans should be considered especially carefully in terms of their costs; perhaps the earmarked funds can be channeled into more productive research and development efforts.

After bewailing the failure of some evaluation analyses to take account of the possible differential effects of an educational program on the individuals in a class, it is appropriate to return to consideration of whether the usual notion of compensatory education, itself, includes appropriate recognition of the individual. Much reasoning in this field proceeds this way: Any disadvantaged child is an appropriate candidate for compensatory education; you can tell a disadvantaged child by the income of his family, the color of his skin, the language spoken at home, etc. Yet no amount of compensatory education removes the signs by which a school child is labeled disadvantaged. (A few years ago, as Julian Stanley was fond of pointing out, a child was not labeled disadvantaged if he was reading two years above grade level regardless of his color or the economic condition of his family. But that state of affairs seems to have changed.)

Our earlier analysis of the whats and hows of compensatory education failed to indicate many distinctive (or distinguished) features of compensatory education as it is practiced. Furthermore, it clearly pointed to some dangers of categorizing children for educational purposes on *non*educational variables. Sigel pleads for time for conceptual model building; I hope that time can also be made available for a more thorough examination of the concept of compensatory education itself. Jablonsky (1971) reports that, of the 244 compensatory education efforts listed in the Gordon and Wilkerson book (1966), only 51 were still identifiable four to five years later "by title, purpose or key person"; I suspect that failures or discontinuances of compensatory education programs are as much attributable to their weak conceptual foundations as to other kinds of difficulties that are given more publicity (bureaucratic red tape, community agitation, funding, etc.). I have personally come to the conclusion that "compensatory education," as presently understood, is counterproductive. It seems to stem, on the one hand, from the kinds of motivations Winschel (1970) describes—prejudice, do-goodness, conscience-salving, and maintenance of the status quo—and, on the other hand, from a reluctance to tackle the larger project of revamping our entire educational structure. Compensatory education also reflects, as Sigel points out, an expectation of failure from alternative patterns for breaking the "poverty cycle."

In recent years we have had many reminders that our schools were created for a different time and place (for example, Jackson 1968; Reimer 1971; and Silberman 1970). Coleman (1972) has pointed out that schools no longer function as the window on the world for a majority of people. In our present information-rich society, he suggests, it is necessary at least to change the goals of the schools. Perhaps the change could encompass the set of survival or participation goals put forward by Gordon and Wilkerson (1966; see also Gordon 1972):

Mastery of Basic Communication Skills
Problem-Solving
The Management of Knowledge
Employment, Leisure, and Continuing Education
Self Management

Perhaps, too, such goals could be sought in a context that engages the learner affectively, is suited to his individual needs and styles, and has societal relevance (Gordon 1970). Such an educational scheme would seem to be applicable to almost all citizens, regardless of income, race, creed, color, or sex. And it should have the beneficial side effect of alleviating the need for compensatory education and even of exposing it as an institution as anachronistic as the *non*compensatory education of the nineteen sixties and seventies.

REFERENCES

Anderson, S. B. 1970. From textbooks to reality: Social researchers face the facts of life in the world of the disadvantaged. Pp. 226–37, in J. Hellmuth (ed.), *Disadvantaged child, Vol. 3: Compensatory education: A national debate*. New York: Brunner/Mazel.

Ausubel, D. P. 1967. How reversible are the cognitive and motivational effects of cultural deprivation? Implications for teaching the culturally deprived child. Pp. 306–26, in A. H. Passow, M. Goldberg, and A. J. Tannenbaum (eds.), *Education of the disadvantaged: A book of readings*. New York: Holt, Rinehart and Winston.

Ball, S., and Bogatz, G. A. 1970. *The first year of Sesame Street: An evaluation*. Princeton, N.J.: Educational Testing Service, PR-70-15.

Birren, J. E., and Hess, R. D. 1968. Influences of biological, psychological, and social deprivations upon learning and performance. Pp. 91–183, in U.S. Department of Health, Education, and Welfare, the National Institute of Child Health and Human Development, *Perspectives on human deprivation: Biological, psychological, and sociological*. Washington, D.C.: U.S. Department of Health, Education, and Welfare.

California Education. 1963. New compensatory education project established by McAteer Act. 1: 17–18.

Campbell, D. T. 1957. Factors relevant to the validity of experiments in social settings. *Psychological Bulletin* 54: 297–312.

——. 1969. Reforms as experiments. *American Psychologist* 24: 409–29.

Campbell, D. T., and Frey, P. W. 1970. The implications of learning theory for the fade-out of gains from compensatory education. Pp. 455–63, in J. Hellmuth (ed.), *Disadvantaged child, Vol. 3: Compensatory education: A national debate*. New York: Brunner/Mazel.

Campbell, D. T., and Stanley, J. C. 1966. *Experimental and quasi-experimental designs for research*. Chicago: Rand McNally.

Chazan, M. 1968. Compensatory education: Defining the problem. Pp. 7–27, in *Compensatory education: An introduction*. Occasional Publication Number 1, University College of Swansea Department of Education, Schools Council Research Project in Compensatory Education. Swansea, Wales: Schools Council Publishing Company.

Cohen, D. K. 1970. Politics and research: Evaluation of social action programs in education. *Review of Educational Research* 40: 213–38.

Coleman, J. S. 1972. The children have outgrown the schools. *Psychology Today* 5(9): 72–75, 82.

Coleman, J. S., and Campbell, E. Q., Hobson, C. J., McPartland, J., Mood, A. M., Weinfeld, F. D., and York, R. L. 1966. *Equality of educational opportunity*. Washington, D.C.: U.S. Government Printing Office, OE-38001.

Dyer, H. S. 1966. Overview of the evaluation process. Pp. 17–21, in *On evaluating Title I programs*. Princeton, N.J.: Educational Testing Service.

Gordon, E. W. 1970. Problems in the determination of educability in populations with differential characteristics. Pp. 249–67, in J. Hellmuth (ed.), *Disadvantaged child, Vol. 3: Compensatory education: A national debate*. New York: Brunner/Mazel.

——. 1972. Toward defining equality of educational opportunity. Pp. 423–24, in F. Mosteller and D. P. Moynihan (eds.), *On equality of educational opportunity*. New York: Vintage (Random House).

Gordon, E. W., and Wilkerson, D. A. 1966. *Compensatory education for the disadvantaged*. New York: College Entrance Examination Board.

Guba, E. G. 1969. Comments appearing in the significant differences column. *Educational Researcher* 20(3): 4–5.

Jablonsky, A. 1971. Directory of selected ongoing compensatory education programs. *IRCD Bulletin* 7(3).

Jackson, P. W. 1968. *Life in classrooms*. New York: Holt, Rinehart and Winston.

Messick, S. 1969. Can you do real research in the real world? Pp. 21–26, in S. B. Anderson and J. Doppelt (Chmn.), *Untangling the tangled web of education*. Princeton, N.J.: Educational Testing Service, RM-69-6.

—— · 1972. Research methodology for educational change. Pp. 69–81, in *Proceedings of the 1971 Invitational Conference on Testing Problems*. Princeton, N.J.: Educational Testing Service.

Reimer, E. 1971. *School is dead: Alternatives to education*. Garden City, N.Y.: Doubleday.

Silberman, C. E. 1970. *Crisis in the classroom: The remaking of American education*. New York: Random House.

Stanley, J. C. 1969. Controlled experimentation: Why seldom used in evaluation? Pp. 104–8, in *Proceedings of the 1969 Invitational Conference on Testing Problems*. Princeton, N.J.: Educational Testing Service.

Winschel, J. F. 1970. In the dark ... reflections on compensatory education, 1960–1970. Pp. 3–23, in J. Hellmuth (ed.), *Disadvantaged child, Vol. 3: Compensatory education: A national debate*. New York: Brunner/Mazel.

Young, M., and Willmott, P. 1957. *Family and kinship in East London*. London: Routledge and Kegan Paul.

INDEX OF NAMES

(Pages in boldface denote articles in this volume.)

Clark, D. H., 193
Clark, E. T., 185, 192
Coates, S. W., 160, 192
Cohen, D. K., 201, 206
Coleman, E., 195
Coleman, J. S., 6, 10, 199, 205, 206
Cook, T., 13, 23
Cronbach, L. J., 175, 182, 192

Damarin, F. L., 187, 192
Daniels, L. G., vii
Datta, L., 65, 67, 70, 105, 106
Day, D., 193
Degerman, R., 194
Di Lorenzo, L. T., 67, 86, 105
Dingman, H. F., 194
Dittmann, L., 72, 105
Dodd, C., 194
Doppelt, J., 150, 191, 207
Dowley, E. M., 106, 194
Dunn, L. M., 160, 192
Dyer, H. S., 201, 206
Dyer, J. L., 67, 86, 106

Ekstein, R., 145, 193
Emmerich, W., 51, 61, 174, 185, 193
Engelmann, S., 65, 67, 69, 90, 105, 112,
   113, 115, 116, 117, 118, 119, 120, 121,
   122, 123, 124, 125, 126, 127, 128, 129,
   130, 133, 143
Erickson, E. L., 87, 105
Erlebacher, A., 189, 192
Eska, B., 182, 187, 193

Farber, B., 112, 143
Ferguson, G. A., 179, 193
Fiedler, M., 195
Fifer, G., 193
Fillerup, J., 92
Finucci, J., vii
Flavell, J. H., 184, 193
Forman, G., v, 4, **25–62**, 25
Fox, L. H., 8, 10
Freeman, H. E., 13, 24
Frey, P. W., 199, 206

Froebel, F., 17
Frostig, M., 119, 120, 121, 127, 143

Garrett, H. E., 182, 193
Geoffrion, L., vii
Gilkeson, E., 91
Ginsburg, H., 30, 61
Glass, G. V., 1, 10
Goldberg, M., 205
Goldberg, S., 194
Golden, M., 30, 61, 188, 193
Goodenough, D. R., 195
Gordon, E. W., 204, 205, 206
Gordon, I. J., 67, 68, 76, 92, 106
Gray, S. W., 6, 7, 10
Grim, V., vii
Grinder, R., vii
Grotberg, E. H., 65, 105, 106
Guba, E. G., 201, 206
Guilford, J. P., 139, 143, 174, 179, 193
Guthrie, J., vii
Guttman, L., 175, 194

Hagen, J., 106, 194
Harvey, D. L., 112, 143
Heber, R., 8
Hein, G., 91
Hellmuth, J., 62, 105, 192, 205, 206, 207
Hertzig, M. E., 72, 73, 80, 82, 106
Hess, R. D., 7, 10, 73, 83, 106, 159, 170,
   176, 190, 192, 193, 199, 206
Hobson, C. J., 10, 206
Hodgkins, A. S., 106, 143
Hoffman, L., 105
Hoffman, M. L., 31, 62
Hughes, M., 68
Hunt, J. McV., 29, 62, 111, 143, 179, 193
Hurst, J. G., 179, 193

Ingersoll, G., 21, 24
Inhelder, B., 30, 62

Jablonsky, A., 204, 206
Jackson, P. W., 205, 207
Jacobson, L., 180, 194

Library of Congress Cataloging in Publication Data

Hyman Blumberg Symposium on Research in Early Childhood
Education, 2d, Johns Hopkins University, 1972.
Compensatory education, ages two to eight.

Includes bibliographies.
1. Compensatory education-United States–Congresses.
2. Education, Primary--United States–Congresses.
3. Education, Preschool–United States–Congresses.
I. Stanley, Julian C., ed. II. Title.
LC4091.H93   1972   371.9'67   72-12355
ISBN 0-8018-1457-X
ISBN 0-8018-1461-8 (pbk.)

This book was composed in Press Roman Medium
text and Times Roman display type. It was
printed on 60-lb. Neutratext Natural Wove
paper and bound in Joanna Arrestox cloth
by LithoCrafters, Inc.